The S

WORDPERFECT 5
INSTANT
REFERENCE

Ray Fry
20 Aug '90

The SYBEX Prompter Series

We've designed the SYBEX Prompter Series to meet the evolving needs of software users, who want essential information presented in an accessible format. Our best authors have distilled their expertise into compact *Instant Reference* books you can use to look up the precise use of any command—its syntax, available options, and operation. More than just summaries, these books also provide realistic examples and insights into effective usage drawn from our authors' wealth of experience.

The SYBEX Prompter Series also includes these titles:

DOS Instant Reference
Greg Harvey and Kay Yarborough Nelson

dBASE Instant Reference
Alan Simpson

Turbo BASIC Instant Reference
Douglas Hergert

Lotus 1-2-3 Instant Reference
Greg Harvey and Kay Yarborough Nelson

HyperTalk Instant Reference
Greg Harvey

The SYBEX Prompter™ Series

WORDPERFECT®5 INSTANT REFERENCE

Greg Harvey
and
Kay Yarborough Nelson

San Francisco • Paris • Düsseldorf • London

Editor in Chief: Rudolph S. Langer
Managing Editor: Barbara Gordon
Series Editor: James A. Compton
Editor: Eric M. Stone

Cover design by Thomas Ingalls + Associates

Screen printing in this book was produced with XenoFont from XenoSoft, Berkeley, CA.

dBase III is a registered trademark of Ashton-Tate.
Hercules Graphics Card Plus, Incolor Card, and RamFont are trademarks of Hercules
Computer Technology, Inc.
IBM and PC-DOS are trademarks of International Business Machines Corp.
LaserJet is a trademark of Hewlett-Packard Co.
Lotus 1-2-3 is a trademark of Lotus Development Corp.
Mace Utilities is a trademark of Paul Mace Software.
MS-DOS is a trademark of Microsoft Corp.
Norton Utilities is a trademark of Peter Norton Computing.
PostScript is a trademark of Adobe Systems, Inc.
SideKick is a trademark of Borland International.
WordPerfect is a trademark of WordPerfect Corp.
WordStar is a trademark of MicroPro Corp.

SYBEX is a registered trademark and Prompter Series is a trademark of SYBEX, Inc.

SYBEX is not affiliated with any manufacturer.

Every effort has been made to supply complete and accurate information. However, SYBEX
assumes no responsibility for its use, nor for any infringements of patents or other rights of
third parties which would result.

Library of Congress Card Number: 88-61753
ISBN 0-89588-535-2
Printed by Haddon Craftsmen
Manufactured in the United States of America
10 9 8 7 6 5

ACKNOWLEDGMENTS

Thanks are due to the following people at SYBEX:

Dr. R. S. Langer and Alan Oakes for furnishing the inspiration for this series over dim sum; Jim Compton, the Prompter Series editor; Barbara Gordon, managing editor; Eric Stone, copy editor; Brian Atwood, technical editor; Bob Myren, word processor; Ingrid Owen, series designer; Cheryl Vega, typesetter; Lynne Bourgault, proofreader; Suzanne Albertson, book designer and paste-up artist; Gary Macaluso, paste-up artist; Sonja Schenk, graphics technician; and Jonathan Rinzler, production coordinator.

TABLE OF CONTENTS

Overview

The idea behind this book is simple. When you are stymied by a function that does not work as you intended in WordPerfect 5.0 or a command that produces unpredicted results, or when you want a quick refresher about a certain procedure, you need a single source of information that can quickly help you solve the problem at hand and get on with your work.

This *Instant Reference* is intended to fill just that need: to give you in as short a space as possible the essential information necessary to get the most from WordPerfect's numerous features—both the basic commands and the sophisticated functions that you may not use on a daily basis. It covers version 5.0 of the program, which is somewhat different from earlier versions of WordPerfect, as discussed in the "Update Notes" section of this Overview.

Basic Program Functions

WordPerfect is a screen-oriented word processor, which means that as you create and edit your document, it appears on your screen pretty much as it will when it is printed: What you see is what you get. As soon as you issue the **WP** startup command and press ←, an initial startup screen appears briefly. After the initial startup screen, you will be presented with the editing screen. On it, a default *status line* indicates the document window you are in (Doc 1 or Doc 2) as well as the current page, line, and horizontal cursor position. Page breaks are indicated by a line of hyphens extending across the width of the screen.

To keep the screen view of your document as similar as possible to the printed version, WordPerfect does not display any of the special codes it uses to format the text, nor does it show any menu selections until you issue the appropriate command.

To see the formatting codes that are being used in your document, you press Reveal Codes (Alt-F3). You close this Reveal Codes window by pressing Alt-F3 again. In version 5.0, you can add and edit text while in Reveal Codes.

You issue commands to WordPerfect by pressing the function keys at the left of your keyboard alone or in combination with the Ctrl, Shift, and Alt keys. To see how these assignments differ from those in previous versions of the program, refer to the "Update Notes" section below.

Update Notes

In version 5.0, you select menu choices by pressing either the corresponding number *or* a mnemonic letter, which is usually but not always the first letter of the option name.

One other major difference between version 5.0 and earlier versions of WordPerfect is that document format commands are saved with the document and take precedence over any initial setup default settings that may have been specified. In effect, this means that you can retrieve a WordPerfect 5.0 document into any copy of WordPerfect 5.0, and it will retain the format under which it was created.

If you have been using an earlier version of WordPerfect, you will find that version 5.0 has been somewhat reorganized, primarily for ease of use. As a result, some of the functions have been reassigned to different keys. If you are a previous user of WordPerfect, you may find the following quick summary helpful:

- **F1**—The Super/Subscript commands have been moved to the Font key (Ctrl-F8), which was itself previously the Print Format key. (All format functions are now on Shift-F8, which is the Format key.) Shift-F1 is Setup, which replaces the old WP/S option. Shell (Ctrl-F1), Thesaurus (Alt-F1), and Cancel (F1) remain the same.

- **F2**—Search (F2), Replace (Alt-F2), Reverse Search (Shift-F2), and Spell (Ctrl-F2) are still on this key, but some of their functions have been enhanced.

- **F3**—Help remains as F3, as do Reveal Codes as Alt-F3 and Switch as Shift-F3. On the Screen key (Ctrl-F3), Colors and Auto Rewrite have been moved to the Setup key (Shift-F1), and the Ctrl/Alt key's functions are now covered through new Keyboard Layout and Compose commands.

- **F4**—Indent (F4) and Left/Right Indent (Shift-F4) remain the same. Move (Ctrl-F4) and Block (Alt-F4) are still assigned to this key, although you will find that some of their menu items have been reassigned and made easier to use.

- **F5**—This is basically a new key in version 5.0. The Text In/Out key (Ctrl-F5) now consists of five submenus. Document Summary functions are now on the Format key (Shift-F8). Date is changed to Date/Outline (Shift-F5), and Outline and Paragraph Numbering have been moved from Mark Text (Alt-F5) to this key. Mark Text itself has been reorganized: It now contains Master Document, Document Compare, and Automatic Reference features. Redline and Strikeout are now on the Font key (Ctrl-F8). List Files (F5) has been enhanced, and new types of word searches are now possible.

- **F6**—The functions of this key remain essentially the same.

- **F7**—Exit (F7) is the same; however, the other functions of this key have been enhanced. Footnote (Ctrl-F7) now has footnotes and endnotes on different submenus, with new features. Print (Shift-F7) is divided into Print and Options, with renamed menu choices and new options that combine the old Print Options and Printer Control options while adding new ones. The process of installing printers has been streamlined.

- **F8**—This is also basically a new key in version 5.0. Only Underline (F8) remains the same. The program's formatting features are now on Format (Shift-F8), which combines the old Line Format, Page Format, Print Format, and Document Format options. You will find that many format commands are easier to use and that new options have been made available. The Font key (Ctrl-F8) is a new feature that allows you to change the size and style of text directly instead of having to insert a Font Change code, as you did previously. Style (Alt-F8) is another new feature that allows you to create format style sheets for the documents you write.

- **F9**—Merge Codes is now Shift-F9 instead of Alt-F9, and a new feature, Graphics (Alt-F9), which allows you to combine graphics and text, has been added. Merge E is now chosen from Merge Codes instead of being assigned to a key of its own.

- **F10**—Save (F10), Retrieve (Shift-F10), and Macro (Alt-F10) are the same; Macro Define (Ctrl-F10) now contains a macro editor.

In addition to these reassignments of the command keys, Word-Perfect 5.0 contains many new features. They are listed alphabetically here; for more information on any of them, refer to the appropriate heading in this *Instant Reference*.

Advance

Automatic Reference

Appearance

Base Font

Beep Options

Cartridges and Fonts

Colors/Fonts/Attributes

Compose

Cursor Speed

Decimal/Align Character

Display Pitch

Display, Setup

Document Comments

Document Compare

Fast Save (Unformatted)

Font

Force Odd/Even Page

Forms

Graphics

Initial Settings

Kerning

Keyboard Layout

Language

Line Height

Line Spacing

Location of Auxiliary Files

Margins, Top and Bottom

Master Document

Print Color

Printer, Select

Setup

Style Sheets

Units of Measure

View Document

Word/Letter Spacing

Using the *WordPerfect 5 Instant Reference*

The entries in this book follow a somewhat flexible format, reflecting variations in the scope and format of the commands that make up WordPerfect. After each command heading you will find a short summary of the function that the command carries out, followed by the key sequence required to carry out that task. As WordPerfect 5.0 is constructed with a hierarchical menu system, these keystrokes are presented vertically on the page to represent the menu structure you will be going through as you carry out the sequence.

If you must press two keys in combination, they are connected by a hyphen. For example,

Shift-F7

indicates that you should press Shift and hold it down while pressing

F7. Variable information that you enter is presented in a lighter, *italic* typeface within angle brackets. For example,

Alt-F6 (Flush Right)

<text> ⏎

indicates that to align text flush right, you press Alt-F6, enter the text you wish to align, and press ⏎. If you need to perform an operation other than keyboard entry, that operation is indicated in *italic* typeface within regular brackets. For example,

Alt-F4 (Block)

[highlight text to be centered]

Shift-F6 (Center)

[Cntr]? (Y/N) **Yes**

indicates that you must highlight a block of text before proceeding with the command sequence, which in this case centers the highlighted text.

If there are two different ways to indicate a menu choice—either by number or by mnemonic letter—they are indicated in **boldface**. For example

4 Append

means that you may press either the *4* key or the *A* (or *a*) key to select that menu option. Number alternatives are presented first, but after you work with WordPerfect for a while and become accustomed to its command names, you may prefer the mnemonic alternatives.

Under the heading "USAGE," you will find a short discussion of the command or option, or in some cases, a step-by-step sequence of instructions you must follow to accomplish a complex task, such as merge-printing or creating an index. If all you need is a quick review of the key sequence that is required, you do not need to read the discussion. If you need additional information, you will usually find enough details in the discussion to allow you to accomplish the task at hand. If you find that your work takes you beyond the scope of the quick advice this *Instant Reference* gives you, you may want to refer to the *WordPerfect 5 Desktop Companion* by Greg Harvey and Kay Yarborough Nelson (San Francisco: SYBEX, 1988); this more comprehensive reference book covers all aspects of WordPerfect in detail.

Finally, where appropriate, you'll find cross-references to commands of related interest under the heading "SEE ALSO."

The appendices are also designed to be used as a quick guide to the program's features. Appendix A summarizes installation procedures for IBM and IBM-compatible computers. Appendix B presents the hidden formatting codes WordPerfect uses in your documents. You may often need to verify the exact abbreviation for these codes or look up what a certain code stands for to determine its effect in your document. Finally, Appendix C introduces WordPerfect's new macro command language and lists each command along with a brief description.

Advance

Advances the printer to a specific line or position on the page.

KEY SEQUENCE

Shift-F8 (Format)

4 – Other

1 – Advance

1 Up; **2 D**own; **3 L**ine; **4 L**eft; **5 R**ight; **6 P**osition

<measurement to advance> ←

F7 (Exit)

USAGE

The Advance feature advances the printer to a specific position on the page. To advance the printer up, down, left, or right of the current printing position (that is, the place where the [Adv] code is entered), you enter a distance that is relative to the cursor's position when you use the command. To advance the printer to a specific line or column, you enter a measurement that is an absolute position on the page. When using the Advance to Line option, you enter the distance from the top of the page. When using the Advance to Position option, you enter the distance from the left edge of the page.

To use the Advance feature, move the cursor to the place where you want the advance to begin and follow the key sequence shown at the beginning of this section. After you press F7 (Exit), type the text to be advanced.

Although the status line will reflect the advance position, the cursor does not move when you use this command. To return to the original position when using Advance Up, Down, Left, or Right, select the opposite Advance option (down if you used up, right if you used left, etc.) and enter the same distance you specified earlier. To return to the original line or column when using Advance to Line or Advance to Position, repeat the advance procedure, selecting the same Advance option but entering the original line or offset position as the distance. To prevent the text from being advanced as indicated, locate the appropriate [Adv] code in the Reveal Codes screen and delete it.

The Advance feature is especially useful in layout work involving text and graphics on a page. You can use it to fine-tune the placement of headings in Text boxes and to position text that overlays other types of graphics on the page (see **Graphics**).

Alignment Character

See **Decimal/Align Character**.

Append Block

Adds a marked block of text to the end of another document.

KEY SEQUENCE ═══════════════════════════

To append a sentence, paragraph, or page:

Ctrl-F4 (Move)
——▭——

1 Sentence; **2** Paragraph; **3** Page
——▭——

4 Append
——▭——

Append to: <*file name*>

To append a marked block, column, or rectangle:

Alt-F4 (Block)
——▭——

[highlight block of text with cursor keys]
——▭——

Ctrl-F4 (Move)
——▭——

1 Block; **2** Tabular Column; **3** Rectangle
——▭——

4 Append
——▭——

Append to: <*file name*>

USAGE ═══════════════════════════

When you append a block of text, WordPerfect adds it to the end of a document saved on disk. You can append a discrete block of text like a sentence, paragraph, or page without using Block (Alt-F4) to mark it first. When appending any other type of block (like several words but not an entire sentence, several lines but not an entire paragraph) or a tabular column or rectangle, you must use Block to mark the text to be appended before you use Move (Ctrl-F4).

When using either method, you indicate the type of block and select the Append option. You are then asked for the name of the file to which this text will be appended. Type in the file name. If this file is not in the current (default) directory, include the path name. After entering the name, press ⏎ to have the text added to the end of the disk file.

NOTE

You can also append the text of a disk file to the end of the document currently in the editing screen. To do this, you move to the end of the document (Home Home ↓), select Retrieve Text (Shift-F10), and enter the name of the document whose text you want appended. The same thing happens when you use the Retrieve option on the List Files menu and have a document on the editing screen.

SEE ALSO

Block Operations

Cut and Copy Text

Retrieving Documents

Automatic Reference

Allows you to mark references in the document to a figure, table, footnote, or page; automatically updates them.

KEY SEQUENCE

To mark both the reference and target:

[move to the place where the reference is to appear]

Alt-F5 (Mark Text)

1 Auto **R**ef

3 – Mark **B**oth Reference and Target

    1 – **P**age Number
    2 – Paragraph/**O**utline Number
    3 – **F**ootnote Number
    4 – **E**ndnote Number
    5 – **G**raphics Box Number

[position cursor immediately after the target] ←

Target Name: *<target name>* ←

To mark only the reference:

[move to the place where the reference is to appear]

Alt-F5 (Mark Text)

1 Auto **R**ef

1 – Mark **R**eference

1 – **P**age Number
2 – Paragraph/**O**utline Number
3 – **F**ootnote Number
4 – **E**ndnote Number
5 – **G**raphics Box Number

Target Name: *<target name>* ←

To mark only the target:

[position the cursor immediately after the target]

—▭—

Alt-F5 (Mark Text)

—▭—

1 Auto **R**ef

—▭—

2 – Mark **T**arget

—▭—

Target Name: *<target name>* ↵

To generate the automatic references for those where the reference and target were marked separately:

Alt-F5 (Mark Text)

—▭—

6 **G**enerate

—▭—

5 – **G**enerate Tables, Indexes, Automatic References, etc.

—▭—

Existing tables, lists, and indexes will be replaced.
Continue? (Y/N) ↵ *or any key except N*

USAGE

The Automatic Reference feature maintains and automatically updates references to areas of text, footnotes, endnotes, headers, footers, graphics boxes, or the captions attached to graphics boxes. The place in the document where the reference number will appear when the document is printed is the *reference*. The place in the document that contains the text referred to is the *target*.

You can mark the reference and target at the same time except when referencing a graphics box caption. In this case, you must mark the reference and the target separately. When you mark a reference only, a question mark appears in place of the reference number. This question mark is replaced with the actual figure, note, or page number when you generate the references.

SEE ALSO

Graphics

Mark Text

Master Document

Backup, Timed and Original Document

Automatically saves your document at intervals of your choosing or saves a copy of the original document each time you save the document on the editing screen.

KEY SEQUENCE

Shift-F1 (Setup)

1 – Backup

1 – Timed Document Backup
Minutes Between Backups
2 – Original Document Backup

F7 (Exit)

USAGE

WordPerfect periodically saves your document to a temporary backup file if you turn on the Timed Document Backup feature. This guards against a loss of edits should you experience either a machine failure or a loss of power when working. When you exit WordPerfect normally, these backup files are deleted.

The document being edited in document window 1 is saved as WP{WP}.BK.1, and the one being edited in document window 2 is saved as WP{WP}.BK.2. If you should be prevented from exiting normally, you can retrieve either of these documents from the directory where they are stored. Then, you can save them under a new name using Save (F10) or Exit (F7).

With the Original Document Backup option, you can have Word-Perfect save a copy of the document before your most recent editing changes to it. When you activate this feature, any time you save a document under the same name (by answering Yes to the Replace? (Y/N) question), it first saves a copy of the document as it was last saved, using the same file name with the extension .BK!. Then it saves the document on your editing screen, with all of the changes you have made, to disk.

To specify where the backup files made by the Timed Document Backup and Original Document Backup are to be stored, you need to set the Backup Directory from the Setup menu (see **Location of Files**). Note that even when using both of these backup methods, you should still keep backup copies of your work on a different disk. See **Copying Files** for information on how to make these backup copies from within WordPerfect.

SEE ALSO

Copying Files

Location of Auxiliary Files

Base Font

Changes the basic font used in printing the document from the cursor's position forward.

KEY SEQUENCE ═══════════════════

Ctrl-F8 (Font)

—▭—

4 Base Font

—▭—

[highlight font with cursor keys]

—▭—

1 Select; **N** Name Search

USAGE ═══════════════════════════

The *current font* represents the font in which the text is normally printed. This font depends upon the printer that you have selected and the initial font that you have assigned to it (see **Printer Selection**). To switch to a new basic font in the document, you use the Base Font option on the Font menu (Ctrl-F8). When you select a new font in this way, it becomes the new current font from the cursor's position forward in the document.

The current font also determines what sizes will be used when you select different font size options such as Fine, Small, or Large, or different attribute options like Bold or Italics (see **Font**). For example, if you select a new base font of Times Roman 10 point, WordPerfect will use Times Roman 10 point bold to print boldfaced text in the document, Times Roman 10 Italic to print italicized text, and so on. Likewise, when you make a change to the size, it will use different sized fonts in the Times Roman family, such as Times Roman 6 point for Fine, Times Roman 8 point for Small, Times Roman 12 point for Large, and so forth. The actual sizes chosen for each change in size depend upon the fonts your printer supports and the fonts you have selected for that printer. Moreover, the font choices available when you change the current font with the Base Font option are determined by the fonts you have selected for the printer you are using (see **Cartridges and Fonts**). To prevent a font change from taking place, locate the [Font] code in the Reveal Codes screen and delete it.

SEE ALSO

Cartridges and Fonts

Font

Printer Selection: Initial Font

Beep Options

Determines whether WordPerfect beeps when an error occurs, a word is to be hyphenated, or a search fails.

KEY SEQUENCE

Shift-F1 (Setup)

5 – Initial Settings

1 – **B**eep Options

1 – Beep on **E**rror
2 – Beep on **H**yphenation
3 – Beep on **S**earch Failure

F7 (Exit)

USAGE

By default, WordPerfect beeps only when prompting you to hyphenate a word if you are using the Hyphenation feature (see **Hyphenation**). You can, however, also have it beep when an error occurs or when a search operation fails. If you don't want to be disturbed by any beeps, you can turn off the beep on the Hyphenation option and leave the others off.

Binding

Shifts text to the right on odd-numbered pages and to the left on even-numbered pages.

KEY SEQUENCE

Shift-F7 (Print)

B – **B**inding *<measurement for binding width>* ←

F7 (Exit)

USAGE

You use the Binding option on the Print menu (Shift-F7) when your document is going to be reproduced on two-sided copies to ensure that there is sufficient room to bind the document. You set a binding width to determine how far the text is shifted to the right on odd-numbered pages and to the left on even-numbered pages.

The binding width is entered as an absolute measurement from the left or right edge of the paper and overrides the left and right margin settings that are in effect. You can enter the binding width any time prior to printing the document.

If you intend to reproduce the document on just one side of the paper, you can ignore the Binding option; just increase the left margin setting to allow sufficient room for binding.

To remove the binding width before printing a document during the same work session, you need to select the Binding option from the Print menu and enter **0** as the binding width measurement.

Block Operations

Defines a block of text on which you can then perform any of a number of operations.

KEY SEQUENCE

Alt-F4 (Block)

[highlight block with cursor keys]

[select the operation to be performed on the block]

USAGE

The Block command (Alt-F4) is used to highlight (mark) a section of text for use with other WordPerfect commands. Once you have marked a block of text, you can use any of the following Word-Perfect features:

Bold

Center

Delete

Flush Right

Font: Appearance and Size

Format

Macro

Mark Text: Index, List, Table of Authorities, Table of Contents

Move: Block, Tabular Column, Rectangle

Print

Replace

Save

Search

Shell (if using the WordPerfect Library)

Sort

Spell

Style

Switch

Text In/Out

Underline

Marking a Block

To mark a block of text, you position the cursor at the beginning of the block and press Block (Alt-F4). The message

Block on

appears at the bottom left of your screen. Position the cursor at the end of the block; as you move the cursor, the text included will be highlighted. Then select the operation you want applied to the block.

When marking the block, you have several options for positioning the cursor. You can use the Search feature to move the cursor forward or backward to a particular place in the document. Press ⏎ to extend the block to the next [HRt] code (hard return). Type a particular character to extend the block to that character—like a period to include text up to the end of the sentence. Press ↑ or ↓ to extend the block up or down to include a number of lines. Press Ctrl-→ to extend the block to include several words.

Many WordPerfect commands behave differently if you have marked the text before using them. The differences are summarized in Table 1.

KEY	BLOCK ON	BLOCK OFF
F1 (Cancel)	Cancels block	Cancels; Undeletes
Alt-F2 (Replace)	Replaces in block	Replaces in document
Ctrl-F2 (Spell)	Checks block	Checks word, page, or document; Changes dictionary, Looks up word; Gets word count
Shift-F3 (Switch)	Uppercases or lowercases block	Switches to other window
Ctrl-F4 (Move)	Cuts, copies, or appends block; Cuts/ copies column or rectangle	Moves sentence, paragraph, or page; Retrieves column, text or rectangle
Alt-F5 (Mark Text)	Marks for ToC, list, paragraph numbering	Turns outlining, redline, strikeout, index numbering on/ off; Enters short form for ToA; Other options define styles for paragraph and outline numbering, ToC, index, and lists; Deletes redline; Edits ToA; Generates ToC and lists

Table 1: Block Commands

KEY	BLOCK ON	BLOCK OFF
F6 (Bold)	Bolds block	Bolds as text is entered
Alt-F6 (Flush Rt)	Moves block flush right	Moves text flush right as entered
Shift-F6 (Center)	Centers block	Centers text as entered
Shift-F7 (Print)	Prints block	Prints full text or page as on screen; Accesses print options and printer control; Type-thru; Print preview
F8 (Underline)	Underlines block	Underlines text as entered
Shift-F8 (Format)	Protects block	Accesses page format options
Ctrl-F9 (Merge/Sort)	Sorts block	Merges; Sorts; Specifies sort sequence
F10 (Save)	Saves block in new file	Saves document

Table 1: Block Commands (continued)

Rehighlighting a Block

After you mark the block and select a WordPerfect feature, the highlighting and the *Block on* message will disappear. To rehighlight the block you just used, you press Block (Alt-F4) and then Go To (Ctrl-Home) twice. To move the cursor directly to the beginning of the block, press Go To (Ctrl-Home) followed by Block (Alt-F4).

Press Cancel (F1) or Block (Alt-F4) to turn off the *Block on* prompt and cancel the intended block operation.

SEE ALSO

Bold

Center

Cut and Copy Text

Mark Text

Save Text

Sort

Speller

Underline

Block Protect

Prevents a marked block of text from being split by a page break.

KEY SEQUENCE

Alt-F4 Block

—▭—

[highlight text of block with cursor keys]

—▭—

Shift-F8 (Format)

—▭—

Protect block? (Y/N) **Y**

USAGE

You can use block protection to ensure that any block of text is not split between pages. If you make editing changes that would split the protected text between pages, WordPerfect will shift the entire block to the following page. This feature can be used effectively to keep tables on a single page.

To block-protect text, move the cursor to the beginning of the block, press Block (Alt-F4), and move the cursor to the end of the block. Then, press Format (Shift-F8). WordPerfect will display the prompt

   Protect block? (Y/N) No

Type **Y** to have the block protected.

To remove block protection, locate the [BlockPro:On] or [BlockPro:Off] code in the Reveal Codes screen and delete it.

SEE ALSO

Conditional End of Page

Page Breaks

Widow/Orphan Protection

Bold

Enhances the selected text by printing it in a boldface font or with doublestrike.

KEY SEQUENCE

To boldface text as you type it:

F6 (Bold)

[type text to be boldfaced]

F6 (Bold)

To boldface existing text:

Alt-F4 (Block)

[highlight text to be boldfaced]

F6 (Bold)

USAGE

WordPerfect allows you to enhance portions of text with boldfacing by placing the text between a pair of Bold formatting codes. Boldfacing is indicated on the screen by double-intensity or a different color. When printing the boldfaced text, the program will either select a bold version of the font in use or doublestrike the text, depending upon the type of printer you have.

You can also boldface text by using Font (Ctrl-F8), selecting the Appearance option (**2** or **A**) and then selecting the Bold option (**1** or **B**).

To remove boldfacing, locate either the [BOLD] or [bold] code in the Reveal Codes screen and delete it. You only have to delete one of the pair to delete both and remove the boldfacing.

When the cursor is located on a boldfaced character in the text, the number at the Pos indicator is shown in the same attribute used by your monitor to display bold text (double-intensity or a new color). As soon the cursor is moved ahead of or behind the Bold code, this number returns to the normal attribute. Thus, you can refer to the Pos indicator to locate a Bold code for deletion without using the Reveal Codes screen.

When you are about to delete a Bold code in this way (either on purpose or unintentionally), WordPerfect displays the prompt

Delete [Bold]? (Y/N) No

You must type **Y** for Yes to delete—if you simply press ←, the bold-facing will remain.

SEE ALSO

Base Font

Cartridges and Fonts

Font

Canceling a Command

Terminates almost any WordPerfect command that is being carried out.

KEY SEQUENCE

F1 (Cancel)

USAGE

You can use F1 almost any time you wish to cancel the command you have initiated. There are a few exceptions. For example, merge operations are canceled by pressing Merge R (F9). In certain cases, you can press the Esc key two or more times to cancel a particular command.

When you have not initiated a WordPerfect command, the Cancel key has the function of undeleting text. For information about this use of Cancel, see **Undelete**.

SEE ALSO

Esc Key

Keyboard Layout

Undelete

Canceling Printing

See **Print Job, Cancel**.

Cartridges and Fonts

Allows you to select the fonts you want to use in the document.

KEY SEQUENCE

To select fonts:

Shift-F7 (Print)

S – **S**elect Printer

[highlight the printer that uses the fonts]

3 – **E**dit

5 – **C**artridges and Fonts

[highlight Cartridge Fonts *or* Soft Fonts*]*

1 Select **F**onts

[mark fonts with * *if they will be present when job begins or with*
+ if WordPerfect must load them during print job]

F7 (Exit) *five times*

To designate where the soft fonts are located:

Shift-F7 (Print)

S – **S**elect Printer

[highlight the printer that uses the fonts]

3 – **E**dit

7 – Path for **D**ownloadable
Fonts and Printer
Command Files *<drive/directory path>* ⏎

F7 (Exit) *three times*

USAGE

If your printer can use different cartridges or soft fonts, you need to select them before you use them in the document (by selecting a new base font or changing the size or appearance on the Font menu). The Cartridges and Fonts menu will show you the number of cartridges that the selected printer supports. It will also show you how much memory is available for downloading soft fonts. At the bottom of the screen, there are three options:

   1 Select Fonts; **2** Change **Q**uantity; **N** Name search: 1

If your laser printer has more than 512K of memory, select the Quantity option (**2** or **Q**). Enter the amount of additional memory in kilobytes above the standard configuration for your printer (512K for the LaserJet), plus the amount of memory available for soft fonts, shown on the screen. For example, if you equip your LaserJet with 1.5Mb of total memory (1Mb or 1024K additional), you enter **1374** for the quantity—1024K extra memory plus the 350K currently available for soft fonts.

To select cartridge fonts, be sure that the highlight cursor is on *Cartridges* and then choose the Select Fonts option (**1** or **F**). Mark the cartridges you wish to use by highlighting them and typing an asterisk (*). Press Exit (F7) twice and WordPerfect will update the printer definition file.

To select soft (downloadable) fonts, move the highlight cursor to Soft Fonts and then choose the Select Fonts option (**1** or **F**). To quickly locate the font you want to add from the list, use Name Search by pressing F2 and typing in the first few letters of the font name.

Mark with an asterisk (*) all of the fonts that will be present (that is, downloaded) before the print job begins. Mark all of the fonts that will be downloaded during the print job with a plus (**+**). Press Exit (F7) twice and WordPerfect will update the printer definition file.

If you have marked fonts that are to be downloaded by Word-Perfect during the print job, you must indicate the directory that contains the fonts. Note that before printing you must manually load any fonts marked with *, using the Initialize Printer option on the Print menu (Shift-F7 7 or I)—then WordPerfect will download them for you. To indicate this directory, select the Path for

Downloadable Fonts and Printer Command Files option (**7** or **D**) and enter the complete path name.

The fonts you have selected will appear on the Base Font menu and may be used in the document either by selecting a new base font or by selecting a new size or appearance (see **Base Font** and **Font**).

To unmark fonts, repeat the procedure for editing the fonts for the selected printer. If you marked a font with an asterisk (*), highlight it again and type another * to unmark it. If you marked the font with a plus (+), type + again to unmark it.

SEE ALSO

Base Font

Font

Printer Selection

Case Conversion

Converts a marked block of text to uppercase or lowercase letters.

KEY SEQUENCE

Alt-F4 (Block)

[highlight text to be converted]

Shift-F3 (Switch)

1 Uppercase; **2** Lowercase

USAGE

To convert a block of text to all uppercase or all lowercase letters, you simply mark it as a block with Block (Alt-F4) and then select Switch (Shift-F3). To convert the marked text to uppercase, select the Uppercase option by typing **1** or **U**. To convert it to lowercase, select the Lowercase option by typing **2** or **L**.

Note that converting text to lowercase will not affect a capital letter at the beginning of a sentence. For example

...and John Smith. He...

becomes

...and john smith. He...

Center

Centers text on a line between the left and right margins.

KEY SEQUENCE

To center text as you type it:

Shift-F6 (Center)

<text to be centered> ⏎

To center existing text:

Alt-F4 (Block)

———□———

[highlight text to be centered]

———□———

Shift-F6 (Center)

———□———

[Cntr]? (Y/N) **Yes**

USAGE

To center text on a line between the left and right margin settings, press Center (Shift-F6), type the text, and press the Enter key. To center text after it has been entered, mark the text (this can include several lines) with Block (Alt-F4) and then select Center (Shift-F6). WordPerfect will display the prompt

[Cntr]? (Y/N) No

To have the marked text centered, simply type **Y** for Yes.

To remove centering, locate either the [Cntr] or [C/A/Flrt] code in the Reveal Codes screen and delete it.

SEE ALSO

Block Operations

Flush Right

Center Page (Top to Bottom)

Centers text on a page between the top and bottom margins.

KEY SEQUENCE

Home Home Home ↑

——▭——

Shift-F8 (Format)

——▭——

2 – **Page**

——▭——

1 – Center Page (top to bottom) **Y**

——▭——

F7 (Exit)

USAGE

The Center Page (Top to Bottom) command is used when you want to print less than an entire page of text so that it is centered vertically between your top and bottom margins. This is most often used for title sheets of reports and papers.

When using this command, you must remember to position the cursor at the very top of the page before entering the [Center Pg] code.

Most often, when you want text centered vertically, you also want it centered horizontally (see **Center**).

To remove centering on the page, locate and delete the [Center Pg] code in the Reveal Codes screen.

SEE ALSO

Center

Codes

Instruct the printer on how to format the text and graphics in your document.

```
KEY SEQUENCE ═══════════════════
```

Alt-F3 (Reveal Codes)

[view or edit codes and text in the Reveal Codes screen]

Alt-F3 (Reveal Codes)

```
USAGE ═══════════════════
```

WordPerfect enters formatting codes into your document as you use various commands. These codes are then sent to your printer when you print the document. They instruct the printer on how to accomplish various formatting changes in the document.

Some codes, like those used to boldface and underline text, are inserted in pairs, with one code turning on the effect and the other one turning it off.

WordPerfect keeps the formatting codes hidden from view on the editing screen. To see them, you must press Reveal Codes (Alt-F3). This causes the program to split the screen into two windows. The lower window shows the text with all of the codes inserted by Word-Perfect commands. WordPerfect indicates the position of the cursor in the Reveal Codes screen by highlighting the code or character. When using Reveal Codes, you can use all of the standard Word-Perfect editing features (including Undelete). When you want the Reveal Codes screen to disappear, press Reveal Codes (Alt-F3) a second time.

Most of the time you use the Reveal Codes screen to locate the position of a code that you wish to delete or change (you can't always tell when the cursor is on a code just by looking at the regular editing screen). To quickly locate the position of a code, you can use Word-Perfect's Search feature (see **Search: Searching for Codes**).

You can prevent a formatting change that you have introduced in the document by locating and deleting the code in the Reveal Codes screen. If the cursor is located on the code, press the Del key to remove it. If the cursor is after the code, press the Backspace key to remove it. If you delete a code in error, press Cancel (F1) and select the Restore option (**1** or **R**).

Appendix B shows you all of the codes used in WordPerfect.

SEE ALSO

Appendix B: Formatting Codes

Colors/Fonts/Attributes

Allows you to change the way particular text attributes are displayed on your screen.

KEY SEQUENCE

Shift-F1 (Setup)

3 – Display

2 – Colors/Fonts/Attributes

[select colors/fonts/attributes from menu(s)—varies according to display card and monitor]

Shift-F3 (Switch) to set Doc 2

F7 (Exit)

USAGE

Colors/Fonts/Attributes allows you to choose how the 16 font attributes available from the Size and Appearance menus (accessed with

Font—Ctrl-F8), as well as the attribute used to show a marked block of text, are displayed on your screen. The on-screen display selected for each attribute is independent of the way it will be produced by your printer.

The settings selected with the Colors/Fonts/Attributes option are in effect each time you start WordPerfect. The settings assigned to the Doc 1 screen are saved independently of those for the Doc 2 screen. After selecting your settings for the Doc 1 screen, you can use Switch (Shift-F3) to make the selections for the Doc 2 screen. You can also use Move (Ctrl-F4) to copy the settings from Doc 1 to Doc 2. After using Switch and Move, WordPerfect will display the prompt

Copy attributes from other document? (Y/N) No

Type **Y** for Yes to have the settings from Doc 1 copied to Doc 2.

The choices available for displaying different attributes are determined by the type of display card and monitor you are using. The differences are outlined in the following sections.

Monochrome

If you are using a monochrome monitor with a display card other than the Hercules Graphics Card Plus (with RamFont capabilities—see below), you can only set the attributes using underlining, double-intensity (bold), blinking, and inverse video (blocked). When you select the Colors/Fonts/Attributes option from the Display menu of the Setup key, you are presented immediately with the Set Attributes screen. Here, you may alter some of the default settings by changing the Y(es) or N(o) settings for each attribute. You can use the space bar to toggle between Y and N when changing a particular attribute. As you make a change, you can see its effect by looking at the sample in the far right column of the table.

Color

If you have a color monitor, you can set different foreground/background color combinations to represent different attributes.

The number of color combinations available depends upon the type of color display card you are using. If you are using an EGA (with sufficient memory) or VGA card, you can select among five different fonts (for showing italics, underline, small caps, etc.), or increase the number of displayable characters from 256 to 512. When you use these options (instead of Normal Font Only), the number of colors is limited to eight.

When using the Colors/Fonts/Attributes option for a color system, you can modify the Fast Text Display option. If you set this to Yes, WordPerfect will rewrite the screen faster, although you may experience "snow" on the screen.

If you have a CGA, PC3270, or MCGA (or EGA with limited memory or in a mode that displays more than 25 lines), you select colors for each attribute on the Set Screen Colors menu by assigning new foreground and/or background colors. To set a new color combination, move to the foreground color and type the letter of a listed color, then move to the background color and type its letter. As you make the change, the Sample column will immediately reflect it.

If you have an EGA (with sufficient memory) or VGA card, you select one of the fonts available by typing an asterisk (*). If the asterisk doesn't appear, there is a problem in loading the appropriate .FRS file (make sure that all .FRS files that begin with EGA have been copied to your WordPerfect directory).

When you select the Screen Colors option (**1** or **S**), you set the color combinations just as described for the CGA card. If you have selected a font, you assign it to an attribute by typing **Y** for Yes or **N** for No (or use the space bar to toggle between the two) in the appropriate column.

Hercules Graphics
Cards with RamFont

If you have a Hercules Graphics Card Plus or InColor Card with RamFont, when you select the Colors/Fonts/Attributes option you are presented with the following menu that includes three Font/

Color options (when you select one of these options, the program marks it with an asterisk.)

1 – **S**creen Attributes
2 – 12 Fonts, 256 Characters
3 – 6 Fonts, 512 Characters
4 – **N**ormal Font only

Choose option 2 to use 12 fonts with 256 characters or option 3 to use 6 fonts with 512 characters. If you select option 4, Normal Font Only, your display will act as though you have a standard Hercules Graphics card (even if you have a color monitor) and you must follow the procedure for a monochrome system (see **Monochrome** above).

After selecting the number of fonts, select option 1 if you wish to change any of the predefined attributes. There are five capabilities that you can set for certain attributes, starting with Font. To change the number of the font, you can type a number between 1 and 6 if using 6 fonts or 1–9 and A–C if you are using 12 fonts. You can also use the space bar or the plus (+) and minus (−) keys on the numeric pad to cycle through available font choices. Of course, you can change the other capabilities as well as the font for certain attributes.

```
NOTE
```

Changing the screen colors in no way affects the colors used in printing. If you have a color printer, select the Print Color option on the Font menu (see **Print Color**).

```
SEE ALSO
```

Display, Setup: Graphics Screen Type
Font: Size and Appearance

Columns, Text (Newspaper and Parallel)

Allows you to format your text using either newspaper or parallel columns.

KEY SEQUENCE

To define newspaper or parallel text columns:

Alt-F7 (Math/Columns)

4 Column **D**ef

1 – **T**ype
2 – **N**umber of Columns
3 – **D**istance Between Columns
4 – **M**argins

F7 (Exit)

To turn text columns on and off in the document:

Alt-F7 (Math/Columns)

3 Column On/Off

To change the display of text columns on the screen:

Shift-F1 (Setup)

3 – **D**isplay

8 – **S**ide-by-side Columns Display **Y** or **N**

F7 (Exit)

USAGE

WordPerfect can automatically format two different types of text columns: *newspaper* (sometimes called "winding" or "snaking" columns) and *parallel* (or "comparison") columns. Neither of these is to be confused with tabular columns, which are set simply by pressing Tab to go the next tab stop. Newspaper columns are used with continuous text (as in a newsletter), for which it does not matter where the material in the column ends, because the program wraps the text to the top of the next column. Parallel columns are used when the material consists of separate items that should remain together on a page (such as scripts).

There are several basic steps involved in using either type of text column:

1. Position the cursor at the beginning of the area to be formatted in columns or anywhere before this point in the document.

2. Define the columns.

3. Turn on the columns.

4. Enter the text for the columns.

5. Turn off the columns.

Defining the Columns

The steps involved in defining Newspaper and Parallel columns are very similar

1. Press Math/Columns (Alt-F7).

2. Select the Column Def option (**4** or **D**).

3. Select the Type option (**1** or **T**). WordPerfect displays the options

   Column Type: **1** Newspaper; **2** Parallel; **3** Parallel with **B**lock Protect: **0**

4. Select the appropriate column type: **1** or **N** for newspaper, **2** or **P** for parallel (without block protection), or **3** or **B** for parallel with block protection.

5. Select the Number option (**2** or **N**) and enter the number of columns you want (the default is 2 and you can set up to 24).

6. WordPerfect automatically calculates the distance between columns depending upon the number and the margin settings. If you wish to override this distance, select the Distance Between Columns option (**3** or **D**) and enter the distance you want to use.

7. WordPerfect automatically calculates the left and right margin settings for the columns depending upon the number of columns, the distance between them, and the margin settings. If you wish to have unequal columns, select the Margins option (**4** or **M**) and the the left and right margin settings for the column (or columns) you wish to change.

8. Press Exit (F7) to save your column definition.

When you define text columns, WordPerfect inserts a [Col Def] code in your document. This code includes the number (but not the type) of columns followed by the left and right margin setting of each column defined.

Turning On the Columns

After defining the columns, you are returned to the Math/Columns menu. If you wish to use your columns at the cursor's present position, select the Column On/Off option (**3** or **C**). If you wish to use the columns somewhere later on in the document, exit from this menu, move the cursor to the place where you want your columns to begin, and then return to this option. When you turn on columns, WordPerfect inserts the code [Col On] in the document.

You can't use the Column On/Off option on the Math/Columns menu until after you have defined your columns. If you have defined several different columns in a document, WordPerfect will use the one whose [Col Def] code immediately precedes the [Col On] code.

Editing the Text Columns

When typing or editing the text for your columns, you can use most WordPerfect editing features. However, you can't sort, add footnotes, or change the margin settings. In addition, movement between columns is a little different in Column mode; these techniques are summarized in Table 2. The delete keys work within a single column. This means that pressing Delete to the End of Page (Ctrl-Page Down) deletes from the cursor to the end of the column.

KEY SEQUENCE	RESULT
Ctrl-Home → or ←	Moves cursor between columns
Ctrl-Home Home ←	Moves to the first column
Ctrl-Home Home →	Moves to the last column
→	Moves to the first character of the next column when the cursor is on the last character in one column
←	Moves to the last character of the previous column when the cursor is on the first character in one column
Ctrl-Return	Ends a column and moves to the next column; In a rightmost newspaper-style column, also creates a page break

Note: Other cursor control key sequences work as they do in Editing mode and scroll all columns simultaneously.

Table 2: Cursor Movement in Column Mode

You can use Move (Ctrl-F4) to cut or copy a sentence or paragraph in a single column. However, to cut or copy an entire column (equivalent to a page), you must use Block (Alt-F4) with Block Move or Copy. Do not try to use the Tabular Column option to move a column, as a text column is not defined by Tab stops and can't be properly retrieved as a tabular column.

Newspaper Columns

When entering text in newspaper-style columns, WordPerfect inserts a Soft Page code [SPg] when you reach the bottom margin of the page and the cursor moves to the top of the next column. To end a column before you reach the bottom margin, press Hard Page (Ctrl-Enter) to insert a Hard Page code [HPg]. To shorten the length of all newspaper columns on the page, increase the bottom margin.

Parallel Columns

When entering text in parallel columns, you press Hard Page (Ctrl-Enter) to move to the next column across. When you press Hard Page after entering the text for the last column, the cursor returns to the beginning of the first column. If you are using parallel columns without block protection, the codes

    [Col Off]
    [HRt]
    [Col On]

are inserted into the document at this point. If you are using parallel columns with block protection, the codes

    [BlockPro:Off][Col Off]
    [Hrt]
    [BlockPro:On][Col On]

are inserted into the document. All items between the [Block-Pro:On] and [BlockPro:Off] codes are kept together on a page. If the material will be split across pages by a soft page break [SPg], Word-Perfect will move it all to the next page.

Turning Off the Columns

When you are finished entering your columns and wish to return to the normal format of your document, you need to turn off the columns. To do this, press Math/Columns (Alt-F7) and select the

Column On/Off option (**3** or **C**). WordPerfect inserts a [Col Off] code in your document at the cursor's position.

Changing the Display of Columns

When working with text columns, you can speed up scrolling and rewriting the screen by having WordPerfect display each column on a separate page (as opposed to side by side, the default). To turn off the side-by-side display, press Setup (Shift-F1), select the Display option (**3** or **D**), select the Side-by-side Columns Display option (**8** or **S**), type **N** to change Yes to No, and press ← and F7 (Exit). To change the display back to side-by-side, repeat this procedure, this time typing **Y** for Yes.

To delete columns in a document, locate the [Col Def] code in the Reveal Codes screen and delete it.

SEE ALSO

Tabs (for creating tabular columns)

Compose

Allows you to create digraphs and diacriticals or select a special symbol or character from one of WordPerfect's character sets.

KEY SEQUENCE

To create a digraph or diacritical:

Ctrl-2 (Compose)

<first character> <second character>

To select a character from one of WordPerfect's character sets:

Ctrl-2 (Compose)

<character set number>, <character number> ←

USAGE

You can use Compose (Ctrl-2—not to be confused with Ctrl-F2, Spell) to create digraphs like æ or diacriticals like é or ñ. To produce such characters, you press Compose (Ctrl-2) and then enter the two characters that make up the special character. For example, to produce æ, you follow these steps:

1. Press Compose (Ctrl-2).

2. Type **ae** (or **ea**—the order in which the characters are entered doesn't matter).

As soon as you type the *a* and the *e,* the æ will appear at the cursor's position. However, the fact that you can create these special characters on your screen doesn't mean that your printer can reproduce them. This depends upon the printer and fonts that you are using.

You can also use the Compose feature to produce specific characters in one of the many characters sets created by WordPerfect. Each set is assigned a number, as is each character in that set. To view the character sets, you need to retrieve the document CHARACTR.DOC on the Conversion disk. You can also retrieve the document CHARMAP.TST to see which of these characters your printer can produce.

To enter a character from one of these sets, you follow these steps:

1. Press Compose (Ctrl-2).

2. Enter the number of the character set.

3. Type a comma, enter the number of the character in that set, and press ⏎.

For example, to enter the ½ symbol, which is character 17 of character set 4, you press Compose (Ctrl-2), then enter **4,17** and press ⏎. If your printer can't produce the character you entered with Compose, you will see a solid rectangle instead of the desired character in your document.

WordPerfect doesn't enter any codes when you type a special character with Compose. Therefore, to remove the character, you simply delete it as you would any other character in the document.

SEE ALSO

Keyboard Layout

Overstrike

Concordance

See **Indexes: Creating a Concordance File**.

Conditional End of Page

Ensures that a specific number of lines of text remain together on a page.

KEY SEQUENCE

[move the cursor to the line above the lines to keep together]

Shift-F8 (Format)

4 – Other

2 – Conditional End of Page

Number of Lines to Keep Together: <*number of lines*>

F7 (Exit)

USAGE

The Conditional End of Page command is used to keep a group of lines together on a page. Once the group of lines is marked, if subsequent changes to an earlier part of the document result in a soft page break within the block, WordPerfect will move the entire block to the beginning of the next page (resulting in a shorter previous page).

To use the Conditional End of Page command, you must count up the number of lines you want to keep together. Before you begin the command procedure, locate the cursor somewhere on the line above those that are always to remain together. Then, follow the key sequence shown above. To remove the conditional end of page, locate the [Cndl EOP] code in the Reveal Codes screen and delete it.

NOTE

You can also use Block Protect to accomplish the same thing. When you use this command, you don't have to know the number of lines involved, as you indicate the text to stay on a page by marking it as a block.

SEE ALSO

Block Protection

Widow/Orphan Protection

Copying Files

Allows you to copy files between disks and directories from within
WordPerfect.

KEY SEQUENCE

To copy a single file located in the current directory:

F5 (List Files) ←

[highlight file]

8 **C**opy

Copy this file to: *<drive letter/path name>* ←

To copy multiple files located in the current directory:

F5 (List Files) ←

*[type * before each file to be copied]*

8 **C**opy

Copy marked files? (Y/N) **Y**

Copy all files to: *<drive letter/path name>* ←

USAGE

WordPerfect allows you to copy files to a new disk or directory from the List Files menu. To copy a single file, highlight the name on the List Files screen and select the Copy option (**8** or **C**). WordPerfect will display the prompt

Copy this file to:

Enter the drive letter (as in **B:**) if you want to copy the file to a new disk. Enter the entire path name (as in **C:\WP\LTRS**), if you want to copy it to a new directory.

To copy multiple files at one time, mark each file by highlighting it and typing an asterisk (★). To copy all of the files in the list, press Alt-F5 and select the Copy option. The prompt

Copy marked files? (Y/N) No

will appear. Type **Y** for Yes, designate the drive/directory for these copies in response to the prompt

Copy all files to:

and press ◄──┘.

SEE ALSO

Directories: Changing Directories

List Files

Cursor Movement

Allows you to position the cursor (indicating where text or formatting codes are entered) through the document.

KEY SEQUENCE

Refer to Table 3.

TO MOVE	KEY SEQUENCE
Character by character	↑ or →
Word by word	Ctrl-↑ or Ctrl-→
To the beginning of a line	Home ←
To the end of a line	Home →
To the end of the sentence	Ctrl-Home .
To the next occurrence of a character	Ctrl-Home *<character>*
To the top of the screen	Home ↑ or − (minus)
To the bottom of the screen	Home ↓ or + (plus)
To previous screens	Home ↑ or − (minus) repeatedly
To following screens	Home ↓ or + (plus) repeatedly
To the previous page	PgUp
To the next page	PgDn
To the top of the page	Ctrl-Home ↑
To the bottom of the page	Ctrl-Home ↓
To a specified page	Ctrl-Home *<page number>* Return
To the last cursor position before the cursor movement command	Ctrl-Home Ctrl-Home
To the beginning of the last-defined block	Ctrl-Home Alt-F4
To the beginning of the document	Home Home ↑
To the end of the document	Home Home ↓

Table 3: WordPerfect's Cursor-Movement Techniques

WordPerfect has many key combinations that move the cursor through a document, as shown in Table 3. However, you can only use these techniques to move through existing text or codes. Word-Perfect will not allow you to move the cursor beyond the last text character or formatting code.

Arrow Keys

WordPerfect uses the four arrow keys to move the cursor one character at a time in the four directions. If you have the original IBM PC, PC/XT, or PC/AT keyboard, these keys are combined with the numeric keypad. If you have the IBM enhanced keyboard, these keys exist both on the numeric keypad and separately; you may use either set of arrow keys to move the cursor provided that Num Lock isn't engaged (indicated by the flashing Pos indicator on the status line and an indicator light on some keyboards).

Word Right/Left

To go to the beginning of the next word to the right, press Ctrl-→. To go to the beginning of the next word to the left, press Ctrl-←.

Home

You press Home plus one of the arrow keys to move the cursor to the limits of the editing screen: Home-→ to go to the end of the line; Home-← to the beginning; Home-↑ to go to the top of the screen; and Home-↓ to the bottom. You can also move the cursor to the end of the line by simply pressing the End key.

To go to the very beginning of the document, before any codes, you press Home three times followed by the ↑ key. To go to the very end of the document, press Home three times followed by ↓.

Screen Up/Down

To move the cursor by screens and scroll the text, you use the Screen Up key, which is the minus key (−) on the numeric keypad, or the Screen Down key, which is the plus key (+) on the numeric keypad. The first time you press Screen Up, it takes the cursor to the top of the screen. The second time and succeeding times, it scrolls the text down by screenfuls. The Screen Down key works the same way, only in the opposite direction. Note that you can't use the Screen Up and Screen Down keys if you have engaged Num Lock to enter numbers in the document from the numeric keypad.

Page Up/Down

The Page Up key on the cursor pad moves the cursor to the previous page. The Page Down key moves it to the beginning of the following page.

Go To

Go To (Ctrl-Home) moves the cursor to the next occurrence of a specific character, to a specific page or text column, or to the previous cursor position (see **Go To**).

SEE ALSO

Esc Key

Go To

Cursor Speed

Allows you to increase or decrease the rate at which certain keys are repeated.

KEY SEQUENCE

Shift-F1 (Setup)

2 – Cursor Speed

1 15; **2** 20; **3** 30; **4** 40; **5** 50; **6** Normal

F7 (Exit)

USAGE

Many keys in WordPerfect, like the arrow keys, Screen Up/Down, Page Up/Down, and all the ordinary character keys, repeat when you hold them down. The Cursor Speed option on the Setup menu allows you to increase or decrease the rate of the repetition. This rate is measured in characters per second. The normal speed (selected with the Normal option) is the characters per second considered normal for your keyboard. You can increase this up to 50 characters per second. When you select a new rate, it remains in effect each time you use WordPerfect.

NOTE

The Cursor Speed option is incompatible with some memory-resident programs. Also, you may find that this feature doesn't work properly on some IBM-compatible computers.

Cut and Copy Text

Allows you to move or copy text within a document or between two documents.

KEY SEQUENCE

To move or copy a sentence, paragraph, or page:

Ctrl-F4 (Move)

1 Sentence; **2** Paragraph; **3** Page

1 Move; **2** Copy

[move cursor to place where text is to be moved or copied] ←

To move or copy a marked block, column, or rectangle:

Alt-F4 (Block)

[highlight block of text with cursor keys]

Ctrl-F4 (Move)

1 Block; **2** Tabular Column; **3** Rectangle

1 Move; **2** Copy

[move cursor to place where text is to be moved or copied] ←

USAGE

WordPerfect provides you with two methods for moving or copying text. When you move text, it is cut from its original position and relocated in the new position you indicate. When you copy text, it remains in its original position and is copied to the new position you indicate. To move or copy text between document windows, press Switch (Shift-F3) before pressing ←┘ to retrieve the text.

If you want to move or copy a tabular column (see **Marking a Tabular Column**), a rectangle (see **Marking a Rectangle**), or any block that is not an entire sentence, paragraph, or page, you need to mark the block before you move or copy it.

Text that has been moved or copied remains in a special place in the computer's memory (known as a *buffer*) even after it has been retrieved the first time. To retrieve another copy of the text elsewhere in the document, you take these steps:

1. Relocate the cursor to the place where you want the second copy to appear.

2. Press Move (Ctrl-F4).

3. Select the Retrieve option by typing **4** or **R**.

4. Select the appropriate option: **1** or **B** for Block (use this option even if you cut or copied an entire sentence, paragraph, or page); **2** or **C** for tabular column; or **3** or **R** for rectangle.

You can also do this by pressing Retrieve (Shift-F10) and then the ←┘ key.

Marking a Tabular Column

To mark a tabular column for moving or copying, you must have each column separated by at least one tab stop. Move the cursor to the first tab stop in the first line of the column. Press Block, then move the cursor to the beginning of the column in the last line. Then press Move and select the Tabular Column option. Word-Perfect will highlight just the column. Finally, choose either the Copy or Move option and complete the procedure by moving the cursor to the column's new position and pressing ←┘.

Marking a Rectangle

A rectangular block is marked for moving or copying from corner to corner. To mark a rectangle, position the cursor at one corner—either the upper left or the lower right—and press Block. Then move the cursor to the opposite corner and press Move. Select the Rectangle option (**3** or **R**), choose either Copy or Move, and complete the procedure by moving the cursor to the rectangle's new position and pressing ←⏎.

To abandon the move or copy operation that you have initiated, press Cancel (F1). If the marked block disappears from your editing screen when you use Cancel, press Move (Ctrl-F4) and select the Retrieve and Block (or Column or Rectangle) options to have it reappear in its original position.

SEE ALSO

Appending a Block

Deleting Text: Deleting a Block

Date, Inserting the

Inserts the current date either as text or as a function that is updated when the document is retrieved or printed.

To enter the date text or Date code in the document:

Shift-F5 (Date/Outline)

1 Date **T**ext; **2** Date **C**ode

To change the date format:

Shift-F5 (Date/Outline)

3 Date Format

Date format: <*date format codes*> ←

F7 (Exit)

To change the default date format permanently:

Shift-F1 (Setup)

5 – Initial Settings

2 – **D**ate Format

Date format: <*date format codes*> ←

F7 (Exit)

USAGE

You can use the Date Text and Date Code options on the Date/
Outline menu (Shift-F5) to insert the current date and/or time in
your document. If you select the Date Text option (**1** or **T**), the date

is entered as text and doesn't change. If you select the Date Code option (**2** or **C**), the date is entered as a function code that is updated whenever you retrieve or print the document.

You can format the date in a variety of ways by using the Date Format option (**3** or **F**). Table 4 summarizes the format codes and shows you examples of their use. To change the default format code (3 1, 4), follow the steps shown in the key sequence and then enter the date format codes as shown in Table 4.

To insert the current date or time during a merge, use the ^D merge code (see Merge Operations: Merge Codes).

To remove the date inserted as text, delete it as you would any text in WordPerfect. To remove the Date code, locate and delete the [Date] code in the Reveal Codes screen.

SEE ALSO

Merge Operations: Merge Codes

Decimal/Align Character

Allows you to enter a new character for the decimal point (and tab alignment character) and thousands' separator.

KEY SEQUENCE

Shift-F8 (Format)

4 – Other

3 – Decimal/Align Character <*character*> ←
Thousands' Separator <*character*> ←

F7 (Exit)

PATTERN	FORMAT CODES	EXAMPLE
For dates without leading zeros:		
Month DD, YYYY	3 1, 4	March 1, 1989
Weekday Month DD, YYYY	6 3 1, 4	Tuesday March 1, 1989
MM/DD/YYYY	2/1/4	3/1/1989
MM/DD/YY	2/1/5	3/1/89
DD/MM/YY	1/2/5	1/3/89
Report Date: MM/DD/YY	Report Date: 2/1/5	Report Date: 3/1/89
For dates with leading zeros:		
Month, DD, YYYY	3 %1, 4	March 01, 1989
MM/DD/YY	%2/%1/5	03/01/89
For time without leading zeros:		
HH:MM AM/PM	8:9 0	1:7 PM
HH:MM (24 hr. clock)	7:9	13:7
For time with leading zeros:		
HH:MM AM/PM	%8:%9 0	01:07 PM
For date and time:		
MM/DD/YY - HH:MM AM/PM	%2/%1/5 - 8:%9 0	03/01/89 - 1:07 PM

Table 4: Date Format Options

WordPerfect uses the period as the decimal and alignment character and the comma as the thousands' separator. To change these, follow the key sequence shown above. A change to the decimal/align character affects how Tab Align and totals calculated with the Math feature work.

Math

Tab Align

Deleting Files

Allows you to delete files from within WordPerfect without having to exit to DOS.

To delete a single file in the current directory:

F5 (List Files) ↵

[highlight file name]

2 Delete

Delete <*file name*>? (Y/N) **Y**

To delete several files in the current directory at one time:

F5 (List Files) ↵

*[Enter * before each file to be deleted]*

2 Delete

Delete marked files? (Y/N) **Y**

USAGE

By using the Delete option on the List Files menu, you can delete unneeded document files from within WordPerfect without having to use the DOS delete commands.

To delete a document form the List Files menu, press F5, and enter a new drive/directory if the files aren't in the current directory; otherwise, just press ↵. Move the highlight cursor to the file to be deleted. If you want to delete several files, mark each one by typing an asterisk (*) by its name. Then select the Delete option (**2** or **D**) and confirm the deletion by typing **Y** for Yes.

You can't restore a deleted file in WordPerfect as you can deleted text. Therefore, use the Delete option on List Files with care. If you do delete a file in error, turn to DOS utilities like Norton Utilities or Mace Utilities to restore the file.

SEE ALSO

Directories: Changing Directories

Deleting Text

Allows you delete any amount of text in the document.

KEY SEQUENCE

See Table 5.

TO DELETE	PRESS
Character by character	Backspace (deletes to left of cursor); Del (deletes character or space the cursor is on)
Word by word	Ctrl-Backspace
Several words	Esc *n* (*n* = number of words to left of the cursor) Ctrl-Backspace
The word to the left of the cursor	Ctrl-← Ctrl-Backspace
The word to the right of the cursor	Ctrl-→ Ctrl-Backspace
From the cursor left to the beginning of a word	Home Backspace
From the cursor right to the end of a word	Home Del
To the end of a line	Ctrl-End
A marked page	Ctrl-PgDn
A sentence	Ctrl-F4 S D
A paragraph	Ctrl-F4 P D
A page	Ctrl-F4 A D
A marked block	Alt-F4 Backspace or Del Y

Table 5: Methods for Deleting Text in WordPerfect

WordPerfect includes a wide variety of methods for deleting text in the document or formatting codes in the Reveal Codes screen (see **Codes**). All methods are summarized in Table 5 and the most common are discussed in the following sections.

To restore the text you just deleted, press Cancel (F1) and select the Restore option (**1** or **R**).

Backspace   Press the Backspace key to delete the character or code to the left of the cursor's position.

Del(ete) Key   Press the Del key to delete the character or code at the cursor's position.

Delete Block   Press the Backspace or Del key and type **Y** for Yes in response to the prompt

   Delete Block? (Y/N) No

to delete a marked block of text (see **Block Operations**).

Delete Word   Press Ctrl-Backspace to delete the word the cursor is on. If the cursor is positioned on a space between words when you press Ctrl-Backspace, the word to the left of the cursor is removed.

Delete to End of Line   Press Ctrl-End to delete the text and codes from the cursor's position to the end of the line.

Delete to End of Page   Press Ctrl-PgDn and type **Y** for Yes in response to the prompt

   Delete Remainder of page? (Y/N) No

to delete from the cursor's position to the end of the page.

Delete to Word Boundary   Press Home Backspace to delete left of the cursor's position to the word boundary (a space). Press Home Del to delete right of the cursor's position to the word boundary (a space).

SEE ALSO

Codes

Undelete

Directories

Allows you to create and delete directories from within WordPerfect and to change the current (or default) directory.

KEY SEQUENCE

To create a new directory:

F5 (List Files) =
or
F5 (List Files) ←⎯ **7**–**O**ther Directory

⎯▭⎯

<drive/directory path name> ←⎯

⎯▭⎯

Create *<drive/directory path name>*? (Y/N) **Y**

To make an existing directory current (the default):

F5 (List Files) =
or
F5 (List Files) ←⎯ **7** – **O**ther Directory

⎯▭⎯

New directory = *<drive/directory path name>* ←⎯

⎯▭⎯

Dir: *<drive/directory path name>*\ * . *

⎯▭⎯

Cancel (**F1**) – to return to screen
or ←⎯ – to obtain a directory listing

To delete a directory (after removing all its files):

F5 (List Files) ⏎

[highlight directory name]

2 – Delete

Delete *<drive/directory path name>*? (Y/N) **Yes**

USAGE

WordPerfect allows you to manage your document files by saving them in different directories. Most often these directories contain your documents and are organized as subdirectories of the WordPerfect directory (such as C:\WP\Files) that contains the WordPerfect program files. You can create and remove such directories from within WordPerfect instead of resorting to the DOS Make Directory commands. However, WordPerfect won't let you delete any directory until you have removed all of the files within it (see **Deleting Files**).

Creating Directories

To create a new directory, you perform the procedure to change directories (outlined in the key sequence above). When WordPerfect finds that the directory doesn't exist, it prompts you to create it. If you type **Y** for Yes, the program creates the directory for you.

Path Names

When entering the path name for the directory, begin with the drive letter and a colon (such as **B:**, **C:**, or **D:**) if it is on another drive and then list all of the directories in the hierarchy, separated by the back slash (\). If the directory is on the same disk, you need only enter the directory names separated by back slashes.

Changing Directories

You can change the current (or default) directory in WordPerfect using List Files (F5) from either the editing screen or the List Files menu. To change the directory from the editing screen, press List Files (F5) and type = . Then enter the new drive/directory path in response to the *New directory* = prompt and press ←. You can edit the current path name that is placed after this prompt; you don't have to retype it from scratch unless the new one is totally different.

WordPerfect responds by showing you the new default directory, terminated by *.* (the global wild cards for listing all files in the directory). To return to the editing screen, press Cancel (F1). To obtain a listing of all of the files in the new default directory, press ←.

If you don't know the name of the directory or where it is located on the path, you can change the default directory using the Other Directory option on the List Files menu by pressing List Files (F5) and ←. If the name of the desired directory appears at the top of the list, move the highlight cursor to it. If it is located on a level above that of the current directory, highlight .. *<PARENT> <DIR>* and press ← twice. Then locate and highlight the directory name on the new list. If the desired directory is a subdirectory of one shown on the list, highlight that directory, press ← twice, then move the highlight cursor to its name on the new list. Select the Other Directory option (**7** or **O**), and WordPerfect will supply the path to the highlighted directory as the new directory to change to; to accept it press ←. To return to the editing screen, press Cancel (F1) twice. To obtain a directory listing of all of the files in the new default directory, press ←.

Deleting Directories

To delete a directory, first make sure that there are no files in it. You can do this by changing to the directory and listing the files as outlined above. With the highlight cursor on the directory name, select the Delete option (**2** or **D**) on the List Files menu (F5 ←) and answer Yes to the prompt to delete the directory.

SEE ALSO

Deleting Files

Looking at the Contents of Files and Directories

Display Pitch

Adjusts the amount of space that one character occupies on the display screen.

KEY SEQUENCE

Shift-F8 (Format)

3 – Document

1 – Display Pitch - Automatic Y *or* **N**
Width *<width>* ⏎

F7 (Exit)

USAGE

WordPerfect displays all characters on the screen in a monospaced pitch of 10 characters per inch, regardless of what font you are using. Sometimes, when you're setting up complex tables or using the Advance feature, some characters will overlap and therefore not be visible on the screen. To help you see the spacing between characters, you can change the display pitch on the Document menu, accessed from Format—Shift-F8.

There are two options attached to Display Pitch: Automatic, which is set to Yes or No, and Width, which allows you to enter a measurement for increasing or decreasing the display pitch. When Automatic is set to Yes, you can only decrease the Width setting, to display the text closer together. If you set Automatic to No, you can increase the Width setting, to display the text farther apart. Doing this may make it necessary to scroll the text horizontally, as it may expand the line length past the right edge of the screen.

You can change the display pitch from anywhere in the document; the new pitch affects the entire document. To return the document to the normal display width of one-tenth of an inch, return to the Display Pitch option and enter **Y** for the Auto setting and **.1** as the Width measurement.

| SEE ALSO |

Unit of Measurement

Display, Setup

Enables you change the settings for a variety of screen display options.

```
KEY SEQUENCE
```

Shift-F1 (Setup)

3 – Display

1 – Automatically Format and Rewrite
2 – Colors/Fonts/Attributes
3 – Display Document Comments
4 – Filename on the Status Line
5 – Graphics Screen Type
6 – Hard Return Display Character
7 – Menu Letter Display
8 – Side-by-side Columns Display

F7 (Exit)

```
USAGE
```

The Setup Display menu allows you to change a number of default options having to do with the editing display screen. The purpose of each option is outlined below.

Automatically Format and Rewrite

The default for the Automatically Format and Rewrite option is Yes. This means that WordPerfect rewrites the screen and reformats the text as you edit it (however, word wrap still happens only when you use ↑ or ↓ to move to a new line or one of the other cursor movement techniques to move somewhere else in the text).

If you change this option to No, the program rewrites the screen and reformats the text only when you scroll through enough of the text that WordPerfect is forced to rewrite the screen or when you press Screen (Ctrl-F3) and select the Rewrite option (**1** or **R**). You can also force the screen to be rewritten at any time by pressing Screen (Ctrl-F3) twice.

Colors/Fonts/Attributes

This option allows you to select the way various attributes, like bold-facing, underlining, marked block, and others, are displayed on the screen. The options available from this menu vary according to the display card and monitor you are using. See **Color/Fonts/Attributes** for details on selecting new attributes.

Display Document Comments

If you change the default of Yes to No for this option, all comments you have entered in the document will no longer be visible. Although they can't be seen, they still exist in the document. See **Document Comments** for information on how to enter comments in the document.

Filename on Status Line

After you save your document the first time, WordPerfect displays the document file name in the lower left corner of the editing screen (unless you switch to Typeover). To suppress this display, change the setting for this option from Yes to No.

Graphics Screen Type

WordPerfect automatically selects the correct graphics driver for the display card and monitor installed in your system. However, you may need to use this option when you have two monitors connected to your system and wish to change to a new one. When you select this option (**5** or **G**), the program displays a listing of the various screen types it supports. To change the screen type, move the highlight cursor to the driver name and choose it by entering **1** or **S**. The currently selected screen type is marked with an asterisk (*) before its name.

If the graphics screen type you wish to use is not shown on the list, you may find it on the Fonts/Graphics disk. All screen type files have the extension .WPD. To make a new screen driver available, copy the appropriate .WPD file from the Fonts/Graphics disk to the directory that contains the WP.EXE (WordPerfect startup) file and then return to this menu to select it.

Hard Return Display Character

When you press ⏎ to end a paragraph or short line in WordPerfect, the program inserts a Hard Return code [HRt] in the document. However, because WordPerfect uses a space as the default hard return display character, you can't see the location of hard returns on the editing screen.

To make hard returns visible, you select this option (**6** or **H**) and enter the character to be used. If you want to use a character that can be entered directly from the keyboard (like <), just type it in. If you want to use a character that can't be entered directly (like ¶), use Compose (Ctrl-2) and the appropriate character set numbers to enter it (see **Compose**).

To restore the hard return to the default of a space, return to this option and press the space bar before pressing ⏎ and Exit (F7).

Menu Letter Display

To let you know which letter of a menu option name can be pressed to select the option, WordPerfect displays this letter in bold (either double-intensity or the color selected for boldfacing). You can change this attribute to any of the 16 size and appearance choices on the Font menu (see **Font**). To change the menu letter display, select this option (**7** or **M**). WordPerfect displays the menu choices

1 Size; **2** Appearance; **3** Normal: **0**

To select a new size for the menu letters, choose the Size option and select the desired size from this menu. To change the appearance of the menu letter, select the Appearance option and select the desired appearance (e.g, underlining, italics, etc.). To have WordPerfect use no special enhancement for the menu letters (so you won't be able to tell which letter can be used), select the Normal option.

Side-by-Side Columns Display

When working with text columns (newspaper or parallel), WordPerfect displays the columns side by side on the screen as they will be printed. However, you can scroll through columns more quickly if they are displayed as separate pages on the screen. To turn off the side-by-side column display, change this option from Yes to No. See **Columns, Text (Newspaper and Parallel)** for more information on working with text columns.

SEE ALSO

Colors/Fonts/Attributes

Columns, Text (Newspaper and Parallel)

Compose

Document Comments

Hard Return

Rewrite, Screen

Document Comments

Places nonprinting comments in your document.

KEY SEQUENCE

To create or edit a comment or convert a comment to text:

Ctrl-F5 (Text In/Out)

5 – **Comments**

1 Create; **2 E**dit; **3** Convert to **Text**

To convert text to a comment:

Alt-F4 (Block)

[highlight text to be placed in comment]

Ctrl-F5 (Text In/Out)

Create a comment? (Y/N) **Y**

To turn on and off the display of comments in the document:

Shift-F1 (Setup)

3 – **D**isplay

3 – **D**isplay Document Comments **Y** *or* **N**

F7 (Exit)

USAGE

WordPerfect allows you to enter nonprinting comments anywhere in the text of your document. These comments can be used as reminders of editing changes that still remain to be done. You can use the Search feature to quickly locate comments in the text because WordPerfect inserts the code [Comment] in the document when you create a comment (see **Search: Searching for Codes**).

On the editing screen, the text entered as a comment is displayed within a double-lined box. If you create the comment in the middle of a line, the comment box will split the sentence on different lines, although the cursor will bypass the comment box when moving from the part of the sentence before the comment to the part after it.

WordPerfect allows you to convert the text entered into a comment box into document text, which will be printed. To do this, you follow the procedure for editing a comment except that you select the Convert to Text option (**3** or **T**) on the Comment menu. The box surrounding the comment disappears, and WordPerfect reformats the text as required.

You can also convert document text to comment text, so that it is no longer part of the document, nor is it printed, as indicated in the key sequence. When you do this, the prompt

Create a comment? (Y/N) No

will appear. When you type **Y** for Yes, the text will be enclosed in a comment box.

To remove a comment from the document, locate and delete the [Comment] code in the Reveal Codes screen.

SEE ALSO

Document Summary

Document Compare

Compares the copy of your document on the editing screen with the disk version and marks the differences.

KEY SEQUENCE

To compare a document on screen with a document on disk:

Alt-F5 (Mark Text)

6 – **G**enerate

2 – **C**ompare Screen and Disk Document
and Add Redline and Strikeout

Other Document: <*file name*> ←┘

To remove all redline markings and strikeout text added when using Document Compare:

Alt-F5 (Mark Text)

6 – **G**enerate

1 – **R**emove Redline Markings and
Strikeout Text from Document

Delete redline markings and strikeout text? (Y/N) **Y**

USAGE

This feature checks the document on the editing screen against any version of the document on disk. This feature compares only phrases in the two documents and automatically indicates any discrepancies between the two by marking the document on your screen. WordPerfect considers a phrase to be any text between markers, including any punctuation marks, hard returns, hard page breaks, Footnote and Endnote codes, and the end of the document.

If phrases that don't exist in the disk version have been added to the document on screen, WordPerfect redlines the text in the screen version. If phrases that still exist in the disk version no longer exist in the document on screen, the program marks the text with strike-out. If phrases have been moved in the document on screen from their position in the disk version, WordPerfect inserts

THE FOLLOWING TEXT WAS MOVED

on a line before the text and

THE PRECEDING TEXT WAS MOVED

on a line after the text. These messages are displayed in strikeout, and the text in between them may be displayed in either redline or strikeout, depending on the version in which it exists.

After running the Document Compare procedure as outlined by the key sequence above, you can locate the Redline codes and strike-out text by using the Search feature (see **Search: Searching for Codes**). After examining the changes, you can remove all Redline and Strikeout codes as indicated in the key sequence above.

SEE ALSO

Redline/Strikeout

Document, Format

See **Format**.

Document Summary

Enables you to add a nonprinting summary to your document.

KEY SEQUENCE

To create or edit a document summary:

Shift-F8 (Format)

3 – Document

5 – Summary

1 – Descriptive Filename
2 – Subject/Account
3 – Author
4 – Typist
5 – Comments

F7 (Exit)

To create a document summary on Save/Exit or change subject search text:

Shift-F1 (Setup)

5 – Initial Settings

3 – Document Summary

1 – Create on Save/Exit **Y** *or* **N**
2 – Subject Search Text *<search text>* ↵

F7 (Exit)

USAGE

You can add a document summary to any document that you create in WordPerfect. The document summary can be added or edited from any place within the document. Unlike version 4.2,

WordPerfect 5.0 no longer inserts a Document Summary code in the document and, therefore, provides you with no way to remove a document summary once it has been created. The document summary is never printed. The only way to obtain a hard copy of the summary is to use Shift-PrtSc when the Document Summary menu is on the editing screen.

The document summary can include the following statistics on the document (note that the first two are entered automatically by WordPerfect and the rest are entered by you):

- The system file name—the program inserts *Not Named Yet* if the document has never been saved.

- The date that the document was created (WordPerfect uses the current date as supplied by DOS). This date doesn't change when you save editing changes on subsequent dates.

- A descriptive file name that can contain up to 40 characters. If you enter a descriptive file name and no system file name has yet been assigned, the first part of the descriptive name is used as the system file name, and this name will be suggested as the file name the first time you save the document.

- The subject of the document or account assigned to it. If the Subject Search Text characters defined for the document summary (the default characters are *RE:*) occur within the first 400 characters of the document, the word or phrase following them is automatically inserted after the Subject/Account heading in the document summary. You can also enter your own word or phrase.

- The initials of the typist and/or author of the document.

- Comments containing up to 780 characters. The first 400 characters in the document are automatically displayed in the comment box.

If you wish to keep document summaries for all documents that you create, you can have WordPerfect automatically prompt you to create a summary when you save the document or exit the program. This procedure is outlined in the key sequence above.

Locating a File Using Its Document Summary Statistics

When you use the Look option (**5** or **L**) on the List Files menu (F5 ←┘) to view the contents of a document that contains a document summary, the summary statistics are always the first text displayed on the screen. You can also use the Word Search option on the List Files menu to locate a file according to particular statistics in the document summary.

If you select the Conditions option (**4** or **C**) under Word Search (**9** or **W**), you can enter the matching conditions for any of the document summary statistics, including a range of creation dates (see **Word Search** for more information).

To make it easier to locate documents of a particular subject-type using Word Search, you should enter a consistent subject description or account number for the Subject/Account statistic. If the characters *RE:* occur in the first 400 characters of the document, the program will automatically enter the word or phrase that follows (up to hard return). You can change this default subject search text from the Setup menu (refer to the key sequence above) to enter a more suitable search word or phrase. Then, you can locate the files that contain the search text by entering it after the Subject/Account heading in the Word Search Conditions menu.

SEE ALSO

Looking at the Contents of Files and Directories

Word Search

Esc Key

Repeats a character (other than a number) or cursor movement key pressed a specified number of times.

| KEY SEQUENCE |

To repeat a character or cursor movement for the default repeat value:

Esc *<character or cursor movement key>*

To repeat a character or cursor movement for a new repeat value:

Esc *<number of times to repeat> <character or cursor movement key>*

To reset the default repeat value for the Esc key:

Shift-F1 (Setup)

5 – Initial Settings

5 – Repeat Value *<repeat number>* ←┘

F7 (Exit)

| USAGE |

The Esc(ape) key in WordPerfect is used primarily to repeat a keyboard character (other than a number) or a cursor movement command. It is only secondarily used to cancel the current WordPerfect command (see **Cancel**). When you press the Esc key, WordPerfect displays the prompt

Repeat Value = 8

If the next key you press is a keyboard character other than a number (like !), WordPerfect will enter that character eight times (entering !!!!!!!!). If the next key you press is a cursor movement key (like ↓ or PgDn), WordPerfect will repeat the cursor movement eight times (moving eight lines or pages down).

You can vary the number of times a character or cursor command is repeated by entering a new repeat number before typing the character or pressing the cursor movement key. WordPerfect uses the new repeat value only that time and then returns to the default number.

To change the default repeat value permanently, you change the repeat value from the Setup menu (Shift-F1) as outlined in the key sequence.

NOTE

If you press the Del(ete) key after pressing Esc, WordPerfect will delete the next eight characters from the cursor's position to the right. If you press the space bar after the Esc key, it will insert eight spaces.

SEE ALSO

Cancel

Exit

Quits WordPerfect and returns to DOS or clears the document editing screen to begin a new document.

F7 (Exit)

—⊏⊐—

Save document? (Y/N) **Yes**

—⊏⊐—

Document to be saved: <*file name*> ◄—┘

—⊏⊐—

Replace <*file name*> (Y/N) **No** or **Yes**

—⊏⊐—

Exit WordPerfect? (Y/N) **No** or **Yes**

| USAGE |

Exit (F7) is used to clear the current editing screen when you want to begin a new document, or to quit WordPerfect when you are finished using the word processor. You also use Exit to leave menus such as Setup, Format, and so on, and after entering the text of headers, footers, footnotes, and endnotes.

Saving and Exiting

When you press Exit during normal document editing, you see the prompt

Save document? (Y/N) Yes

Press ◄—┘ to accept the default setting of Yes, unless you wish to abandon the document and any editing you have made to it (thereby exiting without saving the document). When you press ◄—┘, WordPerfect will prompt you for the name of the document. Enter the document name if you haven't saved it before (see **Save Text**) and press ◄—┘. If you have already saved the document at least once, the prompt will contain the document name. If you want to save the document under a new name, type it in or edit the existing name.

If you want to save it under the same name, simply press ←. Word-Perfect will respond with the prompt

Replace <*file name*>? (Y/N) No

If you change your mind and decide to rename the document, press ←. Otherwise, type **Y** for Yes. After the document is saved, Word-Perfect will prompt you either to exit the current document editing screen (if you are using both Doc 1 and Doc 2) or to exit WordPerfect. The default response is No, so that you can press ← to remain in the current editing screen. If you decide you don't want to have your document cleared from the editing screen, press Cancel (F1) to retain it and return to editing its text.

If you answer Yes to exiting WordPerfect, you will be returned to DOS or to the WordPerfect Library shell, if you use this utility. If you answer Yes to exiting the current document editing screen (either Doc 1 or Doc 2), you will be returned to the other editing screen. If you answer No to exiting WordPerfect or the current document editing screen, you will remain in it, and you can begin creating a new document (using the WordPerfect formatting defaults) or retrieve another document for editing.

Quitting WordPerfect without Using Exit

In WordPerfect it is important that you exit the program properly before you turn off the computer. WordPerfect automatically keeps special files, referred to as *overflow files,* that are not emptied and closed until you press F7 (Exit).

If you simply use Save (F10), and then turn off the power, Word-Perfect will detect the presence of these files the next time you start the program and will beep and display this prompt on the initial startup screen:

Are other copies of WordPerfect currently running? (Y/N)

Responding No tells WordPerfect to erase the contents of the over-flow files and move on to the standard editing screen.

SEE ALSO

Go To DOS/Shell

Save

Fast Save (Unformatted)

Saves an unformatted version of your document at a faster rate.

KEY SEQUENCE

Shift-F1 (Setup)

4 – **Fast Save** (unformatted) **Y** *or* **N**

F7 (Exit)

USAGE

Fast Save saves a copy of the document on the editing screen without formatting it when you use Exit (F7) and save before quitting or Save (F10). A document which has been fast-saved, however, can't be printed from disk unless the cursor was located at the very end of the document when you saved it.

If you aren't concerned with the time it takes to save your document and want to be able to use any of WordPerfect's printing methods at any time, you can leave the Fast Save option turned off.

If you use Fast Save and find that you can't print a document on disk because of it, retrieve the document, press Home Home ↓, and save it again. Then, issue the command to print it from disk.

SEE ALSO

Printing: Printing a Document on Disk

Flush Right

Aligns your text flush with the right margin setting.

KEY SEQUENCE

To align text flush right as you type it:

Alt-F6 (Flush Right)

<text> ⏎

To align existing text flush right:

Alt-F4 (Block)

[highlight all lines to be flush right]

Alt-F6 (Flush Right)

[Flsh Rt]? (Y/N) **Yes**

USAGE

To align text on a line with the right margin setting, follow the key sequence shown above. To right-align text after it has been entered (this can include several lines), mark the text to be flush right with

Block (Alt-F4) and then select Flush Right (Alt-F6). WordPerfect will display the prompt

[Flsh Rt]? (Y/N) No

To have the marked text right-aligned, simply type **Y** for Yes.

To remove the right alignment, locate and delete the [Flsh Rt] or [C/A/Flrt] code in the Reveal Codes screen.

SEE ALSO

Center

Font

Allows you to change the size or appearance of the current fonts used in your document.

KEY SEQUENCE

To change the size of a font:

Ctrl-F8 (Font)

1 Size

1 Supscrpt; **2 S**ubscpt; **3 F**ine; **4 S**mall; **5 L**arge;
6 Vry Large; **7 E**xt Large

To change the appearance of a font:

Ctrl-F8 (Font)

━━▭━━

2 Appearance

━━▭━━

1 Bold **2 U**ndrln **3 D**bl **U**nd **4 I**talc **5 O**utln
6 Shadw **7 S**m **C**ap **8 R**edln **9 S**tkout

To return to the initial font defined for the selected printer:

Ctrl-F8 (Font)

━━▭━━

3 Normal

USAGE	═════════════

Font (Ctrl-F8) controls a variety of options, all of which affect the way your text appears when printed. This section contains information on how to enhance the currently selected font by changing either its size or its appearance. For information on changing the current font, see **Base Font**. For information on using Font to select colors for printing, see **Print Color**. In addition, the options Bold, Undrln, Redln, and Stkout on the Appearance menu are discussed under their own reference entries in this book (see **Bold**, **Underline**, and **Redline/Strikeout**).

All of the options on the Size and Appearance menus accessed from Font (Ctrl-F8) insert a pair of formatting codes (see **Appendix B**) and place the cursor between them. You are then free to enter the text that you want enhanced by the particular attribute selected. To return to the normal text font, you either press the → key once to move the cursor beyond the last code of the pair or select the Normal option (**3** or **N**) on the Font menu (this does the same thing as pressing →). To apply one of these attributes to existing text, mark it as a block using Alt-F4 (Block) before selecting the appropriate Size or Appearance menu option.

To delete any size or appearance attributes assigned to text, locate the pair of codes in the Reveal Codes screen and delete either one of them.

Changing the Size of the Font

When you select the Size option (**1** or **S**) on Font, you are presented with seven options. The first two are used for superscripting and subscripting characters. Superscripted text is printed a half-line above the baseline of the normal text, while subscripted text is printed a half-line below. To change the amount of adjustment up or down, use the Advance feature (see **Advance** with either option).

The five remaining size options are used to change only the size of the current font. The actual point size or pitch used to produce the text that is assigned the attributes Fine, Small, Large, Very Large, and Extra Large depends upon the capabilities of the printer that is currently selected and the range of fonts that have been installed for that printer.

When you change the size of the text using one of these options, WordPerfect automatically adjusts the line spacing to accommodate the larger or smaller size. To overrule this adjustment, you need to use the Line Height option on the Line Format menu (see **Line Height**).

Changing the Appearance of the Font

When you select the Appearance option (**2** or **A**) on the Font menu, you are presented with nine options to enhance your text. The first two attributes, Bold and Undrln, can also be accessed by pressing F6 or F8 respectively (see **Bold** and **Underline**). The remaining attributes can only be accessed from this menu.

The attributes of double underlining (Dbl Und), italics (Italc), outline, shadow, and small caps can't be produced by every printer. To determine whether your printer is capable of producing these effects, print the PRINTER.TST file that is supplied with the program. If you select an enhancement that your printer doesn't support, WordPerfect will ignore it (unless you have specified italics, in which case the program will substitute underlining).

NOTES

The Small Caps option (Sm Cap) produces all uppercase letters in a smaller font size. They are most commonly used with acronyms and with times like 9:00 A.M. When entering text after selecting the Sm Cap option, you don't need to use the Shift key to capitalize the text.

See **Color/Fonts/Attributes** for ways that you can define how these size and appearance attributes are displayed on your editing screen.

SEE ALSO

Base Font

Bold

Cartridges and Fonts

Colors/Fonts/Attributes

Line Height

Print Color

Redline/Strikeout

Underline

Footnotes and Endnotes

Allows you to add footnotes that appear at the bottom of the page or endnotes that appear at a place of your choice in the document.

KEY SEQUENCE

Ctrl-F7 (Footnote)

1 Footnote; **2** Endnote

1 Create; **2** Edit; **3** New Number; **4** Options

Notes to the text are automatically numbered for you in WordPerfect. If you want the text of the note to appear on the same page as its reference number, you create a footnote. If you want the text of all of the notes to appear together somewhere in the document, you create an endnote.

The text of footnotes and endnotes is not shown in the text, only their reference numbers. To see the notes before printing, you must use the View Document option on the Print menu (see **View Document**).

Creating Notes

To create a footnote or endnote in the text, follow these steps:

1. Move the cursor to the position where you want the footnote or endnote reference number to appear.

2. Press Footnote (Ctrl-F7).

3. Select either the Footnote (**1** or **F**) or Endnote (**2** or **E**) option.

4. Select the Create option, **1** or **C**.

5. Type the text of your note (insert a space between the number on the note editing screen and the text).

6. Press Exit (F7) when you are finished entering the note text.

To delete a footnote or endnote from the document, locate and delete the [Footnote] or [Endnote] code in the Reveal Codes screen.

New Number

WordPerfect automatically begins footnote and endnote numbering from 1. To change the starting number for all notes or to renumber a series of notes from a particular place in the document, you use the New Number option (**3** or **N**) on the Footnote or Endnote menu. This feature is especially useful if the document that contains the notes is a subdocument (like a book chapter) of a master document that requires sequential numbering of the notes in all the documents to be printed together (see **Master Document**).

To enter a new starting note number, follow these steps:

1. Move the cursor to the place in the document where the notes are to be renumbered (the top of the document if all notes are to be renumbered).
2. Press Footnote (Ctrl-F7).
3. Select either the Footnote (**1** or **F**) or Endnote (**2** or **E**) option.
4. Select the New Number option, **3** or **N**.
5. Enter the new starting number and press ↵.
6. Press Screen (Ctrl-F3) and ↵ to have the notes renumbered.

WordPerfect inserts a [New Ftn Num] or [New End Num] code in the document at the cursor's position when you use this option.

Endnote Placement

When using endnotes in the document, you designate where the text of the endnotes is to appear by using the Endnote Placement option (**3** or **P** when you press Footnote). If you don't locate the cursor and use the Endnote Placement option to specify where in your document the endnotes are to be inserted, WordPerfect will automatically place them at the end of your document.

When you use the Endnote Placement option, WordPerfect inserts an [Endnote Placement] code at the cursor's position and prompts you with

Restart endnote numbering? (Y/N) Yes

If you choose to restart the endnote numbering from 1, press ↵ to answer Yes to this prompt (WordPerfect inserts the code [New End Num:1] in the document). If you want to retain sequential numbering from the last endnote number, type **N** for No. After you respond to this prompt, WordPerfect inserts the following comment in the text:

Endnote Placement.
It is not known how much space endnotes will occupy here.
Generate to determine.

It also automatically inserts a hard page break after this comment.

To generate the endnotes at this point, you select Mark Text (Alt-F5), select Generate (**6** or **G**), select Generate Tables, Indexes, Automatic References, etc. (**5** or **G**) and then press ⏎ to the prompt.

> Existing tables, lists, and indexes will be replaced.
> Continue? (Y/N) Yes

After the endnotes are generated, you will see the comment

> Endnote Placement

on the screen. This comment will take up as much space as is required to print all of the endnotes up to that point in the document. To view your endnotes, use the View Document option (**6** or **V**) on the Print menu (Shift-F7).

If you want the text of your endnotes to appear on a new page, be sure to insert a hard page break (Ctrl-⏎) before the Endnote Placement comment box.

Changing the Formatting of Notes

When printing your footnotes and endnotes, WordPerfect makes certain assumptions as how they are to be formatted. You can, however, control their formatting by using Options (**4** or **O**) on the Footnote or Endnote menu. When you select Options on the Footnote menu, you are presented with the options and default values shown in Figure 1. When you select Options on the Endnote menu, you are presented with the options and defaults shown in Figure 2.

When specifying the spacing within footnotes or endnotes, enter **1** for single spacing, **1.5** for one-and-a-half spacing, **2** for double spacing, and so on. You specify the spacing between notes and the amount of note to keep together on a page by entering a measurement in inches.

To change the style of the numbers in the text or note for footnotes or endnotes, you select the appropriate options and enter the commands to insert the attributes that you wish to use. Note that you can insert graphics into a note if you select the Character type for the graphics box (see **Graphics**).

```
Footnote Options
        1 - Spacing Within Footnotes              1
                    Between Footnotes             Ø.16"

        2 - Amount of Note to Keep Together       Ø.5"

        3 - Style for Number in Text              [SUPRSCPT][Note Num][suprscpt]

        4 - Style for Number in Note                       [SUPRSCPT][Note Num][suprscp

        5 - Footnote Numbering Method             Numbers

        6 - Start Footnote Numbers each Page      No

        7 - Line Separating Text and Footnotes    2-inch Line

        8 - Print Continued Message               No

        9 - Footnotes at Bottom of Page       .   Yes


Selection: Ø
```

Figure 1: Footnote Options menu

```
Endnote Options
        1 - Spacing Within Endnotes               1
                    Between Endnotes              Ø.16"

        2 - Amount of Endnote to Keep Together    Ø.5"

        3 - Style for Numbers in Text             [SUPRSCPT][Note Num][suprscpt]

        4 - Style for Numbers in Note             [Note Num].

        5 - Endnote Numbering Method              Numbers




Selection: Ø
```

Figure 2: Endnote Options menu

When you select the option to change the numbering method for footnotes or endnotes, you are presented with these options:

1 Numbers; **2** Letters; **3** Characters: **0**

When you select Characters, you can specify up to five different characters to be used. After all of the characters you entered are used, WordPerfect will double and then triple them, if necessary.

For footnotes, you may designate that your footnotes be renumbered on each new page or change the type of line separator used to demarcate the footnote from the body of the text. When you select Line Separating Text and Footnotes, you are presented with the options:

1 No Line; **2** 2-inch Line; **3** Margin to Margin

The footnote option Print Continued Messages can be used to have WordPerfect print a *Continued...* message on the last line of any footnote that is split across pages (this message will also be printed on the first line of the note on the following page). You can use the Footnotes at Bottom of Page option (No) to have the footnotes moved up on a short page so that they are printed right under the body of the text rather than at the very bottom of the page with multiple blank lines separating the footnotes from the text.

SEE ALSO

Graphics

Mark Text

Master Document

View Document

Force Odd/Even Page

Forces the page to be numbered with either an odd or even number.

KEY SEQUENCE

Shift-F8 (Format)

2 – Page

2 – Force Odd/Even Page

1 Odd; **2 E**ven

F7 (Exit)

USAGE

You can use the Force Odd/Even Page feature to ensure that a particular page will always be given either an odd or even page number (see **Page Numbering** for information on adding page numbers to a document). To use this command, position the cursor at the top of the page that is always to have either an odd or even page number.

The Force Odd/Even Page feature can be used in documents that are to be reproduced on both sides of the paper, to guarantee that a particular page is always either a left-hand (even-numbered) page or a right-hand (odd-numbered) page. When you use this feature, the program inserts either a [Force:Odd] or [Force:Even] formatting code at the cursor's position.

WordPerfect will renumber the page only if its number will be the opposite of the type specified by the Force Odd/Even Page code. For example, if you insert a [Force:Even] code at the top of page 1, it will be renumbered to page 2. However, if this code occurs at the top of page 6, it will not be renumbered. Any change to the page number due to the Force Odd/Even Page code is reflected in Pg indicator on the status line.

To return to regular page numbering, locate and delete the [Force] code in the Reveal Codes screen.

Headers and Footers

Page Numbering

Format

Controls most aspects of the document format using four submenus: Line, Page, Document, and Other.

KEY SEQUENCE

See Figure 3.

USAGE

All of the formatting options (with the exception of font changes— see **Font**) are accessed from Format (Shift-F8). Figure 3 shows the four Format submenus (Line, Page, Document, and Other) and lists all of the options available on each one. To find information about a particular formatting option on these submenus, look it up under the name of the option listed in Figure 3.

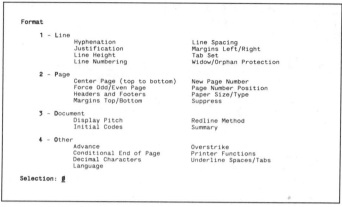

Figure 3: The Format menu

Forms

Allows you to set up a form definition and then use it to print all or part of your document.

KEY SEQUENCE

To define, modify, or delete a form:

Shift-F7 (Print)

S – Select Printer

[highlight printer to print form]

3 – Edit

4 – Forms

1 Add; **2 D**elete; **3 E**dit

F7 (Exit)

To use a form definition:

Shift-F8 (Format)

2 – Page

8 – Paper **S**ize
Type

F7 (Exit)

USAGE

You use the Forms feature on the Select Printer Forms menu to create a form definition, which stipulates such settings as the paper size and type, orientation, offsets, and location of the paper. You can then apply this form definition to a document by specifying the size and type of paper it uses on the Page Format menu.

WordPerfect comes with three predefined forms: Standard letter size in either portrait (narrow) or landscape (wide) mode, Envelope, and ALL OTHERS (invoked when you try to use a form definition that WordPerfect can't find). You can modify the settings of these forms or add new definitions to the list. To remove a form definition, select the Delete option (**2** or **D**) on the Printer Select: Forms menu.

Creating a Form Definition

As indicated by the key sequence, the form definitions that you create are part of the printer definition. When you select the Add option on the Printer Select: Forms menu, you are presented with two full-screen menus: the Form Type menu shown in Figure 4, and the Forms menu shown in Figure 5. When you select the Edit option, you are presented only with the second Forms menu, where you make the modifications to the selected definition.

When adding a new form definition, you must first specify the type of form to be used. The Form Type menu contains the name of seven frequently used forms. To select one of these, simply enter its mnemonic letter or number. If you want to add your own form description, select the Other option (**9** or **O**) and enter its name.

After indicating the type of form to be used, you are presented with the options in the Forms menu (Figure 5). Here, you indicate

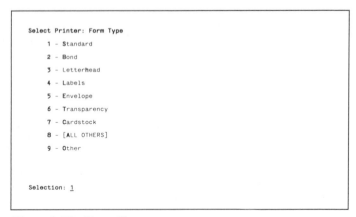

```
Select Printer: Form Type

        1 - Standard

        2 - Bond

        3 - Letterhead

        4 - Labels

        5 - Envelope

        6 - Transparency

        7 - Cardstock

        8 - [ALL OTHERS]

        9 - Other




    Selection: 1
```

Figure 4: The Form Type menu

the paper size, orientation of the text on the form, whether or not it is initially present, its location (that is, type of feed or bin number), and any special page offsets to be used.

If you need to modify the size of the form, select the Form Size option (**1** or **S**). The size options shown in Figure 6 will appear. If none of the predefined size options will do, select the Other option (the letter *O*, not zero) and enter the width and length.

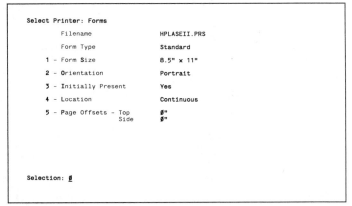

```
Select Printer: Forms

        Filename            HPLASEII.PRS

        Form Type           Standard

1 - Form Size               8.5" x 11"

2 - Orientation             Portrait

3 - Initially Present       Yes

4 - Location                Continuous

5 - Page Offsets - Top      Ø"
                   Side     Ø"




Selection: Ø
```

Figure 5: The Forms menu

```
Select Printer: Form Size
                            Inserted
                            Edge
1 - Standard                8.5"   x   11"

2 - Standard Wide           11"    x   8.5"

3 - Legal                   8.5"   x   14"

4 - Legal Wide              14"    x   8.5"

5 - Envelope                9.5"   x   4"

6 - Half Sheet              5.5"   x   8.5"

7 - US Government           8"     x   11"

8 - A4                      21Ømm  x   297mm

9 - A4 Wide                 297mm  x   21Ømm

0 - Other

Selection: 1
```

Figure 6: The Form Size menu

To modify the placement of the text on the page, select the Orientation option (**2** or **O**). You have three choices:

1 Portrait; **2** Landscape; **3** Both: **0**

If you select Portrait, the text will run parallel to the insertion edge of the form. If you select Landscape, it will run perpendicular to the insertion edge. Select Both only when your printer allows you to manually determine the direction of the insertion edge. For example, to print the text in portrait mode on an 8½" × 11" page, you insert the short edge (8½") in the feeder. To print the text in landscape mode, you insert the long edge (11") in the feeder.

The setting of the third option, Initially Present, should be Yes if the form will be present when the printing begins. If the form must be manually fed to the printer, you should change this setting to No.

The Location option (**4** or **L**) determines the type of paper feed; it has three options attached to it:

1 Continuous; **2** Bin Number; **3** Manual: **0**

If your printer has a sheet feeder with multiple bins, select the Bin Number option and enter its number.

The Page Offsets option (**5** or **P**) is used when the printhead must be positioned in relation to the position of the top and left edge of the paper when the form is loaded in the printer before the printing begins. You can enter either positive or negative offsets for the Top and Side settings. Enter positive offsets for forms which are inserted with their top edge above or their left edge to the right of the printhead position. Enter negative offsets for forms which are inserted with their top edge below or to the right of the printhead position. Note that top and left margin settings for the document are added to the offsets that you specify.

After creating or editing a form definition, always use Exit (F7) instead of Cancel (F1) when leaving the menus. That way, WordPerfect will update the printer definition file with the form's information.

Using a Form Definition

To use a form definition to print your document, you select the appropriate paper size and type from the Page Format menu (refer to the key sequence at the beginning of this entry). After you select the Paper Size option (**8** or **S**) on this menu, you are presented with a full-screen menu that contains the same size options shown in Figure 6. Select the size option here that is appropriate for the form definition you want to use.

After you select the paper size, the Paper Type menu appears. This menu is very similar to the Form Type menu shown in Figure 4. To select a form definition that you named (and defined), choose the Other option (**8** or **O**). This takes you to the Defined Form Types screen, with three options:

1 Select; **2 O**ther; **3 N**ame Search: 1

The screen shows you an alphabetical list of the forms you have defined. Move the cursor to highlight the appropriate name and type **1** or **S** or press ←⏎.

If WordPerfect can't match the paper size and type requested against one of the predefined form definitions, you will see an asterisk (*) in front of the paper size setting on the Page menu and the message

(*requested form is unavailable)

will be displayed beneath the paper type setting. The program will still go ahead and print the document using the paper size specified; however, it will not use any of the formatting instructions attached to the form definition.

SEE ALSO

Page Size/Type

Go To

Moves the cursor to a specific character, page, or text column, or to the previous cursor position.

KEY SEQUENCE

To go to the next occurrence of a character:

Ctrl-Home (Go To) *<character>*

To go to a specific page in the document:

Ctrl-Home (Go To) *<page number>* ↵

To return to the previous cursor position:

Ctrl-Home Ctrl-Home

To move the cursor between text columns:

Ctrl-Home (Go To) → or ←

USAGE

The Go To feature (Ctrl-Home) is used in combination with a particular character or page number to move directly to that character or the top of that page. For example, to move to the next occurrence of a hard return (end of paragraph) in the document, you press Ctrl-Home and press the ↵ key. To go to the next period (end of sentence), press Ctrl-Home and type a period. To move directly to the top of a specific page, press Ctrl-Home, type the page number, and press ↵.

To return the cursor to its previous position in the document, you press Ctrl-Home twice. This is very useful when you're moving a block of text to a new place in the document and you wish to return immediately to the place from which the block was moved.

SEE ALSO

Cursor Movement

Go To DOS/Shell

Allows you to exit WordPerfect temporarily to go to DOS or the WordPerfect Library Shell if you run WordPerfect under this utility.

KEY SEQUENCE

Ctrl-F1 (Shell)

1 Go to DOS

<DOS commands>

EXIT ↵ (to return to WordPerfect)

USAGE

The Go To DOS or Shell feature allows you to leave WordPerfect temporarily and enter DOS commands while the word processor is still loaded in memory. When in DOS, you can issue commands to perform maintenance tasks like copying, renaming files, or formatting disks, as well as to run other software applications. However, when you go to DOS and try to run another program, you may find that your computer doesn't have sufficient memory to load the new program along with WordPerfect. Also, you should not use this feature to load a RAM-resident utility (sometimes called a TSR) like SideKick. Always exit WordPerfect before loading this type of software.

When you have finished executing your commands at the DOS prompt and are ready to return to WordPerfect, type the word **EXIT** (don't press the Exit key—F7) and press ↵. This will return you immediately to the editing screen and any document you have on it.

If you started WordPerfect from the WordPerfect Library shell, you will be returned to the Library Shell menu when you use the Go

To DOS feature. From there, you can go to the DOS prompt by selecting the Go to DOS command on the Shell menu (it too uses the key sequence Ctrl-F1 1). When you are finished with DOS, type **EXIT** to return to the Library Shell menu. To return to WordPerfect, type the program letter you have assigned to WordPerfect 5.0.

Graphics

Allows you to combine graphics created by other programs with the text of your document or to draw rules in the document.

KEY SEQUENCE

To create or edit a graphics box:

Alt-F9 (Graphics)

1 Figure; **2** Table; **3** Text Box; **4** User-Defined

1 Create; **2** Edit; **3** New Number; **4** Options

To create a Horizontal or Vertical Line graphic:

Alt-F9 (Graphics)

5 Line

1 Horizontal Line *or* **2** Vertical Line

1 – Horizontal Position
2 – Vertical Position
3 – Length of Line
4 – Width of Line
5 – Gray Shading (% of black)

The Vertical Position option appears only when you are creating a vertical line.

USAGE

You can use Graphics (Alt-F9) to import a variety of illustrations or graphs created with other graphics programs, as well as digitized images created with scanners, and place them directly in the text of your document. Refer to the Graphics Programs section of the Appendix to your WordPerfect user guide for details on the graphics programs supported. You can also use the Graphics feature to draw vertical and horizontal lines (rules).

In order to insert a graphic image in a document, you must first create a box to contain it. WordPerfect supports four different box types: Figure boxes for any type of graphic image, Table boxes for tables of numbers, Text boxes for any text that is set off from the body of the document (such as sidebars), and User-Defined boxes for any other type of image.

You can use graphics boxes in the body of your document and in its headers, footers, footnotes, and endnotes. If you want to insert a graphics box in a style that you are creating (see **Styles**), the box must either be empty or contain only text.

Defining a Graphics Box

After selecting the appropriate type of box for your graphic, you select the Create option (**1** or **C**). Figure 7 shows you the definition screen for inserting a graphic in a Figure box. The menu options shown here are similar for all types of graphics boxes.

Filename

To retrieve a file that contains an image or graph created with another program, select the Filename option (**1** or **F**) and type in the name of the file, including its extension. Be sure to include the complete path name if the graphics file isn't located in the current directory. Note that you don't have to specify the file at the time you

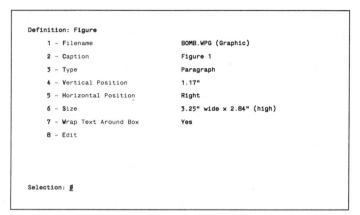

```
Definition: Figure
     1 - Filename                    BOMB.WPG (Graphic)
     2 - Caption                     Figure 1
     3 - Type                        Paragraph
     4 - Vertical Position           1.17"
     5 - Horizontal Position         Right
     6 - Size                        3.25" wide x 2.84" (high)
     7 - Wrap Text Around Box        Yes
     8 - Edit




     Selection: 0
```

Figure 7: The Figure Box Definition menu

create the graphics box to contain it. You can do this later by choosing the Edit option from the box menu, designating the number, and
then choosing the Filename option from the Definition screen.

Caption

If you want to add a caption to your figure or table, select the Caption option (**2** or **C**). This brings you to an editing screen much like
the ones used to enter headers and footers. The screen contains the
name of the box followed by its number. You may delete this text. If
you retain the number, it will automatically be updated if you later
define or delete graphics boxes (of the same type) that precede it in
the document.

Type

There are three possible types of graphics boxes associated with the
Type option (**3** or **T**): Paragraph, which keeps the graphics box adja-
cent to the paragraph text; Page, which is affixed to a stationary position on the page; and Character, which is treated like a single
character. WordPerfect will always wrap the text of a line that contains a Character box so it is below the boundary of the box, on the
next line. Note that Character boxes are the only type that may be
added to footnotes and endnotes.

Vertical and Horizontal Position

The Vertical Position (**4** or **V**) and Horizontal Position (**5** or **H**) options allow you to control the placement of the graphics box on the page. The settings available for them differ according to the type of graphics box chosen.

For the paragraph type, the vertical position setting represents the vertical distance from the first line of the paragraph. The default is 0", which places the graphic even with the paragraph's first line. For the page type, you can align the box vertically with the top or bottom margin, center it on the page, or enter an offset measured from the top edge of the page. If you select Full Page, the graphics box expands to the margin settings for that page. For the character type, you can have the graphics box positioned so that the text of the line it's on is aligned with the top, center, or bottom of the box.

You can position a Paragraph box horizontally so that it aligns with the left or right edge, or is centered between the edges of the area that contains its associated paragraph text. As long as the Wrap Text Around Box option is set to Yes (see below), the text of the paragraph will wrap around the graphics box. In addition, you can have the box fill this entire area from left to right by choosing the Both Left & Right option.

For a Page box, you have three options for setting the horizontal position of the graphics box: Margins, which allows you to left-align, right-align, center, or expand the box to left and right margins; Columns, which allows you to select a text column or range of columns (see **Columns, Text [Newspaper and Parallel]**), using the same alignment options as with Margins; and Set Position, which allows you to position the box a specific measurement in from the left edge of the page. When using the Column option, you can designate a range of text columns by entering their column numbers separated by a hyphen (as in *2–3*).

When using the character type of graphics box, you don't assign a horizontal position because WordPerfect automatically places the box to the left of the character that contains the cursor at the time you define it.

Size

Use the Size option (**6** or **S**) to modify the size of the graphics box. When you select this option, you have three choices:

1 Width (auto height); **2 H**eight (auto width);
3 Both Width and Height: **0**

If you want to set both dimensions for the graphics box, select Both Width and Height (**3** or **B**), then enter the two dimensions. Word-Perfect will automatically calculate the opposite dimension if you change the width of the box with the Width option (**1** or **W**) or the height with the Height option (**2** or **H**).

Wrap Text Around Box

WordPerfect will flow the text around the borders of the graphics box if the Wrap Text Around Box option (**7** or **W**) is set to Yes. On the editing screen, it draws the outline of the graphics box (without displaying the illustration or graph) as you enter the text of the document. If you change this setting to No, the text will go through the graphic and the box outline will not appear on the editing screen. You can preview the positioning of the text around the graphics box by using the View Document feature (see **View Document**).

Edit

Use the Edit option (**8** or **E**) to enter or edit the text for the graphics box or to modify the position or size of an illustration imported from the graphics file designated in the Filename option (see **Filename** above).

When the graphics box contains only text, you can enter or edit as you would any other text in WordPerfect after selecting the Edit option. You can change the font, size, alignment, or attributes of the text by using the appropriate WordPerfect commands.

When the graphics box contains an illustration or graph created in another program, and you select the Edit option, WordPerfect displays it in graphics mode (if your computer has a graphics card) on the screen surrounded by an outline representing the size and shape of the graphics box that contains it. From here, you can modify its size, its position, or both. Note that you can't add text to an illustration or graph when editing it; this must be done in the program that produced the graphics file. Figure 8 shows you these options along with a simple graphic imported from a clip art file included with the program.

To move the graphic image in the box, you can press any of the four cursor movement keys. To enlarge the image in the box, you press PgUp; to shrink it, you press PgDn. You can change its proportions by selecting the Scale option and entering a Y-scale (or vertical scale) percentage and an X-scale (horizontal) percentage. To rotate the image clockwise, press the Screen Up key (− on the numeric keypad). To rotate the image counterclockwise, press the Screen Down key (+ on the numeric keypad). You can also rotate the image by selecting the Rotate option and entering the percentage of rotation (where 100% is 360 degrees). When using this option, you can also designate that the image be flipped, by answering Yes to the *Mirror Image? (Y/N)* question that appears after a percentage is entered.

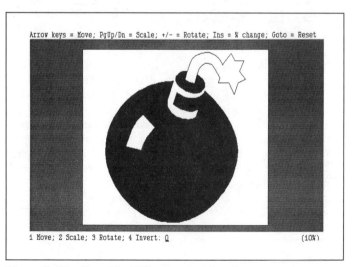

Figure 8: The Graphics Edit screen and options

The % Change option is activated by pressing the Ins (Insert) key. The percentage of change affects the amount that the image is moved, scaled, or rotated when applying the techniques discussed above. You can choose among 1%, 5%, 10%, or 25% change by pressing the Ins key until the percentage you want to use appears in the lower right corner of the screen.

You can use the Invert option (**4**) on the Edit screen to reverse the image if it is a bitmap graphic rather than a line drawing. When you use it, each white dot (or *pixel*) is changed to black and each black dot to white. Graphics imported from .WPG files (the clip art files included with WordPerfect) and .PIC files (which contain Lotus 1-2-3 graphs) are considered line drawings and, therefore, can't be inverted, while EPS (Encapsulated PostScript) and TIFF (Tagged Image File Format—created by scanners) files can be inverted.

After you have made all the desired modifications to your graphic, press F7 (Exit) to return to the Definition screen. If you want to return the image to the original settings, press the Go To key combination, Ctrl-Home.

Adjusting the Settings for a Graphics Box

WordPerfect allows you to modify many of the default settings for the graphics boxes you insert in the document. These include the style of the border of the graphics, the inside space between the image and the borders of the box, the outside space between the text and the borders of the box, level numbering methods, the position of the caption, and the gray shading used in the box.

To change any of these settings, you move the cursor to the place in the document that contains your graphics box, press Alt-F9 (Graphics), select the option that corresponds to the type of box used there, and then select Options by pressing **4** or **O**. Figure 9 shows you the Options screen that appears when you select the Figure box type. When you change any of the options on this screen, they affect the style of any of the graphics boxes of the same type from the position of the cursor when you made the changes forward in the document.

Creating Horizontal and Vertical Lines

WordPerfect's Graphics feature allows you to create horizontal and vertical lines (rules) of various thicknesses. Use these lines instead of those created with the Line Draw feature when you need to draw rules that use a proportionally spaced font, as lines created with Line Draw will not print correctly unless you are using a mono-spaced font. To draw a rule in the document, position the cursor on the line

```
Options:    Figure

    1 - Border Style
            Left                        Single
            Right                       Single
            Top                         Single
            Bottom                      Single
    2 - Outside Border Space
            Left                        Ø.16"
            Right                       Ø.16"
            Top                         Ø.16"
            Bottom                      Ø.16"
    3 - Inside Border Space
            Left                        Ø"
            Right                       Ø"
            Top                         Ø"
            Bottom                      Ø"
    4 - First Level Numbering Method    Numbers
    5 - Second Level Numbering Method   Off
    6 - Caption Number Style            [BOLD]Figure 1[bold]
    7 - Position of Caption             Below box, Outside borders
    8 - Minimum Offset from Paragraph   Ø"
    9 - Gray Shading (% of black)       Ø%

Selection: Ø
```

Figure 9: The Figure Options screen

where you want the rule to start and follow the key sequence shown at the beginning of this entry.

WordPerfect can draw either a vertical line that extends up and down part of or the entire the length of the page or a horizontal line that extends across part of or the entire the width of the page. After selecting the type of line you want, you are presented with line options that allow you to specify the horizontal position (and vertical position if you are creating a vertical line), the length of the line, its thickness, and the amount of gray shading to be applied to it (100% is black).

When specifying the horizontal position of a horizontal line, you can have it aligned with the left or right margin or centered between them. You can also position the line by entering an offset measurement from the left edge of the page or have it extend from the left to the right margin.

When specifying the horizontal position for a vertical line, you can have it drawn slightly ahead of the left margin or after the right margin, or drawn between columns (indicated by number). You can also position the line by entering an offset measurement from the left edge of the page. You can specify the vertical position of the line as centered between the top and bottom margins (Full Page), aligned with either the top or bottom margin, or placed at a specific distance from the top of the page.

Use the Length of Line option to determine how long the rule is to be. If you have specified a horizontal rule whose position is Left and Right, the line length is automatically calculated by the margin settings. For other horizontal lines, the default length (which you can override) is determined by the cursor's position when you created the line.

The Width of Line option allows you to specify how thick the line is to be. To enter this measurement in points, even if the measurement is given in inches by default, follow the number with a *p*.

The Gray Shading option allows you to draw rules in other gradations that are not totally black. To decrease the contrast of the line, enter a percentage (10% is the lowest shading you can specify).

SEE ALSO

Line Draw

View Document

Hard Page Break

See **Page Break, Soft and Hard**.

Hard Return

Terminates paragraphs and short lines of text or enters blank lines.

KEY SEQUENCE

←┘ (Enter)

USAGE

You use the Enter key (←┘) to terminate a paragraph of text, to terminate a short line that does not extend as far as the right margin, or to add blank lines to a document. When you press ←┘, WordPerfect places an invisible hard return in the document, shown by the code [HRt] in the Reveal Codes screen.

When entering the text of a paragraph, you don't press ←┘ to begin a new line when you come to the right margin setting, as is the case when using a typewriter. WordPerfect automatically wraps any text that extends beyond the right margin to the next line. At the end of a line where word wrap occurs, the program inserts a soft return, whose code appears as [SRt] in the Reveal Codes screen.

To separate the text of one paragraph into two paragraphs, you locate the cursor on the first character to be in the new paragraph and press ⏎ (it doesn't matter whether you are in Insert or Typeover mode). To join two paragraphs together, you locate the cursor at the beginning of the second paragraph and press the Backspace key to delete the [HRt] code. To make it easier to locate these Hard Return codes, you can choose a character to display their location on the editing screen (see **Display, Setup: Hard Return Display Character**).

SEE ALSO

Display, Setup: Hard Return Display Character

Hard Space

Prevents individual words from being separated by word wrap.

KEY SEQUENCE

Homespace

USAGE

The hard space, entered between two words by pressing the Home key before pressing the space bar, prevents WordPerfect from separating those words by word wrap. It can be used as the space character in any phrase that should never be separated by word wrap. A hard space code appears as [ ] in the Reveal Codes screen. To convert a hard space to a regular space (subject to word wrap), locate this code, delete it, and press the space bar.

Headers and Footers

Enters running heads at the top or bottom of the pages of your document.

KEY SEQUENCE

Shift-F8 (Format)

2 − Page

3 − Headers *or*
4 − Footers

1 Header **A**; **2** Header **B** *or*
1 Footer **A**; **2** Footer **B**

1 Discontinue; **2** Every **P**age; **3** Odd Pages;
4 Even Pages; **5** Edit

[enter or edit text of header or footer]

F7 (Exit)

USAGE

WordPerfect allows you to create up to two different headers (running heads printed at the top of the page) and two different footers (running heads printed at the bottom of the page) in your document. You can have these headings printed on every page, or just on even or odd pages of the document. Before adding a header or footer to your document (as outlined in the key sequence), position the cursor at the top of the first page that the header or footer is to appear on.

You create two headers (or footers) A and B if you want their text to alternate on even- and odd-numbered pages of a bound document. When using two headers or footers on every page, place one flush left and the other flush right or place them on separate lines.

When creating a header or footer, after selecting its number and type, you are presented with a full editing screen on which to enter the text of the header (or footer). Your header or footer can use as many lines as you need. You can also add any text enhancements (such as boldface or a new font) or formatting (such as centering or flush right) that you wish. To insert automatic page numbering into your headers and footers, press Ctrl-B (or Ctrl-N) at the position in the header or footer where you want the page number to appear.

Headers begin printing on the first line below the top margin, and WordPerfect places 0.16" between the last line of the header and the body of the text. Footers begin printing on the first line above the bottom margin, and the program places 0.16" between the first line of the footer and the body of the text.

To see how your headers and footers will appear when printed, use the View Document feature. To discontinue a header or footer from a specific page to the end of the document, select the Discontinue option after selecting the appropriate header or footer on the Page menu. To suppress a header or footer on a specific page, use the Suppress (this page only) option (see **Suppress Page Format**). To edit the text of a header, select its header or footer number and use the Edit option on the Header or Footer menu.

To delete a header or footer, locate and delete the [Header/Footer:] code associated with it. WordPerfect displays the first 50 characters of the header or footer in the Reveal Codes screen.

SEE ALSO

Suppress Page Format

View Document

Help

Gives you on-line help about a function key or WordPerfect command.

To get help on the function keys:

F3 *<function key or combination>*

⎯☐⎯

←⎯ *or* **space bar**

To get help on a WordPerfect command:

F3 *<first letter of the command>*

⎯☐⎯

←⎯ *or* **space bar**

To display the WordPerfect function key template:

F3 F3

⎯☐⎯

←⎯ *or* **space bar**

WordPerfect's on-line help is available any time you are working with the program. To get help about the use of a particular function key or key combination, press F3 (Help) followed by those function keys. To get help about a particular feature by name, press F3 followed by the initial letter of the feature name (such as **S** to get help on Styles). When a letter has more than one Help screen, type **1** to display another screen of entries for that letter. After locating the name of the feature on the Help screen, press the function keys indicated to obtain information about the feature's use.

To display a diagram of the function key assignments in Word-Perfect, press F3 twice. To exit Help, you simply press ⏎ or the space bar (pressing F1—Cancel—simply gives you a screen of help on the Cancel feature).

If you wish to reassign the Help key to F1 as it is commonly assigned by other programs, select the ALTRNAT keyboard that is supplied with your program (see **Keyboard Layout**). This key-board reassigns the Cancel function to the Esc key and the Esc key function to F3.

SEE ALSO

Keyboard Layout

Hyphenation

Hyphenates words according to WordPerfect's hyphenation rules, either automatically or at your discretion.

KEY SEQUENCE

To turn hyphenation on or off:

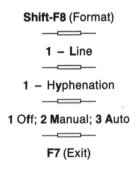

Shift-F8 (Format)

1 – Line

1 – Hyphenation

1 Off; **2** Manual; **3** Auto

F7 (Exit)

To change the hyphenation zone:

Shift-F8 (Format)

――⟨▭⟩――

1 – Line

――⟨▭⟩――

2 – Hyphenation **Z**one – Left <*left zone %*> ↵
Right <*right zone %*> ↵

――⟨▭⟩――

F7 (Exit)

| USAGE | ═══════════════ |

WordPerfect uses three different types of hyphens:

- Soft hyphens, which the program enters; these are not printed if the document is edited and the word no longer requires hyphenation.
- Hard hyphens, which you enter by pressing the hyphen key (-). These will appear on the screen and in print whenever the word appears. A line can break after a hard hyphen.
- Nonbreaking hyphens, which you specify by pressing Home and then pressing the hyphen key (-). This prevents a hyphenated word from being split between two lines.

You insert soft hyphens by pressing Ctrl and the hyphen key or by using the program's Hyphenation feature. The default setting for WordPerfect's Hyphenation feature is off. If you want to use the program's Hyphenation command, you must turn it on and choose between manual and automatic hyphenation as outlined in the key sequence above.

With manual hyphenation, WordPerfect will beep (if the Beep on Hyphenation option is set to Yes—see **Beep Options**) each time a word extends beyond the right margin and starts at or before the left hyphenation zone. You will then see this prompt:

Position hyphen; Press ESC

To the right of this prompt you will see the word as WordPerfect will hyphenate it if you press Esc. To change the place where the word is hyphenated, use the arrow keys to move the hyphen to the position where you want the word to break; then press Esc. If you do not want the word to be hyphenated, press F1 (Cancel).

When automatic hyphenation is on, WordPerfect will hyphenate any word that starts at or before the hyphenation zone and extends beyond the right margin, without giving you a chance to change the place where it is hyphenated.

The Hyphenation Zone option on the Line format menu (**2** or **Z**) is used to change the settings that determine how often WordPerfect will hyphenate a word. If a word begins before or at the left zone boundary and continues past the right zone boundary, WordPerfect will either prompt you for a place to insert the hyphen (if you are using manual hyphenation) or will immediately hyphenate the word (if you are using automatic hyphenation).

The left and right hyphenation zone boundaries are set as a percentage of the line length. This means that the default setting of 10% for the left boundary is 0.6" and that of 4% for the right boundary is 0.24", if the line length is currently 6". To have WordPerfect hyphenate more frequently, decrease the size of the hyphenation zone. To have the program hyphenate less frequently, increase the size of the hyphenation zone.

WordPerfect makes all hyphenation suggestions and decisions according to its own hyphenation rules. You can purchase foreign language hyphenation modules from WordPerfect Corporation. To have the program use one of these foreign language hyphenation modules, you need to change the Language code on the Other format menu (see **Language**). You indicate the location of your hyphenation dictionary (or dictionaries) by using the Location of Auxiliary Files option on the Setup menu (see **Location of Auxiliary Files**).

SEE ALSO

Beep Options

Language

Location of Auxiliary Files

Importing and Exporting DOS Text Files

See **Text In/Out.**

→Indent

Sets a temporary left margin and aligns all text to this indent until you press ↵.

KEY SEQUENCE

F4 (→Indent)

─────☐─────

<text> ↵

USAGE

For a left indent, press F4 (→Indent) at the beginning of your paragraph. It is then indented ½ inch from the left margin, or to the measurement of the first tab stop if you have reset tabs. Press F4 a second time to indent the paragraph 1 inch (or to the next tab stop), a third time to indent it 1½ inches, and so forth. If you press F4 at the beginning of an existing paragraph, it will be reformatted. If you press F4 at the beginning of a paragraph you are typing, it will be indented as you type until you press ↵ again to signal the beginning of a new paragraph. To indent only the first line in a paragraph, use the Tab key instead of F4.

To remove an indentation, locate and delete the [→Indent] code in the Reveal Codes screen.

→Indent←

Margin Release

Tabs

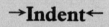

→Indent←

Sets temporary left and right margins and aligns all text to these indents until you press ←⏎.

KEY SEQUENCE

Shift-F4 (→Indent←)

<text> ←⏎

USAGE

For a left and right indent, press Shift-F4 (→Indent←). The paragraph will be indented ½ inch from the left and right margins, or to the first tab setting for both sides. Continue to press Shift-F4 to indent the paragraph in increments of ½ inch or to the tab settings. To indent only the first line in a paragraph, use the Tab key. To delete a left and right indent, locate and delete the [→Indent←] code in the Reveal Codes screen.

| SEE ALSO |

→Indent

Tabs

Indexes

Generates an index from entries marked in the document or stored in a concordance file.

| KEY SEQUENCE |

To mark an entry for the index:

Alt-F4 (Block)

[highlight text to be indexed]

Alt-F5 (Mark Text)

3 Index

Index Heading: ⏎ *to use displayed text*
or <index heading> ⏎

Subheading: ⏎ *to use displayed text*
or <subheading> ⏎

To define the style of the index:

Alt-F5 (Mark Text)

---

5 Define

---

3 – Define Index

Concordance Filename (Enter = none): ◄┘ or <*filename*> ◄┘

---

    1 – **N**o Page Numbers
    2 – **P**age Numbers Follow Entries
    3 – **(**Page Numbers) Follow Entries
    4 – **F**lush Right Page Numbers
    5 – **F**lush Right Page Numbers with **L**eaders

To generate an index:

Alt-F5 (Mark Text)

---

6 Generate

---

   5 – **G**enerate Tables, Indexes, Automatic References, etc.

   Existing tables, lists, and indexes will be replaced.
   Continue? (Y/N) ◄┘ *or any key except N*

USAGE

To create an index, you must first mark the items to be included in it, then define its style and generate it. To mark items for an index:

1. Locate the word or phrase you wish to include in the index. Position the cursor on it or on the space following it. If you are indexing a phrase, you must first mark it by pressing Alt-F4 (Block) and highlighting the phrase.

2. Press Alt-F5 (Mark Text) and then select the Index option (**3** or **I**). The following prompt appears:

Index Heading:

This prompt is followed by the phrase you marked or the word the cursor is on. If you want the entry to appear in the index just as it does where it is highlighted, press ←┘. WordPerfect automatically capitalizes the first letter of an index heading, and it lowercases subheading entries unless the word was capitalized in the text. If you want the word or phrase to appear differently in the index, type it or edit it as you wish it to appear.

3. The program then prompts you for a subheading. If you accepted the default word or phrase as the heading, you can type a subheading or simply press ←┘ for no subheading. If you entered a different word or phrase for the heading, Word-Perfect will present that word or phrase as the default subheading. You can press ←┘ to accept it, type over the word WordPerfect presents and substitute the one you wish to use, or delete the subheading if you do not want one.

4. Repeat this process for each word or phrase you want to include in your index.

Creating a Concordance File

A concordance file is simply a list of all the words and phrases that you wish WordPerfect to search for and mark as index entries. To use a concordance file, you specify its file name when you define the style of your index.

To create a concordance file, you need to start a new document and enter the words or phrases you want to use in the index as headings or as subheadings. Press ←┘ after you enter each one. Then, if you are using subheadings, go back and mark each entry with the appropriate index marks by pressing Alt-F5 (Mark Text) and selecting the Index option (you will need to block phrases first). Otherwise, all entries will be headings. You can then generate the index.

Defining the Style of an Index

WordPerfect allows you to choose among several formatting styles for the indexes it generates. To define the style for an index, follow the steps as outlined in the key sequence. After you select the Define and Index options, you see the following prompt:

Concordance filename (Enter = none):

Type the name of the concordance file, if you are using one; otherwise, press ⏎.

Then you select the option number corresponding to the style you wish to use as shown in the key sequence section. If you want a columnar index, you must insert the column codes and turn the Columns feature on in the text (with Alt-F7) just before the [Def-Mark:Index] code that indicates where the index has been defined.

A [Def Mark] code is inserted in the document when you press F7 (Exit) after selecting a numbering style for the index. This marks the position where the index will be generated (see below).

Generating Tables, Lists, and Indexes

After marking the index entries and indicating the style of the index, you are ready to generate the index. Select first the Generate (**6** or **G**) and then the Generate Tables, Indexes, Automatic References, etc. (**5** or **G**) options. You will receive the following prompt:

Existing tables, lists, and indexes will be replaced.
Continue? (Y/N)

To have WordPerfect generate the index, type **Y** or press any key besides **N**. If you have previously generated an index for the document, it will be completely replaced unless you type **N**. The index is generated at the [Def Mark] code in the document, and the program automatically inserts an [End Def] mark at the end of the index.

| SEE ALSO |

Lists

Mark Text

Tables of Contents

Initial Settings

Allows you to modify the initial settings for the WordPerfect program or just the current document.

| KEY SEQUENCE |

To change the initial (default) settings for the program:

Shift-F1 (Setup)

5 – Initial Settings

1 – **B**eep Options
2 – **D**ate Format
3 – Document **S**ummary
4 – **I**nitial Codes
5 – **R**epeat Value
6 – Table of **A**uthorities

To change the initial format settings for the current document only:

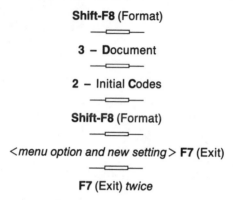

Shift-F8 (Format)

3 – Document

2 – Initial **C**odes

Shift-F8 (Format)

<menu option and new setting> **F7** (Exit)

F7 (Exit) *twice*

To change the initial font for the current document only:

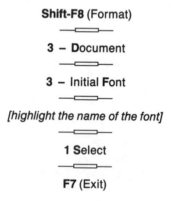

Shift-F8 (Format)

3 – Document

3 – Initial **F**ont

[highlight the name of the font]

1 Select

F7 (Exit)

USAGE

WordPerfect allows you to change the default settings that remain in effect each time you use the program or to change the format default settings just for the document you are creating.

To change the default settings for the program, you select Shift-F1 (Setup) and the Initial Settings option (**5** or **I**). Then select the number or letter of the option you wish to reset. Information on changing the default settings for Beep Options, Date Format, Document Summary, Repeat Value (see **Esc Key**), and Table of Authorities can be found under those reference entries in this guide. Table 6 shows you the default settings in effect when you install WordPerfect.

FEATURE	DEFAULT SETTING
Automatically reformat and rewrite	On
Backup options	
– Timed	Off
– Original	Off
Beep options	
– on Error	Off
– on Hyphenation	On
– on Search failure	Off
Center page, top to bottom	Off
Cursor speed	30 cps
Date format	3 1,4
Decimal/align character	. (period)
– Thousands' separator	, (comma)
Display comments	On
Display pitch	Auto
Document summary	
– on Save/exit	Off
– Subject search	RE:
Fast save	Off

Table 6: WordPerfect's Default Settings

FEATURE	DEFAULT SETTING
File name on status line	On
Forced odd/even page	Off
Hard return display character	Space
Hyphenation	Off
Hyphenation zone	
– Left	10%
– Right	4%
Justification	On
Kerning	Off
Language	EN (English)
Line height	Auto
Line spacing	1 (single)
Margins	
– Left	1"
– Right	1"
– Top	1"
– Bottom	1"
Menu letter display	Bold
Page number position	No page numbers
Paper	
– Size	8½" × 11"
– Type	Standard
Redline format	Printer dependent
Repeat value	8

Table 6: WordPerfect's Default Settings (continued)

FEATURE	DEFAULT SETTING
Side-by-side display of columns	On
Tab set	Every .5"
Table of authorities format	
− Dot leaders	On
− Underlining	Off
− Blank Lines	On
Typeover	Off
Underline	
− Spaces	On
− Tabs	Off
Units of measure	
− Display and entry of numbers	" (inches)
− Status line display	" (inches)
Widow/orphan protection	Off
Word spacing	Optimal
Letter spacing	Optimal
Word spacing justification limits	
− Compressed to	60%
− Expanded to	400%

Table 6: WordPerfect's Default Settings (continued)

To change the initial format or font settings for the current document only, you choose the Initial Codes option on the Document menu (as indicated in the key sequence). The Initial Codes option takes you to a split screen that shows the Reveal Codes screen in the lower half. Then, you press Shift-F8 (Format) and select the appropriate format menu (Line, Page, Document, or Other) and change all of the default settings as you want them for the document on the editing screen.

After you finish making the desired changes on the menus and press F7, you will see their formatting codes in the Reveal Codes screen. When you press F7 again, these formatting changes will be added to the document. When you press F7 a third time to return to the editing screen, the cursor will automatically be located at the beginning of the document. To return to your previous position in the document, press Ctrl-Home (Go To) twice.

You also use this method when using the Initial Codes option on the Initial Settings menu to change the format settings that you want in effect each time you start WordPerfect. All changes to the initial settings are stored with the document when you save it. Changes made to the settings for the current document preempt those made to the program. This means that they will remain in effect even if you retrieve the document on another computer whose copy of WordPerfect has different format defaults in effect.

SEE ALSO

Base Font

Beep Options

Date, Inserting the

Document Summary

Esc Key

Printer, Select

Table of Authorities

Insert

See **Typeover**.

Italics

See **Font**.

Justification

Turns on or off right justification in the document.

KEY SEQUENCE

To turn on or off right justification in the document:

Shift-F8 (Format)

⎯⊏⊐⎯

1 − Line

⎯⊏⊐⎯

3 − Justification N *or* **Y**

⎯⊏⊐⎯

F7 (Exit)

To compress or expand the word spacing:

Shift-F8 (Format)

—⊏⊐—

4 – Other

—⊏⊐—

6 – Printer Functions

—⊏⊐—

4 – Word Spacing Justification
Compressed to (0%–100%) <*compression %*> ↵
Expanded to (100%–unlimited) <*expansion %*> ↵

—⊏⊐—

F7 (Exit)

USAGE

By default, justification is on when you begin a new document in WordPerfect. This means that the program will align the right margin of each line by adjusting the spacing between its words. The program can't display justification on the editing screen (the right margin always appears ragged right). To see justification and the spacing between words in each line, you need to use the View Document feature.

You can turn off justification for the entire document or just part of it. Position the cursor in the document where you want the change to begin and follow the steps indicated in the key sequence. To turn it off for the entire document, be sure to position the cursor at the beginning of the document (Home Home ↑) before following the key sequence. You can also turn off justification for the whole document by using the Initial Codes option on the Document format menu (see **Initial Settings**). When you select No for the Justification option, WordPerfect inserts a [Just Off] code in the document. You can return to the default of justification by locating and deleting this code in the Reveal Codes screen.

WordPerfect provides two methods for controlling the spacing between words when justification is used. You can turn on WordPerfect's Hyphenation feature and adjust the size of the hyphenation zone (see **Hyphenation**) to reduce the amount of space between words.

This is especially useful when you have a short line length, as when using newspaper and parallel columns. You can also adjust the word spacing from the Printer Functions menu (as indicated in the key sequence). The Word Spacing Justification option allows you to modify the minimum and maximum range within which WordPerfect can fit justified text. With a proportionally spaced font, the optimal spacing between words is built into the font (expressed by percentage as 100%). Use the Compressed To option to set the minimum word spacing percentage and the Expanded To option to set the maximum word spacing percentage allowed. When one of these limits is reached, WordPerfect begins to adjust the spacing between letters in the words themselves (see **Word/Letter Spacing**).

SEE ALSO

Hyphenation

Initial Settings

View Document

Word/Letter Spacing

Kerning

Turns on or off automatic kerning, which tightens the letter spacing between specific pairs of letters in a font.

KEY SEQUENCE

Shift-F8 (Format)

4 – Other

6 – Printer Functions

1 – Kerning **Y** *or* **N**

F7 (Exit)

USAGE

When you turn on kerning in a document, WordPerfect reduces space between specific letter pairs in a font from the cursor's position forward in the document. Kerning combinations are determined by the kerning table contained in the printer definition file (ending in .PRS) used by the selected printer (see **Printer, Select**).

If you want to reduce the space between a particular letter pair in a font that is not currently kerned, you can create your own kerning table for the font using the printer definition program that is included on the PTR Program diskette (see *WordPerfect 5 Desktop Companion*, SYBEX, 1988 for details on using the PTR program).

When you turn kerning on in a document, WordPerfect inserts a [Kern:On] code in the document at the cursor's position. If you decide not to use kerning in the final printed document, locate and delete this code in the Reveal Codes screen.

SEE ALSO

Justification

Word/Letter Spacing

Keyboard Layout

Allows you to assign new functions or characters to any key on the keyboard.

To create a keyboard layout:

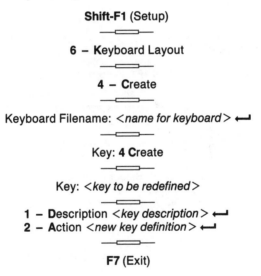

Shift-F1 (Setup)

6 – **K**eyboard Layout

4 – **C**reate

Keyboard Filename: <*name for keyboard*> ←

Key: **4 C**reate

Key: <*key to be redefined*>

1 – **D**escription <*key description*> ←
2 – **A**ction <*new key definition*> ←

F7 (Exit)

To edit a key's function:

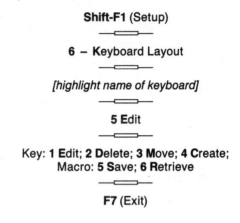

Shift-F1 (Setup)

6 – Keyboard Layout

[highlight name of keyboard]

5 Edit

Key: **1 E**dit; **2 D**elete; **3 M**ove; **4 C**reate;
Macro: **5 S**ave; **6 R**etrieve

F7 (Exit)

To select a keyboard layout:

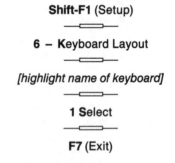

Shift-F1 (Setup)

6 – Keyboard Layout

[highlight name of keyboard]

1 Select

F7 (Exit)

USAGE

You can use the Keyboard Layout feature to change the function of any key on the keyboard. The reassigned key functions are then saved under a file name, which can be selected as indicated in the key sequence. When you select a new keyboard layout, it remains in effect each time you start WordPerfect. To return to the original keyboard layout, select the Original option (**6** or **O**) from the Keyboard Layout menu.

Editing Keyboard Definitions

WordPerfect comes with three predefined keyboards, ALTRNAT, ENHANCED, and MACROS, that you can use as is or edit. To view or change the reassignments made to individual keys, select the Edit option (**5** or **E**) on the Keyboard Layout menu. To modify a key definition, move the highlight bar to the name of the key and select the Edit option (**1** or **E**). This takes you to an edit screen very similar to the one used to modify macros (see **Macros**). To modify the key's function, then select the Action option (**2** or **A**). This positions the cursor inside the key definition window. Once there, you can use the regular WordPerfect editing and cursor movement keys to modify the text or the functions listed there.

To add a new function as part of a key definition, press Ctrl-V or Ctrl-F10 (Macro Define), followed by the function key or key combination to be added. For instance, to add centering to a key definition, you select the Action option, position the cursor in the definition window at the place where centering is to happen, press Ctrl-V, and then Shift-F6. WordPerfect will place the code {Center} in the definition window at the cursor's position. As when editing macros, you must be sure to press Ctrl-F10 a second time if you used it instead of Ctrl-V to enter the function key code. This toggles you back into editing mode so that the editing and cursor movement keys work as usual.

When reassigning a key's function, you can also use the macro commands available in WordPerfect. You add a macro command by pressing Ctrl-PgUp once the cursor is in the definition screen, highlighting the name of the macro command, and then pressing ↵ (see **Appendix C** for a list of the macro programming commands).

After you are finished reassigning the function of the key, press F7 (Exit) to save the definition and exit the key modification screen.

When editing a keyboard layout, you can also delete (**2** or **D**) or move (**3** or **M**) a key definition, or create (**4** or **C**) a new key definition. In addition, you can use the Save option (**5** or **S**) to store a key definition as a macro by highlighting the key, typing **5** or **S**, and entering a macro name. That way, you can invoke the key definition as you would any WordPerfect macro, even if the keyboard layout is not currently selected (see **Macros**).

Finally, you can assign a macro definition to a particular key by typing **6** or **R**, pressing the key or key combination, and then entering the name of the macro to be assigned to it. This option allows you to map macro definitions to specific Ctrl-letter key combinations. For example, if you have defined a macro named *backup*, which makes a backup of the current directory, you can use this option to map its function to the key combination Ctrl-B so that you can make a backup simply by pressing Ctrl-B rather than having to press Alt-F10, type *backup*, and then press ←⎯.

Creating a New Keyboard Definition

Creating a new keyboard layout involves much the same steps as editing an existing one. After you select the Create option (**4** or **C**), you are prompted to enter a name for the keyboard. After naming it, you go on to define the function of the individual keys and key combinations that you wish to add to it. Each key definition is given a description and an action.

You can create all sorts of specialized keyboards to meet your needs. You can add special math/science or foreign language symbols to the keyboard using the Compose feature (see **Compose**). You can rearrange the WordPerfect function keys so that they match some other word processing system. For instance, a user familiar with WordStar could map Ctrl-Backspace onto Ctrl-T so that Ctrl-T deletes the current word as it does in that word processor. You can also create a keyboard that uses a particular set of macros. For instance, you could create a merge keyboard that assigns a set of specialized merge macros to familiar keys.

NOTE

The Keyboard Layout feature replaces the Ctrl/Alt key mapping from version 4.2.

SEE ALSO

Appendix C

Compose

Location of Auxiliary Files

Macros

Language

Allows you to switch between different language versions of the spelling, thesaurus, and hyphenation dictionaries.

KEY SEQUENCE

Shift-F8 (Format)

4 – Other

4 – Language <*language code*> ↵

F7 (Exit)

USAGE

WordPerfect comes with an English language version of the spelling and thesaurus dictionaries. You can, however, purchase foreign language versions of these dictionaries, as well as special hyphenation dictionaries, from WordPerfect Corporation. To have WordPerfect use one of these versions instead of English, you must change the language code default from EN (for English) to its code as indicated in Table 7.

LANGUAGE	CODE
British English	UK
Canadian French	CA
Danish	DA
Dutch	NE
English	EN
Finnish	SU
French	FR
German	DE
Icelandic	IC
Italian	IT
Norwegian	NO
Portuguese	PO
Spanish	ES
Swedish	SV

Table 7: WordPerfect's Language Codes

SEE ALSO

Location of Auxiliary Files

Line Draw

Allows you to draw straight lines and boxes in the document.

Ctrl-F3 (Screen)

2 – Line Draw

1 | ; **2** | | ; **3** *; **4** Change; **5** Erase; **6** Move

F7 (Exit) or **F1** (Cancel)

┌ **USAGE** ┐

To draw simple graphics in WordPerfect, press Ctrl-F3 (Screen) and select the Line Draw option (**2** or **L**). When you are in WordPerfect's Line Draw mode, the following menu appears:

1 | ; **2** | | ; **3** *; **4** Change; **5** Erase; **6** Move: 1

When you are in Line Draw mode, the option you have selected appears at the end of the menu line. Selecting option 1, 2, or 3 allows you to choose among drawing single lines, double lines, or asterisks. Selecting option 4 allows you to select up to eight different types of alternate drawing characters. In addition, you can use any of the characters that your printer can print (see **Compose**). If you select option 5, the cursor will erase each character it passes through. Selecting option 6 allows you to move the cursor through your drawing without changing anything.

To enter text in drawings you have created, you should be in Typeover mode. If you remain in Insert mode, which is Word-Perfect's default setting, lines will be pushed to the right as you type, and pressing ←, Tab, or the space bar will insert spaces into your graphics. You can also type text for your graphics first, then enter Line Draw mode and draw lines around the text you have already entered.

To exit Line Draw mode and enter text, press F7 (Exit) or F1 (Cancel). Pressing F1 does not erase any drawings you have created.

NOTE

When creating horizontal and vertical rules for a desktop publishing application, use the Line option on the Graphics menu (Alt-F9), rather than the Line Draw feature.

SEE ALSO

Graphics: Creating Horizontal and Vertical Lines

Line Format

See **Format**.

Line Height

Allows you to fix the amount of space placed between the baseline of one line and the baseline of the next line in the document.

KEY SEQUENCE

Shift-F8 (Format)

----□----

1 – Line

----□----

4 – Line Height

----□----

1 Auto
2 Fixed *<distance between baselines>* ↵

----□----

F7 (Exit)

USAGE

WordPerfect automatically adjusts the line height—that is, the measurement from the baseline of one line of text to the baseline of the following line of text—to accommodate the largest font used in the line. If you wish to override this automatic adjustment and enter a fixed line height for all of the lines in a part or all of the document, you use the Line Height option on the Line format menu. After you select the Fixed option (as indicated in the key sequence), enter the distance between baselines. You can enter this measurement in points, inches, or centimeters. If you enter the number of points, and inches is the default unit of measurement, be sure to end the number with *p*—WordPerfect will automatically convert this number into corresponding inches (see **Units of Measure**).

When you change the line height measurement, WordPerfect inserts a [Ln Height:] code in the document at the cursor's position. The line height will then be changed from that point forward in the document, although the difference in the line spacing will not be visible on the editing screen. (To see the effect that changing the line height has on your text, you must use the View Document feature.) To return to automatic line height later on in the text, position the cursor at the beginning of the line where the new line height is to begin, repeat the key sequence, and select the Auto option.

SEE ALSO

Line Spacing

Line Numbering

Numbers the lines in the printed version of the document.

KEY SEQUENCE

Shift-F8 (Format)

—▭—

1 – Line

—▭—

5 – Line **N**umbering **Y**

—▭—

1 – **C**ount Blank Lines
2 – **N**umber Every n Lines, where n is
3 – **P**osition of Number from Left Edge
4 – **S**tarting Number
5 – **R**estart Numbering on Each Page

—▭—

F7 (Exit)

USAGE

WordPerfect allows you to specify that lines be automatically numbered in the documents you create. Although the line numbers do not appear on the editing screen, they will be present when your document is printed or when you preview it (see **View Document**).

To number the lines in a document, move the cursor to the first position at the top of the page where you want line numbering to begin. To turn on line numbering at the cursor position, follow the key sequence shown above and type **Y** after choosing the Line Numbering option. To later turn line numbering off, you type **N** in response to this option. You can also locate and delete the [Ln Num:On] code in the Reveal Codes screen.

When you turn on line numbering, you are presented with five suboptions, which are discussed below.

Count Blank Lines   You can select whether to include blank lines in the line count. If you want blank lines to be skipped, select the Count Blank Lines option (**1** or **C**) and type **N**. WordPerfect automatically includes blank lines as it numbers lines unless you tell it not to. The count does not include blank lines in double-spaced text, however.

Number Every n Lines   The Number Every n Lines, Where n Is option allows you to specify the increment for line numbering. For example, suppose you want to number only every other line or every fifth line. To do so, enter the number of lines you want WordPerfect to skip before it numbers the next line. To have the program number every five lines, enter **5**; WordPerfect will count all the lines but will number only lines 5, 10, 15, 20, and so forth.

Position of Number from Left Edge   The Position of Number from Left Edge option allows you to indicate where you want WordPerfect to print the line numbers. Enter the distance from the left edge of the page in inches.

Starting Number   WordPerfect begins line numbering with 1 on each new page unless you change the Starting Number option and enter a new starting number.

Restart Numbering on Each Page   If you want line numbering to continue sequentially throughout your document, enter **N** for the Restart Number on Each Page option.

SEE ALSO

Outlining

Paragraph Numbering

View Document

Line Spacing

Allows you to change the line spacing in half-line increments.

KEY SEQUENCE

Shift-F8 (Format)

1 – Line

6 – Line **S**pacing *<spacing number>* ⏎

F7 (Exit)

USAGE

The default for WordPerfect is single spacing. To change to another spacing from the cursor's position forward in the document, place the cursor where you want the new spacing to begin and follow the key sequence as shown above. You can enter the spacing number in half-line increments (such as 1.5). WordPerfect displays double spacing (and larger whole number spacing like triple, quadruple, and so on) on the screen. To return to the default of single spacing, locate and delete the [Ln Spacing:] code in the Reveal Codes screen.

SEE ALSO

Line Height

List Files

Allows you to obtain an alphabetical listing of all of the files in the current directory and perform common maintenance tasks on them.

KEY SEQUENCE

F5 (List Files) ⏎

1 Retrieve; 2 Delete; 3 Move/Rename; 4 Print; 5 Text In; 6 Look;
7 Other Directory; 8 Copy; 9 Word Search; N Name Search

F1 (Cancel) *or* **space bar** *or* **O**

USAGE

List Files (F5) allows you to obtain a directory listing of files, retrieve or print a particular document, or make a new data directory or drive current. In addition, you can carry out many tasks that you would otherwise have to do in DOS, such as deleting and renaming files, creating directories, and copying files to a new disk or directory. For information on using such options on the List Files menu, refer to the individual reference entry in this book under the option name.

When you press F5, WordPerfect displays the path name of the current directory at the bottom of the editing screen. If you press ⏎, it will display a new screen showing an alphabetical list of all program files in that directory as well as the List Files menu.

To move through the list of file names on the List Files screen, use the ↑, ↓, PgUp, and PgDn keys. To move directly to the last file name in the list, press Home Home ↓. To move to the first file, press Home Home ↑. To move between columns, use the ← and → keys.

To locate a particular file quickly, type **N** and start typing the first few characters of its name to activate the Name Search feature. The program tries to match the letters entered with files in the listing and moves the highlight directly to the first match. Press ⏎ or one of the arrow keys to exit from Name Search.

If you want to view the contents of a different directory, you can edit the displayed path name or enter the path name of the directory you wish to view. If you will be working in a different directory during the current session, you can change the default directory (see **Directories**). Once you have made a particular directory current, all of the documents you create and save will automatically be located in it.

Press Esc, F1 (Cancel), 0, or F7 (Exit) to return to your document after viewing the List Files screen.

SEE ALSO

Copying Files

Deleting Files

Directories

Looking at the Contents of Files and Directories

Name Search

Printing

Renaming a Document

Retrieve

Text In/Out

Word Search

Lists

Generates lists of figures, tables, and so on, from marked entries in
your document.

KEY SEQUENCE

To mark an entry for the list:

Alt-F4 (Block)

[highlight text to be listed]

Alt-F5 (Mark Text)

2 List

List Number: *<number between 1 and 9>*

To define the style of the list:

Alt-F5 (Mark Text)

5 Define

2 – Define **L**ist

List Number (1–9): *<list number>*

1 – **N**o Page Numbers
2 – **P**age Numbers Follow Entries
3 – **(**Page Numbers) Follow Entries
4 – **F**lush Right Page Numbers
5 – Flush Right Page Numbers with **L**eaders

F7 (Exit)

To generate a list:

Alt-F5 (Mark Text)

—▭—

6 Generate

—▭—

5 – Generate Tables, Indexes, Automatic References, etc.

—▭—

Existing tables, lists, and indexes will be replaced.
Continue? (Y/N) ↵ *or any key except N*

USAGE

You can mark up to five separate lists in a document, but an item
may belong to only one list. For each item that you want to include
in a list, follow these steps:

1. Press Alt-F4 and use the cursor movement keys to mark the list
   item as a block.

2. Press Alt-F5 (Mark Text), then select the List option (**2** or **L**).

3. When the List# prompt appears, enter the number of the list
   (from 1 to 5).

When you mark a list entry with this method, WordPerfect places
a [Mark:List,#] and [End Mark:List,#] code around the marked text.
To delete the entry from the list, you need only to locate and delete
the [Mark:List #] code for that entry in the Reveal Codes screen.

In addition to the five lists you mark yourself, WordPerfect automatically maintains separate predefined lists of the captions for figures, tables, text boxes, and user-defined boxes created with the
Graphics feature (see **Graphics**) assigned to the list numbers 6
through 9 respectively. For example, to create a list composed of all
of the captions for the text boxes in a document, you simply define
the style and generate the list for list 8. There is no need to mark any
of the captions assigned to each of these text boxes as you do with the
first five lists.

Defining the Style of the List

WordPerfect allows you to choose among several formatting styles for the lists it generates. To define the style for a list, follow the steps as outlined in the key sequence. After you select the Define and List options and indicate the number of the list (1–9), you select the option number corresponding to the style you wish to use.

A [Def Mark:] code is inserted in the document when you press F7 (Exit) after selecting a style for the list. This marks the position where the list will be generated (*see* below). Therefore, most often you will want to position the cursor at the end of the document before you define the list style to have it generated there.

Generating Tables, Lists, and Indexes

After marking the list entries (if you are creating a list from 1–5) and indicating the style of the list, you are ready to generate it. After selecting the Generate (**6** or **G**) and Generate Tables, Indexes, Automatic References, etc. (**5** or **G**) options, you receive the prompt

Existing tables, lists, and indexes will be replaced.
Continue? (Y/N)

To have WordPerfect generate the list, type **Y** or press any key besides **N**. If you have previously generated an index for the document, it will be completely replaced unless you type **N**. The list is generated at the [Def Mark] code in the document, and the program automatically inserts an [End Def] mark at the end of the list.

SEE ALSO

Graphics

Mark Text

Location of Auxiliary Files

Allows you to indicate to the program where the WordPerfect spelling, thesaurus, and hyphenation dictionaries, as well as the backup, printer, macro, style, and keyboard files, are located.

KEY SEQUENCE

Shift-F1 (Setup)

7 – Location of Auxiliary Files

1 – **B**ackup Directory
2 – **H**yphenation Module(s)
3 – **K**eyboard/Macro Files
4 – **M**ain Dictionary(s)
5 – **P**rinter Files
6 – Style **L**ibrary Filename
7 – **S**upplementary Dictionary(s)
8 – **T**hesaurus

F7 (Exit)

USAGE

You use the Location of Auxiliary Files option on the Setup menu when you first install WordPerfect to indicate where you keep the program's spelling, thesaurus, and hyphenation dictionaries. In addition, you need to use it to indicate what directory will contain the backup files that the program will make if you use the Backup feature (see **Backup, Timed and Original Document**) as well as the printer definition files installed for the printer you use (see **Printer, Select**).

As you work with WordPerfect, you also use this option to indicate the name of the directory that will contain the macro/keyboard layout files (see **Macros** and **Keyboard Layout**), supplementary spelling dictionaries, and style library files that you create (see **Styles**).

When using this option to indicate the location of a particular file or group of files, you select the appropriate option and enter the full path name, including the drive letter and the directory path.

SEE ALSO

Backup, Timed and Original Document

Directories

Hyphenation

Keyboard Layout

Macros

Speller

Styles

Thesaurus

Locking a File

Allows you to protect a document with a password.

KEY SEQUENCE

To add or change a password:

Ctrl-F5 (Text In/Out)

2 Password

1 Add/Change

Enter Password: *<password>* ↵

Re-Enter Password: *<password>* ↵

To delete password protection:

Ctrl-F5 (Text In/Out)

2 Password

2 Remove

USAGE

To lock the file that is displayed on the screen, follow the key sequence and select the Add/Change option. You will then be prompted to enter the password twice. The password can contain up to 24 characters. WordPerfect does not display the password on the screen, so it asks you to enter it twice to protect against typing errors. If the password you enter is not the same each time, you will receive an error message and must begin the file-locking procedure all over again.

As soon as you save the document after assigning a password, it will be saved with the document. Thereafter, you will have to enter the password in order to retrieve, copy, move, or rename the document as well as to print it from disk. If you aren't able to enter the password correctly, you will not be able to retrieve or print it ever again.

Once you have retrieved a locked file, you can edit it just like any other WordPerfect document. If you wish to remove a password from a file after retrieving, you simply press Ctrl-F5 (Text In/Out) and select the Remove option (**2** or **R**). The next time you save the document, it will be saved without the password, which will no longer be required when you retrieve the file or print it from disk.

Looking at the Contents of Files and Directories

Enables you to look at the contents of a file to determine whether it is the one you want to retrieve.

KEY SEQUENCE

F5 (List Files) ↵

[highlight the name of the file to view]

6 Look

F7 (Exit)

USAGE

By selecting the Look option (**6** or **L**) on the List Files menu, you can display the contents of the file whose name is currently highlighted. This feature is helpful when you need to view the contents of a file to see if it is the document you want to edit or print.

When you highlight the name of a file and press ←┘ (or type **6** or **L**), WordPerfect displays the first part of the document on the screen. If you have added a document summary to the file, you will see its statistics at the top of the screen. You can scroll through the document using any of the standard cursor keys. To return to the List Files menu after viewing the contents of the file, press F7 (Exit).

You can also use the Look option to temporarily view a new directory and locate the documents listed there. Highlight the name of the directory whose listing you wish to see and press ←┘ (or **6** or **L** and ←┘).

SEE ALSO

Directories

Macros

Enables you to record keystrokes and replay them at any time by entering the macro name under which they are stored.

KEY SEQUENCE

To define a macro:

Ctrl-F10 (Macro Define)

Define macro: *<macro name>* ←┘

Description: *<description of macro>* ←┘

<keystrokes to be recorded> ←┘

Ctrl-F10 (Macro Define)

To edit an existing macro:

Ctrl-F10 (Macro Define)

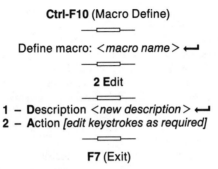

Define macro: *<macro name>* ↵

2 Edit

1 – Description *<new description>* ↵
2 – Action *[edit keystrokes as required]*

F7 (Exit)

To replace an existing macro:

Ctrl-F10 (Macro Define)

Define macro: *<macro name>* ↵

1 Replace

Description: *<new description of macro>* ↵

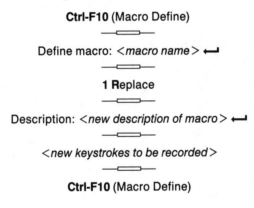

<new keystrokes to be recorded>

Ctrl-F10 (Macro Define)

To execute an Alt-key macro:

Alt-*<letter assigned to macro>*

To execute all other macros:

Alt-F10 (Macro) *<macro name>* ↵

A macro is a recorded sequence of keystrokes that you save in a file and can use repeatedly. Macros can consist of text that you do not want to retype, such as standard paragraphs in a contract or form letter, or they can be complex sequences of commands, such as those that set up a document's format, save the document, and print it. You can even combine text and commands within macros so that you do not have to perform tedious, repetitious procedures, such as searching for formatting codes throughout a document and changing them to other codes.

You can set up macros that repeat themselves, as well as macros that call other macros. In addition, you can specify that a macro be executed only if a certain condition is met.

Creating Macros

The subject of macros is extensive, and it is beyond the scope of this guide to teach you how to use macros. This section presents the rules you need to follow while creating macros but does not make additional suggestions of how you can use them in your work.

To create a macro:

1. Press Ctrl-F10 (Macro Define) to begin the macro definition. WordPerfect will display the prompt

   Define Macro:

   Enter a macro name from one to eight characters long, with no spaces between characters, followed by ←┘, or press the Alt key in combination with a letter from **A** to **Z**, or simply press the Enter key (←┘).

2. WordPerfect will then display the prompt

   Description:

   You may then enter a description of the macro's function, if you wish. It can consist of up to 39 characters. Then press ←┘.

3. WordPerfect then displays the prompt *Macro Def,* which you'll see at the bottom of the screen until you terminate the macro definition. Enter all of the keystrokes that you want to include in the macro.

4. Press Ctrl-F10 a second time to terminate the macro definition. WordPerfect automatically saves the definition in a file. The program appends the extension .WPM to the end of the file name you assigned to the macro. Macro files are automatically saved in the directory that you indicate as the Keyboard/Macro Files directory or in the directory that contains the WordPerfect program files, if you haven't yet specified such a directory (see **Location of Auxiliary Files**).

Executing Macros

To execute a macro whose name consists of one to eight characters, press Alt-F10. WordPerfect displays the following prompt:

Macro:

Enter the name of the macro and press ←┘.

To execute a macro that uses the Alt key and a letter from A to Z, you simply press Alt in combination with the letter key you assigned to the macro.

To execute a macro that was named with the Enter key (←┘), press Alt-F10 and press ←┘. To terminate any macro before it is finished, press F1 (Cancel).

Replacing and Editing Macros

If a macro that you have defined does not work as you intended, you can redefine or edit it. To do either, press Ctrl-F10 (Macro Define) and enter the same name you used when you originally defined the macro. WordPerfect will display the prompt

<*macro name*>.WPM is Already Defined. **1** Replace; **2** Edit: **0**

where *macro name* is the name you entered. To redefine the macro, select the Replace option (**1** or **R**) and reenter the keystrokes you want recorded. Press Ctrl-F10 to terminate and save the new definition when you are finished.

To edit the description or contents of a macro, select the Edit option (**2** or **E**). This takes you to the Macro Editor, which has two options, Description (**1** or **D**) and Action (**2** or **A**). To change the macro's description, select the Description option, edit the comment line, and press ⏎. To edit the contents of the macro, select the Action option (**2** or **A**). This places the cursor inside the macro editing window, which displays the keystrokes already saved in the macro.

Macro programming commands and standard WordPerfect editing commands entered into the macro are both represented by a command or feature name enclosed in a pair of braces. For example, you might see the macro command {BELL}, which sounds the bell, or the editing command {Underline}, which underlines text.

To move the cursor, insert new text, or delete existing text or codes in the Macro Editor, you use the WordPerfect editing and cursor movement keys as usual. However, if you wish to add new WordPerfect commands to the macro, you must press Ctrl-V or Ctrl-F10 (Macro Define) before you press the appropriate function key(s). If you use Ctrl-F10 to enter the Function Key mode, you must press it again to reenter Edit mode before you use any of the editing or cursor movement keys. Otherwise, WordPerfect will insert their codes into the macro (such as {Left} when you press ←) rather than performing their usual function (to move the cursor one character to the left). To insert a macro programming command in a macro, press Ctrl-PgUp. This displays a list of programming commands that you can scroll through. Move the highlight cursor to the command you wish to use and press ⏎ to insert it into the macro.

Once you have finished editing the contents of a macro, press F7 (Exit) to save the new definition and return to the document editing screen. Press F1 (Cancel) if you wish to abandon any editing to the macro.

Enhancing Macros

You can insert a pause into a macro so that you can enter data from the keyboard while the macro is being executed. This makes it possible to write a "general" macro that can be used to accept variable data. For example, you can have a macro that creates a form letter, pausing for you to enter the address and salutation.

To enter a pause for input into a macro, begin the definition of the macro as described above and then press Ctrl-PgUp at the point where you want to insert the pause. The following menu options will appear at the bottom of the screen:

1 Pause; **2** Display; **3** Assign; **4** Comment: **0**

Select the Pause option (**1** or **P**) and then press ◄── and continue with the definition of your macro. When you execute a macro that contains a pause (or pauses) for input, the macro will execute all keystrokes up to the place where you entered the pause and then beep to signal that it has paused. To resume macro execution after you have entered your text, press ◄──.

To make a macro's operation invisible on the screen, you select the Display option (**2** or **D**) after pressing Ctrl-PgUp. The prompt

Display execution? ? (Y/N) No

will appear on the screen. Type **Y** to have the menu options briefly displayed on the document editing screen as WordPerfect commands are selected.

Chaining Macros

A macro can be started from within another macro, or a macro can be made to loop continuously by calling itself. To chain one macro to another, enter the second macro's name at the end of the first macro by pressing Alt-F10 followed by the name of the macro (if you are chaining an Alt macro, you must still press Alt-F10 before pressing Alt and the appropriate letter). When two macros are chained together in this way, all of the keystrokes in the first macro are executed before the keystrokes in the second are executed. By including a search procedure that locates text that you want the macro to process, you can make a macro automatically repeat until it has operated on all occurrences of the search string.

Nesting Macros

You can nest an Alt macro inside of another macro by pressing Alt followed by the appropriate letter key (this time, you don't press Alt-F10 before you press Alt and the letter key). When an Alt macro is nested inside another macro, WordPerfect executes the Alt macro's commands as soon as it comes to its name in the sequence of executing the commands in the first macro. After all of the commands in the Alt macro have been executed, WordPerfect resumes execution of any commands that come after the Alt macro name in the original macro.

The Macro Command Language

WordPerfect now includes sophisticated macro programming commands, which you access by pressing Ctrl-PgUp in the Macro Editor. While it is outside of the scope of this guide to cover their use fully, you will find more information about these commands in Appendix C.

NOTE

WordPerfect 4.2 macros carry the extension .MAC and can't be run under WordPerfect 5.0. You can, however, successfully convert some macros using the MACROCNV.EXE utility (located on the Conversion disk). To convert a 4.2 macro to 5.0 form, go to DOS (you can use the Go To DOS feature) and make the drive/directory that contains this file current, then type

    MACROCNV <macro name>

and press ◄─┘ (enter the full path name if the .MAC file is located on another disk or in a different directory). You don't have to include the .MAC extension as part of the file name. If you are trying to convert an Alt macro, be sure that you don't enter a space between the letters *ALT* and the letter of the key used when you type the macro name (that is, type **ALTP**, not **ALT   P**).

The macro conversion utility will convert as many of the keystrokes in the 4.2 macro into their 5.0 counterparts as possible. It will also rename the macro during conversion by replacing its .MAC extension with .WPM (it won't change the macro name). After the macro has been converted, the utility will display a screenful of statistics. The number of commands that couldn't be successfully converted will be indicated. Also, you will find that these unconverted keystrokes have been changed to comments (by enclosing them in semicolons—used to denote comments in 5.0 macros) when you edit the contents with the Macro Editor.

Because of the degree of change to the menu structure in version 5.0, you will find very few macros that don't require a great deal of manual reworking. Nevertheless, the MACROCNV utility will allow you to transfer the basic structure of the 4.2 macro over to 5.0, and you can then use the Macro Editor to make all necessary manual changes.

SEE ALSO

Keyboard Layout

Appendix C: WordPerfect's Macro Commands

Margin Release

Moves the cursor one tab stop to the left.

KEY SEQUENCE

To release the margin:

Shift-Tab (Margin Release)

To create a hanging indentation:

F4 (→Indent) **Shift-Tab** (Margin Release)

USAGE

To move the cursor one tab stop to the right, you press the Tab key. To move the cursor one tab stop to the left, you press the Margin Release, Shift-Tab. When you use Margin Release to move left, WordPerfect inserts a [←Mar Rel] code in the document in front of the [Tab] code. If you delete the [←Mar Rel] code, only, the [Tab] code will remain, and any text will be indented to its stop.

You can use the Margin Release with Indent to create a hanging indentation. To do this, press F4 to indent the paragraph and then press Shift-Tab to remove the indentation for the first line only. Succeeding lines will be indented, as in the following example:

Hanging indents are often useful to call attention to paragraphs in a series. Sometimes this style of indentation is referred to as an *outdent*.

To delete a hanging indentation, locate and delete the [←Mar Rel] and [→Indent] codes in the Reveal Codes screen.

SEE ALSO

→Indent

→Indent←

Tabs

Margins, Left and Right

Allows you to change the left and right margins of your document.

Shift-F8 (Format)

1 – Line

7 – Margins - Left *<distance from left edge>* ←┘
Right *<distance from right edge>* ←┘

F7 (Exit)

To change the left and right margins for a document, position the cursor at the beginning of the line where you want the new margins to begin and follow the key sequence. The left margin setting is given as the distance from the left edge of the paper, and the right margin setting is given as the distance from the right edge of the paper. Any change to these settings takes effect from the cursor's position forward in the document. To set new left and right margins for the entire document, be sure that the cursor is at the beginning of the file (press Home Home ↑ to get there) before you change them.

WordPerfect automatically adjusts the line length for the current font to maintain the left and right margin settings in effect. Therefore, there is no need to change the left and right margin settings when you change the size of the font in the document.

When you change the left and right margin settings in a document, WordPerfect inserts an [L/R Mar:] code that includes their new settings. To revert to the default left and right margin settings of 1'' each, locate this code in the Reveal Codes screen and delete it.

SEE ALSO

Forms

Margins, Top and Bottom

Page Size/Type

Margins, Top and Bottom

Allows you to change the top and bottom margins of your document.

KEY SEQUENCE

Shift-F8 (Format)

2 – Page

5 – Margins - Top <*distance from top edge*> ◄┘
Bottom <*distance from bottom edge*> ◄┘

F7 (Exit)

USAGE

To change the top and bottom margins for a document, position the cursor at the beginning of the page where you want the margins to change and follow the key sequence. The top margin setting is given as the distance from the top edge of the paper and the bottom margin setting is given as the distance from the bottom edge of the paper. Any change to these settings takes effect from the cursor's position forward in the document. To set new top and bottom margins for the entire document, be sure that the cursor is at the beginning of the file (press Home Home ↑ to get there) before you change them.

WordPerfect maintains the top and bottom margin settings in effect by automatically adjusting the number of lines per page according to the fonts and line heights used. Therefore, there is no need to change the top and bottom margin settings when you change the sizes of fonts or the line height(s) in the document.

When you change the top and bottom margin settings in a document, WordPerfect inserts a [T/B Mar:] code that includes their new settings. To revert to the default top and bottom margin settings of 1" each, locate and delete this code in the Reveal Codes screen.

| SEE ALSO |

Forms

Line Height

Margins, Left and Right

Page Size/Type

Mark Text

Compares documents, removes redline markings and strikeout text, and creates automatic references, master documents, indexes, lists, tables of authorities, and tables of contents.

To access the Mark Text menu:

Alt-F5 (Mark Text)

1 Auto **R**ef; **2** **S**ubdoc; **3** **I**ndex; **4** To**A** Short Form;
5 **D**efine; **6** **G**enerate

To mark a table of contents, list, index, or table of authorities reference:

Alt-F4 (Block)

[highlight text to be marked]

Alt-F5 (Mark Text)

1 To**C**; **2** **L**ist; **3** **I**ndex; **4** To**A**

USAGE

Mark Text is used for automatic references, master documents, document comparison, redline and strikeout removal, outlining, paragraph numbering, indexes and concordances, and tables of contents and authorities. When you press Alt-F5, you see the options shown at the top of the key sequence section. If you have already marked text as a block, the options are slightly different (as shown at the bottom of the key sequence section), because they are designed to allow you to designate which category the marked text is to be in.

For specific information on how Mark Text is used in WordPerfect, refer to the individual reference entries shown in the See Also section below.

SEE ALSO

Automatic Reference
Document Compare

Indexes

Lists

Master Document

Redline/Strikeout

Tables of Authorities

Tables of Contents

Master Document

Allows you to create a master document containing separate documents (specified as subdocuments) that are to be printed together.

KEY SEQUENCE

To insert a subdocument in the master document:

Alt-F5 (Mark Text)

2 Subdoc

Subdoc filename: <*name of file to be inserted*> ↵

To expand the master document:

Alt-F5 (Mark Text)

6 Generate

3 – **E**xpand Master Document

To condense the master document:

Alt-F5 (Mark Text)

⎯ ⊏⊐ ⎯

6 Generate

⎯ ⊏⊐ ⎯

4 – Condense the Master Document

⎯ ⊏⊐ ⎯

Save Subdocs? (Y/N) **N** or **Y**

USAGE	

The Master Document feature allows you to join any number of separate WordPerfect files together so that they are treated as one long document for the purposes of printing and automated references. This feature is most useful when you are creating a long document that consists of a number of discrete sections or parts. For example, you could use this feature to construct a master document for a training manual that is created from separate WordPerfect documents containing the introduction and each section of the manual. By keeping each section in a separate document, you make it easier and more efficient to edit its text. However, because each document is tied to a master document, you can generate a table of contents, list of figures, and index for the entire manual and print it as though it had been created as a single document.

Each WordPerfect document that is tied to the master document is considered a subdocument. To create a master document, you insert Subdocument codes into the master document, indicating where the text of each subdocument is to be inserted. To insert this code, you simply position the cursor in the master document where the text of a subdocument is to occur and follow the steps outlined in the key sequence. When prompted to enter the subdocument file name, type the name of the document. When you press ⏎, WordPerfect displays the name of the subdocument, enclosed in a single-line box. It also enters a [Subdoc:] code into the master document. If you ever want to delete a subdocument from a master document, locate this code in the Reveal Codes screen and delete it—the box containing the subdocument's name in the document editing screen will then disappear.

The master document can contain its own text as well as the Subdocument codes that you enter. If you want to edit the text of a subdocument from within the master document, you can do so by expanding the master document to include the text of all subdocuments within it. Just follow the steps outlined in the key sequence section.

When the master document is expanded, the [Subdoc:] code is replaced by [Subdoc Start:] and [Subdoc End:] codes, which are placed before and after the text of the document (and which are visible on the document editing screen, enclosed in single-line boxes). Once a master document is expanded, you can edit any of its text, including that within the [Subdoc Start:] and [Subdoc End:] codes.

When you use the Exit (F7) or Save (F10) functions on an expanded master document, you receive the prompt

Document is expanded, Condense it? (Y/N) Yes

Press ↵ to condense it before saving it. Type **N** to save it in expanded form. If you press ↵, you receive a second prompt,

Save Subdocs? (Y/N) Yes

Press ↵ to save any editing changes in the subdocument files before the master document is condensed. Type **N**, if you don't want to update the subdocuments with the changes you have made.

You can also condense a master document at any time before saving it. When you condense a master document, as indicated in the key sequence, the text of the subdocuments is replaced with the appropriate [Subdoc:] codes. When you give the command to condense the master document, you receive the same prompt to save the subdocuments as you do when you save the master document.

During editing, be careful that you don't delete any of the [Subdoc Start:] or [Subdoc End:] codes. If you do, WordPerfect won't be able to replace the text that belongs to those codes with the [Subdoc:] code. Therefore, the subdocument's text will remain expanded in the master document. In such a case, delete the subdocument text that can't be condensed and then reinsert the file as a subdocument.

You must expand the master document before you print it, if you want all of the text contained in the subdocument to be included in the printout. If you forget to expand the master document before printing, the printout will contain the Subdocument codes instead of the text stored in the subdocuments.

Prior to generating tables of contents, lists, and indexes for a master document, you should expand it just as with printing. If you forget to expand the master document before generating one of these automatic references, WordPerfect will automatically expand it for you. If this happens, WordPerfect will display the prompt

Update Subdocs? (Y/N) Yes

Press ⏎ to save the subdocuments before condensing the master document. Type **N** if you don't want the changes saved to them.

SEE ALSO

Indexes

Lists

Tables of Contents

Math

Performs calculations on numbers in your document.

KEY SEQUENCE

To turn the Math feature on and off:

Alt-F7 (Math/Columns)

1 Math On/Off

To define math columns:

Alt-F7 (Math/Columns)

—▭—

2 Math Def

—▭—

<*type of columns, negative number display, number of decimal places, and formulas to be used*>

—▭—

F7 (Exit)

USAGE

You can use WordPerfect as a calculator for simple mathematical functions such as addition, subtraction, multiplication, and division. The program can calculate totals, subtotals, and grand totals on numbers down columns. In addition, you can write formulas that perform mathematical operations across columns of numbers.

Turning Math On

To get totals, subtotals, and grand totals from simple columns of numbers (not predefined as Math columns):

1. Clear and then reset the tabs (see **Tabs**). When Math mode is on, WordPerfect aligns tabs on the decimal/alignment character, which is the period (.) unless you change it (see **Decimal/Align Character**).

2. To turn the Math feature on, Press Alt-F7 (Math/Columns) and select the Math On option (**1** or **M**). The following prompt appears in the lower left corner of the screen:

   Math

3. Press the Tab key to move to the first column, then enter the numbers you wish to work with. When you press the period (.)

to indicate a decimal point, the numbers will align on that decimal point. When Math mode is on, WordPerfect treats the tab stop as a decimal tab, like the Tab Align key.

4. Wherever you want a subtotal to be calculated in that column, insert a plus sign (+), either from the numeric keypad or from the top row of your keyboard. WordPerfect will subtotal each number in the column after the previous plus sign. Where you want a total of the subtotals, enter an equal sign (=). If you want any numbers to be considered as subtotals or totals even if no calculation has been performed on them—which may be useful if you are working with imported data on which totals and subtotals have already been calculated—enter **t** before any additional subtotals and **T** before any additional totals. If you want to calculate a grand total—the total of all the totals—enter an asterisk (★).

5. To tell WordPerfect to make the calculations you have specified, press Alt-F7 (Math/Columns) and select the Calculate option (**2** or **A**). (You can select this option at any time to have the program perform calculations—for example, as you enter the numbers.) WordPerfect displays double question marks (*??*) if it cannot make a calculation. If this occurs, recheck your Math Definition screen to make sure that the column references in any formulas you have written are correct.

6. Turn Math mode off by selecting the Math Off option (**1** or **M**) from the Math/Columns menu.

When Math mode is on, you move between columns by using a combination of the Ctrl key and the → and ← keys. Pressing Home ← after the Ctrl-Home (Go To) sequence takes you to the beginning of the first text column.

Defining Math Columns

If you want to perform calculations across columns of numbers, you need to define math columns.

For each column, you define three things: the type of column (calculation, text, numeric, or total), the symbol to be used with negative numbers (either parentheses or the minus sign), and the number of decimal places that are to be displayed (0–4). To do this, press Alt-F7 and select the Math Def option (**2** or **E**) to use the Math Definition screen. Each row under the letters A through X corresponds to a column.

All columns are predefined as numeric columns (type 2). To change a column's definition, move the cursor to its letter by using the arrow keys. Enter **0** if the column is to contain a formula, enter **1** if the column is to contain only text, and enter **3** if the column is to contain a total calculated from other columns. If you have defined the column as type 0, the cursor moves down to the Calculation Formulas section of the screen to allow you to enter the formula for the calculation. Only four columns can be defined for calculations. Press F7 to exit to the menu and save the definition. Press F1 to cancel.

Displaying Totals in Separate Columns

If you have defined Math columns, you can display subtotals, totals, and grand totals in separate columns. To do so, you simply define the column or columns that you wish to hold the total calculations as total columns (type 3) and type the **+** , **=** , or **∗** symbol in your document in the column where you want the calculation to appear.

Using Special Operators for Row Calculations

To use certain special operators in computing the totals and averages of rows, define the column that is to hold these special operators as a calculation column (type 0). Then, when the cursor moves to the Calculation Formulas area of the Math Definition screen, enter any one of the special operators listed here.

- The addition symbol (**+**) calculates the total of all the numbers in the row that are in numeric columns (type 2).

- The **+ /** symbol calculates the average of all the numbers in the row that are in numeric columns (type 2).

- The **=** symbol calculates the total of all the numbers in the row that are in total columns (type 3).

- The **=** *I* symbol calculates the average of all the numbers in the row that are in total columns (type 3).

These special operators work on numbers to their right and left, across the entire row—not just on numbers to the left.

Revising Math Definitions

You will often want to change the definitions of math columns so that you can add new columns of data, delete columns, or move columns to new locations. With your cursor positioned before the [Math On] code in the Reveal Codes screen, you can delete the old [Math Def] code. Then press Alt-F7 (Math/Columns) and select the Math Def option (**2** or **E**) to change any column definitions that you wish. Recalculate by using the new definition before you move to another part of your document.

If you want to revise a Math Definitions screen that you have already defined, position the cursor to the right of the [MathDef] code before you press Alt-F7 and select the Math Def option. You can then use the cursor movement keys to position the cursor on the settings you wish to change. To edit a formula, place the cursor on the *0* that defines the column holding the formula and reenter **0**. The cursor will move to the Calculation Formulas section of the screen, where you can edit the formula or delete it by pressing F1 (Cancel).

Remember that if you add, delete, or move columns, you will also need to revise the formulas that involve them.

SEE ALSO

Decimal/Align Character

Tabs

Merge Operations

Merges data stored in lists in a secondary document into the appropriate places in a primary document.

To designate a field from the secondary file to be merged in the primary file:

Shift-F9 (Merge Codes)

^F

Field: *<enter field number>* ←

To insert other Merge codes:

Shift-F9 (Merge Codes)

^C; **^D**; **^E**; **^F**; **^G**; **^N**; **^O**; **^P**; **^Q**; **^S**; **^T**; **^U**; **^V**

To separate fields in the secondary file with Merge R:

F9 (Merge R)

To separate fields in the secondary file with Merge E:

Shift-F9 (Merge Codes)

^E

To perform a merge:

Ctrl-F9 (Merge/Sort)

———◻——

1 Merge

———◻——

Primary File: *<name of primary file>* ←┘

———◻——

Secondary File: *<name of secondary file>* ←┘

USAGE

Merge operations in WordPerfect can become quite complex, as the program contains many sophisticated merge features. It is beyond the scope of this guide to present a complete tutorial in merge-printing with WordPerfect; instead, this guide briefly summarizes the rules for working with merge operations.

To perform a basic merge operation, such as a form letter, you usually create and use two separate files: a secondary file that contains all of the data to be substituted into each merged document (such as names and addresses), and a primary file (such as a letter) that indicates by special codes where each item from the secondary file is to be placed.

When the program performs the merge, it takes each record that you have specified from the secondary file and inserts its contents into the appropriate place in the primary file, creating a new merge file consisting of one filled-out standard document for each record.

The same record can be used more than once in a primary file. In addition, you do not have to use each record in the secondary file but can use only those that your primary file requires. You also can use several different primary files with the same secondary merge file. For example, you might want to prepare a form letter to go out to all your customers and use that same set of customer data to generate a set of mailing labels.

However, if you do not need to save the variable data to use again, you can skip the process of creating the secondary file and instead enter each variable item from the keyboard as it is needed. You do this by using the ^C code, which instructs WordPerfect to pause for input from the keyboard. Whenever the program encounters this code in your primary document, it will wait for you to type information into the document. (For details about each of the special Merge codes, see **Merge Codes** below.)

The Primary File

Any primary file you use must indicate where the contents (or fields) of the records in the secondary merge file are to be inserted. You do this by pressing Shift-F9, typing **F**, entering the number of the field (*n*), and pressing ◄─┘. Each time the program encounters an *n* in a primary file, it inserts the corresponding data from the *n*th field in the record that is current in the secondary merge file. For example, if the code were 1, WordPerfect would insert the contents of the first field in the current record. WordPerfect numbers fields sequentially beginning with 1 for the first data item.

If you are not using a secondary file but are instead entering data from the keyboard, enter a ^C merge code at each point in the document where you want to insert variable data.

Creating a Primary File

To create a primary merge file:

1. Begin a new document, such as a letter. Enter all of the text that is not to vary from merge document to merge document.

2. Indicate any places where you want information to be supplied from the secondary merge file by entering an ^F merge code; enter a ^C code for input from the keyboard.

You can type a question mark (**?**) at the end of the field number after you enter the ^F merge code to keep the program from inserting blank spaces or lines for empty fields. In fact, if you want to make sure that no blank lines are printed and do not want to bother with keeping track of which fields may be blank, you can simply enter **?** after each code as you enter it. That way, if there are any blank fields in your records, you can be sure that WordPerfect will not leave blanks for them.

WordPerfect places the field number inside a pair of caret symbols (^) in the document. For instance, if you enter **2** after the Field prompt, it will appear as ^F2^ in the text when you press ⏎. To delete a field from the primary file, you must delete the entire field designation, including the caret symbols.

The Secondary File

The secondary merge file contains the data that will be inserted into the final merged documents. To prepare a secondary merge file, which is basically a database consisting of records and fields, you must follow a certain set of rules so that the program can accurately locate the data you want to use:

- Each item of data (field) must start on a separate line.

- Each line must be terminated by a Merge R code, which indicates the end of a field. To insert this code, press F9.

- Each record must end with a Merge End code, which indicates the end of a record. To insert this code, press Shift-F9 and type **E**. WordPerfect will insert ^E and a hard page break into the document.

- Each record must have the same number of fields, although some of them can be empty. This way, WordPerfect can always locate the correct data for, say, item 9, which would be in the ninth field. If records had variable numbers of fields, that data would not always be in the field with the same number.

- A field can contain more than one line of data. For example, you can use a field to contain an entire standard paragraph or clause in a contract and simply insert it each time it is needed.

- A field can contain several different items of information, as long as you are willing to use this information as a unit. For example, a field may contain a complete street address, such as *2345 Polk St.*, or a name, such as *Rev. Evelyn Barker*, but you will not be able to break that unit into smaller units in your final documents.

You can also begin a secondary merge file with a dummy record that indicates all of the fields in each record. This record does not actually contain data; instead, you can use it as you set up your primary document to see which fields contain what information.

Creating a Secondary File

To create a secondary merge file:

1. Begin each information item (field) on its own line and terminate it with a Merge R code. Even if you do not have information for a particular field, you must still press F9 to enter a Merge R code to mark its position in the record because each record in the secondary file must contain the same number of fields.

2. Indicate where each record to be used in the merge operation ends by entering a Merge E code on a separate line.

The following two records illustrate the correct usage of the ^R and ^E codes:

Woody Nelson^R
Creative Enterprises^R
115 South St.^R
Orem, UT 84057^R
^E
================================
Toby Wilson^R
^R
1205 East 15th Ave.^R
Berkeley, CA 94704^R
^E
================================

Performing a Merge

To perform a merge operation, press Ctrl-F9 (Merge/Sort) and select the Merge option (**1** or **M**). You are then prompted to enter the name of the primary merge file to use:

Primary file:

Enter the file name of your primary merge file and press ↵. You are then prompted to enter the name of the secondary merge file:

Secondary file:

As soon as you enter the name of the file containing the secondary merge data you wish to use, WordPerfect begins the merge operation.

While data from the two files are being processed and the new file is being generated, you will see the message *Merging* displayed in the lower left corner of the screen. When the merge operation is completed, the cursor will be at the end of the file. Scroll through the file to make sure that the correct data are in each field; then save the file.

You can abort a merge operation at any time before it is finished by pressing F1 (Cancel). This causes WordPerfect to stop merging and to write any letters or forms that have been completed to the screen. (This is useful if you are using a large secondary file and you do not need to print documents for all the records.) To reexecute the merge operation, press F7 (Exit) and answer **N** to the prompt about saving the new document. You can then edit either the primary or secondary merge file and reissue the Merge command.

WordPerfect doesn't automatically save a newly created merge file. When WordPerfect completes a merge, it sends the merged file (all of it, including any separate documents it contains) to the screen and simply holds it in RAM. If you have a large number of records in your secondary merge file, it is possible to run out of RAM before WordPerfect generates all of the merged copies. If this occurs, the program stops the merge operation when no more memory is available and processes only part of your secondary merge file.

You can get around this limitation by using the technique Word-Perfect calls *merging to the printer.* A special code, ^T, instructs the program to send each standard document to the printer as it is completed and then to clear its contents from RAM. If you are working with a large number of records, you may want to use this technique. However, when you merge to the printer, you are no longer performing a simple merge, and you may need to insert additional codes that tell WordPerfect specifically which primary and secondary file to use for each merge, which records to use, and so forth (see **Merge Codes** below).

Merge Codes

WordPerfect offers many optional Merge codes that you can use to adapt the merge operation to special requirements. To insert a Merge code in a document, press Shift-F9 (Merge Codes) followed by the letter of the code.

The ^C (Console) Merge Option

The ^C code temporarily halts the merge operation in progress, allowing you to enter data for a field directly from the keyboard into the merge documents being created. To continue the merge operation once you have finished adding text, press F9. You insert the Merge code into your primary or secondary document by pressing Shift-F9 and typing **C**.

The ^C pause is often combined with paired ^O Merge codes, primarily to keep a user-created message prompt or menu options on the screen and to allow you to enter your response. Insert the ^C code immediately after the final ^O Merge code.

For example, to create the prompt

Enter name of addressee:

you would enter it as

^OEnter name of addressee:^O^C

The ^C code can also be combined with the ^G, ^P, and ^S Merge codes, primarily to allow you to specify the name of a macro or a primary or secondary file to use. In this case, it is entered within any of these paired codes.

The ^D (Date) Merge Option

The ^D code inserts the system date (the date entered in DOS when you start the computer) into your merge file. Usually you will use this code to insert the date in a primary merge file instead of entering the date manually or with WordPerfect's Date Insert function (see **Date, Inserting the**). When you execute the merge operation, WordPerfect will substitute the full date wherever ^D appears. This date is automatically updated to the current date each time you execute a merge operation using a primary document that contains it. To enter this Merge code into your merge file, press Shift-F9 and type **D**.

The ^G (Go To Macro) Merge Option

The ^G merge option is always paired. Between the pair of ^G merge codes, you place the name of the macro that is to be executed when the merge operation terminates. For example, if you want the macro Alt-M to be executed as soon as the merge operation called for in a primary file is complete, enter

```
^GALTM^G
```

in the primary file. If your macro does not use the Alt key with a single alphabetical letter, you enter its name between the ^G codes. To enter these codes, press Shift-F9 and type **G**, enter the name of the macro (do not enter the .WPM file extension), and press Shift-F9 and type **G** again.

You can enter only one macro in a merge file.

The ^N (Next Record) Merge Option

When you merge to the printer (by using the ^T code), the ^N Merge code tells WordPerfect to use the next record in the designated secondary file. If the program does not find a next record in the file, WordPerfect terminates the current merge operation. To enter the ^N merge code, press Shift-F9 and type **N**.

You can place the ^N code above a particular record in the secondary file to cause WordPerfect to skip that record in the merge operation.

The ^O (On-Screen Message) Merge Option

The ^O Merge code is always paired. Between the pair of ^O codes, you place the text of the message or prompt you want displayed in the lower left corner of the screen. To enter these Merge codes, press Shift-F9, type **O**, enter the text of your message as well as any other Merge codes to be included, and press Shift-F9 and type **O** again.

The ^O code is combined with a ^C pause code to keep a message on the screen until you type the data and press F9. For example, if you enter

^OEnter the date of sale: ^O^C

in a primary file when you perform the merge operation, WordPerfect will pause the operation and display

Enter the date of sale

on the last line of the screen in double intensity. This message will remain on screen until the user presses F9.

The ^O codes can also be used to display a menu of options on the screen by including the menu, with all of its options, between a pair of ^O Merge codes. Also within the ^O codes you could include a pair of ^G codes (to execute the macro associated with the menu selection) plus a ^C code (to allow the user to indicate a selection).

The ^P (Primary File) Merge Option

When you merge to the printer (with the ^T code), WordPerfect neither assumes that you are using the same primary file throughout the merge nor automatically merges all records in the secondary file.

The ^P code designates the primary file to be used. It is always paired. Between the pair of ^P Merge codes, you place the complete name of the primary merge file that you want to use. If you do not specify a file name between the pair of ^P codes to switch to a different primary file, WordPerfect uses the current primary file. To insert these codes, press Shift-F9 and type **P**, enter the file name (if you are using other than the current file), and press Shift-F9 and type **P** again.

You can combine ^P Merge codes with the ^T and ^N codes to cause the current merge operation to continue until all of the records in the designated secondary file are processed.

For example, you might want to send each merged document to the printer as it is created, clear it from memory, advance to the next record, and use the same primary document. In such a case, you enter these codes at the end of the primary document:

```
^T^N^P^P
```

The ^Q (Quit) Merge Option

The ^Q Merge code terminates a merge operation. You may enter this code into either a primary or secondary merge file. However, most often you will use it to restrict the records to be processed in a merge operation. In such a case, you place the code in the secondary merge file on its own line immediately before the beginning (first field) of the first record that you do not want included. When WordPerfect encounters this Merge code, it terminates the merge operation, thus ignoring all records that come after the ^Q code. To enter the ^Q Merge code, press Shift-F9 and type **Q**.

The ^S (Secondary File) Merge Option

The ^S Merge code is always paired. Between the pair of ^S codes, you place the complete name of the secondary merge file that you want inserted. If you do not specify a file name between the pair of ^S codes, WordPerfect uses the current secondary file. To insert these codes, press Shift-F9 and type **S**, enter the file name, and press Shift-F9 and type **S** again.

You use the ^S Merge codes to designate a new secondary file to be used during the current merge operation. Enter the complete file name between a pair of ^S codes in the primary file at the place where new data are to be substituted.

When WordPerfect encounters the ^S codes, it uses the designated secondary document in the merge operation and follows the codes it contains until its merge operations are complete.

The ^T (Type) Merge Option

The ^T Merge code sends all of the text that has been merged up to the location of the code directly to the printer. After the text is sent to the printer, it is cleared from the computer's memory.

This code is used to print each merged document as it is generated. To enter the ^T code, press Shift-F9 and type **T**.

Usually you will combine the ^T Merge code with the ^N code and a pair of ^P codes. This combination, ^T^N^P^P, ensures that each record in the second document is processed, and prevents extra form feeds from being inserted between the documents as they are printed.

The ^U (Update) Merge Option

The ^U Merge code rewrites the screen, causing the merge document that is currently being generated to be displayed on the screen. To enter this code, press Shift-F9 and type **U**.

This option is often combined with the ^O, ^C, and ^P Merge codes. It is used for applications in which the merge document is assembled from several merge files.

The ^V (Insert Code) Merge Option

The ^V Merge code is always paired. It inserts any merge codes enclosed within a pair of ^V codes into the document currently being created. You enter these codes by pressing Shift-F9, typing **V**, pressing Shift-F9 again, typing the letter of the Merge code to be inserted, pressing Shift-F9, and typing **V** a second time.

The ^V code is quite useful for setting up a complex merge operation that adds records that you can transfer to an existing secondary merge document. To summarize the process briefly, by combining the ^O and ^C Merge codes with the ^V code, you can essentially automate the procedure of adding records to any of your secondary merge files. The ^V code (which stands for *Insert*, the usual assignment for *Ctrl-V*) inserts Merge codes into the file you are creating. This is sometimes called a *dual merge*.

Move/Rename File

Allows you to move a file to a new directory or rename it.

KEY SEQUENCE

F5 (List Files) ←┘

──────

[highlight file to move or rename]

──────

3 Move/Rename

──────

<new path name to move and/or file name to rename> ←┘

USAGE

The Move/Rename option (**3** or **M**) on the List Files menu allows you to rename files in the directory listing or to move them to a new disk or directory on your hard disk. When you select this option after highlighting the file to be moved or renamed (as indicated in the key sequence), you receive the prompt

New name:

followed by the current file name. To rename it, edit or retype the file name. To move it to a new directory, edit the path name and leave the file name as is. To move a file and rename it simultaneously, edit both the path name and the file name. After making these changes, press ←┘. If you renamed the document, the new name will appear in the directory listing after you press ←┘. If you moved the document, its name will no longer appear in the listing (you must change directories to see it).

You can use the Move/Rename option to relocate multiple files in one operation. Mark all of the files to be moved with an asterisk (*)

by moving the cursor highlight to each one and typing ★ (you can mark all of the files in the List Files listing at one time by pressing Alt-F5). After marking the files to be moved, select the Move/ Rename option (**3** or **M**), enter the name of the drive/directory that they are to be moved to, and press ◄—▪ .

SEE ALSO

Copying Files

Move Text

See **Cut and Copy Text**.

Name Search

Moves the highlight cursor directly to the file or font name whose initial characters match those you enter.

KEY SEQUENCE

To locate a file or font from a list on a menu screen:

N Name Search *or* **F2** (→Search)

< character(s) to search for >

◄—▪ *or arrow key to exit*

USAGE

The Name Search feature positions the highlight cursor on the first
file or font whose name matches the character or characters entered.
It enables you to locate and select a particular file or font in a long
listing with just a few keystrokes.

You can initiate a name search on the List Files screen by typing **N**
or by pressing F2 (→Search). Even on a screen like the Cartridges
and Fonts screen that doesn't list a Name Search option, you can initiate such a search by pressing F2. As you type your first character,
the highlight cursor jumps to a file or font name that matches that
character. As you continue to type characters, the search narrows,
moving the highlight to the first file whose name begins with the
matching characters. To exit a name search, press ⏎ or one of
the four arrow keys.

SEE ALSO

Word Search

Outlining

Creates an outline by automatically numbering paragraphs as you
enter each level.

To create an outline:

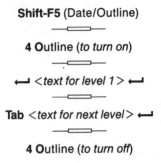

Shift-F5 (Date/Outline)

4 Outline (*to turn on*)

⏎ *< text for level 1 >* ⏎

Tab *< text for next level >* ⏎

4 Outline (*to turn off*)

To define the outlining style:

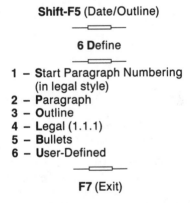

Shift-F5 (Date/Outline)

6 Define

1 – **S**tart Paragraph Numbering
(in legal style)
2 – **P**aragraph
3 – **O**utline
4 – **L**egal (1.1.1)
5 – **B**ullets
6 – **U**ser-Defined

F7 (Exit)

After you have turned on Outline mode, each time you enter characters or a space and then press ⏎, a new outline number is generated in your text. To generate a number at a lower level, press the Tab key after pressing ⏎.

While you are in Outline mode, the prompt

Outline

appears in the lower left corner of your screen. To turn off Outline mode, press Shift-F5 (Date/Outline) and select the Outline option (**4** or **O**), again. Outline mode must be on (the Outline message must be visible on the screen) in order for automatic outline numbering to work.

To indent text without entering an outline number or letter when you are in Outline mode, press the space bar before you press the Tab key. You can also use →Indent (F4) or →Indent← (Shift-F4) to indent text without inserting outline numbers.

Defining the Style of Paragraph/Outline Numbering

WordPerfect's default outlining style (which is option 3, Outline, on the Paragraph Numbering Definition screen) is as follows:

I.
  A.
    1.
      a.
        (1)
          (a)
            i)
              a)

You can use more than eight levels; the eighth-level definition is used for the levels after the eighth, and each level is indented one additional tab stop. There are also three other numbering styles built into the program: paragraph style, which uses the system 1., a., i., (1), (a), (i), 1), a); legal style, which numbers each paragraph and level sequentially as 1, 1.1, 1.1.1, and so forth, and bullet style, which uses a system of symbols that not all printers can produce. You can also change the system of numbering and punctuation by using the User-Defined option (**6** or **U**) and specifying a custom style.

SEE ALSO

Line Numbering

Paragraph Numbering

Overstrike

Prints two (or more) characters or fonts in the same position.

KEY SEQUENCE

Shift-F8 (Format)

4 – Other

5 – Overstrike

1 Create; **2 E**dit

[enter or edit characters or fonts] ←

F7 (Exit)

USAGE

You can use the Overstrike feature to create composite characters such as foreign language characters that use accent marks or special math/science symbols. This is helpful if your printer is unable to print characters in WordPerfect's Character sets created with the Compose feature (see **Compose**). You can also use Overstrike to have your printer combine attributes available from the Font, Size, or Color menus that appear when you press Ctrl-F8 (Font).

When you enter the characters and/or font attributes for Overstrike (as shown in the key sequence), you see all of the characters and attribute codes as you enter them. When you press F7 (Exit) to return to the editing screen, you see there only the last character entered. WordPerfect prints all of the characters and attributes included in the Overstrike definition in the same position in the document.

To edit a composite character created with Overstrike, bring up the Reveal Codes screen with Alt-F3, position the cursor immediately following the [Ovrstk:] code, and select the Edit option (**2** or **E**) as indicated in the key sequence. Enter the new characters and/or attributes, press ←┘, and then press F7 (Exit) to return to the editing screen.

To delete a composite character created with Overstrike, locate and delete the appropriate [Ovrstk:] code in the Reveal Codes screen.

SEE ALSO

Compose

Page Break, Soft and Hard

Divides pages automatically according to the top and bottom margins, the size of the page, and the printer selected (soft page break), or ends a page at the discretion of the user (hard page break).

KEY SEQUENCE

To enter a hard page break in the document:

Ctrl-←┘

USAGE

WordPerfect automatically adjusts soft page breaks as you edit your document. They are displayed as a line of dashes on the screen. To change the placement of a soft page break, change the top and bottom margins, or delete lines of text on the page.

You insert hard page breaks by pressing Ctrl-← at the point where you want a page break to occur. For example, you might want to end a short page at the end of one section of a report so that the next main topic would begin a new page. Hard page breaks are represented by a line of equal signs across the screen.

Hard page breaks are also used to indicate the end of a column when you are using WordPerfect's Columns feature.

To delete a hard page break, position the cursor next to the line of equal signs that represents it and press Backspace or Delete, or locate and delete the [HPg] code in the Reveal Codes screen.

SEE ALSO

Columns

Conditional End of Page

Widow/Orphan Protection

Page Format

See **Format**.

Page Numbering

Adds page numbers that are automatically updated when you make editing changes that affect pagination.

To turn on and off page numbering:

Shift-F8 (Format)

2 – Page

7 – Page Numbering

<page number position, 1–8> or
9 – No Page Numbers

F7 (Exit)

To select a new starting page number:

Shift-F8 (Format)

2 – Page

9 – New Page Number *<page number>* ↵

F7 (Exit)

USAGE

You can turn on page numbering at any point in your document by using the Page Numbering option (**7** or **P**) on the Page Format menu as indicated in the key sequence. When you select Page Numbering, you will see the Page Numbering Position menu (shown in Figure 10), from which you can select where you want page numbers to appear on the page. Choose options 1–3 and 5–7 for page numbers to appear in the same place on every page. Options 4 and 8 will insert page numbers in different locations on alternating left and right pages. Option 9 turns off page numbering.

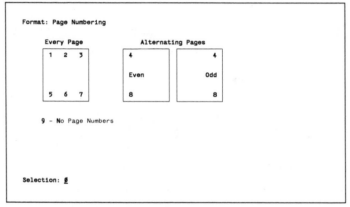

Figure 10: Page Numbering Position menu

When you return to your document by pressing F7 (Exit), you will not see page numbers on the screen, but they will appear when the document is printed. You can use the View Document feature to view page numbers in position on the screen.

You can also turn on page numbering by inserting the code ^B in your document. For example, if you want your headers or footers to contain page numbers, enter a ^B (Ctrl-B) at the position where you want the page number to occur. To specify the position of page numbers in headers and footers, press Alt-F6 (Flush Right) or Shift-F6 (Center) before you enter the ^B.

To start page numbering with a number that you specify, use the New Page Number option (**9** or **N**) on the Page Format menu. If you have saved parts of a document in separate files, this option enables you to number the pages sequentially. When you type the number that you want numbering to start with, you can use either Arabic numerals (1, 2, 3, etc.) or Roman numerals (i, ii, iii, etc.).

When you begin numbering with a new page number, you will see the change reflected on the status line. Be sure to move the cursor to the beginning of the page where you want numbering to start when you use either the Page Numbering or New Page Number option.

To suppress page numbering on any given page, use the Suppress option (**9** or **U**) of the Page Format menu. To turn off page numbering, use option **9** or **N** (No Page Numbers) on the Page Numbering Position menu.

SEE ALSO

Headers and Footers

Suppress Page Format

Page Size/Type

Instructs WordPerfect to use a new page size or form definition in printing.

KEY SEQUENCE

Shift-F8 (Format)

2 – Page

8 – Paper **S**ize *<paper size option, 1–9 or O>* ←

Type *<paper type option, 1–8>* ←

F7 (Exit)

| USAGE |

Depending on your printer's capabilities, you can use the Paper Size/Type option (**8** or **S**) on the Page Format menu, as indicated by the key sequence, to instruct WordPerfect to format pages for a specific paper size, such as 8.5 by 14 inches (legal) or 5.5 by 5.8 inches (half sheet), and different types of paper, such as bond, letterhead, or transparency masters. WordPerfect comes with five predefined forms: Envelope, Standard letter size portrait (or narrow), Standard letter size landscape (wide), Standard legal size, and an ALL OTHERS form. You can modify the settings of any of these forms or add new definitions to the list by using the Forms feature on the Select Printer: Edit menu.

When you use the Paper Size/Type option, you first select the paper size and then the type from the list of options. For example, if your document is an envelope, you would select the Paper Size/Type option (**8** or **S**) and then select Envelopes (**5** or **E**) for the paper size; then select the Envelopes option (**5** or **E**) from the Paper Type submenu shown below.

1-Standard

2-Bond

3-Letterhead

4-Labels

5-Envelope

6-Transparency

7-Cardstock

8-Other

You can use the Other option (**O**) on the Paper Size menu to enter the dimensions for a custom paper size if it is not listed and if your printer is capable of handling it.

When the program reaches a Paper Size/Type code in your document, it matches it with either a predefined form definition that your printer supports or a form definition that you have set up by using the Forms option (**F** or **4**) on the Select Printer: Edit menu.

SEE ALSO

Forms

Paragraph Numbering

Automatically numbers paragraphs as you enter them.

KEY SEQUENCE

To number a paragraph:

Shift-F5 (Date/Outline)

5 Para Num

Paragraph Level (Press Enter for Automatic): *<level number,1–8>* or ←

<text of paragraph> ←

USAGE

To number paragraphs automatically, press Shift-F5 (Date/Outline) and select the Paragraph Number option (**5** or **P**). You will be prompted to enter a paragraph level number or to simply press ← for automatic paragraph numbering. When you press ←, WordPerfect will insert a paragraph number. Each level of numbering is associated with a tab stop. To enter progressively lower levels of paragraph numbers, press the Tab key until you reach the level you want. Then press Shift-F5, select the Paragraph Number option, and press ←.

You can also use *fixed numbering,* in which a particular numbering style will be inserted no matter which tab stop you are on. To use fixed numbering, enter the level (1–8) you want to use when you are prompted for the paragraph level.

Defining the Style of Paragraph Numbering

WordPerfect is preset to use the outline style of numbering (I., A., 1., etc.). It also has a built-in paragraph numbering style (1., a., i., etc.) and a legal numbering style (1., 1.1., 1.1.1., etc.). To select the paragraph or legal numbering style:

1. Press Shift-F5 (Date/Outline) and select the Define option (**6** or **D**).
2. When the Paragraph Numbering Definition screen appears, select a numbering style from the options on the screen or create a style of your own by entering any combination of styles and symbols from the choices available.

SEE ALSO

Line Numbering

Outlining

Pitch and Font

See **Font**.

Preview Document

See **View Document**.

Print Color

Allows you to select the color of the text (when printed), if you have a color printer.

KEY SEQUENCE

Ctrl-F8 (Font)

5 – Print Color

1 – Black		7 – Magenta
2 – White		8 – Cyan
3 – Red		9 – Orange
4 – Green		A – Gray
5 – Blue		N – Brown
6 – Yellow		O – Other

F7 (Exit)

USAGE

If you have a color printer, you can use the Print Color option (**5** or **C**) on the Font menu (Ctrl-F8) to select different colors of text for the printed page. For example, you might want to print cover sheets for each section of a document or chapter of a book in a different color, or you might want to highlight a specific section of text by printing it in color.

To return to black printing after having selected a different color, select the Black option (**1** or **K**) from the list of color options and press Exit (F7).

To specify a custom color, you can select the Other option (**O**) and enter an intensity percentage for red, green, and blue.

The Print Color option controls the color the document is printed in, not the color of the characters on the screen. To change the screen colors, use the Colors/Fonts/Attributes command.

Print Format

See **Font** *and* **Format**.

Print Job, Cancel

Allows you to remove a print job from the print queue.

Shift-F7 (Print)

4 − Control Printer

1 Cancel Job(s) <*job number*> *or*
* Y (*to cancel all jobs*)

F7 (Exit)

Selecting the Cancel Job(s) option (**1** or **C**) while the Control Printer screen is displayed allows you to cancel a specific print job in the print queue. When WordPerfect prompts you for the job to cancel, enter the job number of the document that is being printed or the job you want to cancel and press ←⤶. You may need to press ←⤶ again if your printer does not respond. If you are using a large printer buffer, several seconds may elapse before your printer stops printing what has already been sent to it. To cancel all print jobs, enter an asterisk (*), answer **Y** to the prompt *Cancel all print jobs?*, and press ←⤶.

If you cancel all print jobs, you may get a message informing you that you will need to initialize your printer before you can continue printing. You may also need to adjust the paper in the printer before you resume printing.

Printer Control

Print Job, Display

Print Job, Rush

Print Job, Display

Allows you to see the remaining print jobs in the queue beyond the three displayed on the Control Printer screen.

KEY SEQUENCE

Shift-F7 (Print)

⎯⊏⊐⎯

4 – Control Printer

⎯⊏⊐⎯

3 Display Job(s)

⎯⊏⊐⎯

<any key>

⎯⊏⊐⎯

F7 (Exit)

USAGE

Each time you send a document to the printer, WordPerfect assigns it a job number. The first three print jobs are listed on the Control Printer screen; an *Additional jobs not shown* message indicates that there are additional print jobs that are not listed on the Control Printer screen. You can use the Display Jobs option (**3** or **D**) to see all of the current print jobs, if there are more than three.

   Viewing the print job numbers is useful if you are selecting a print job to cancel or bring to the head of the print queue.

SEE ALSO

Print Job, Cancel

Print Job, Rush

Print Job, Rush

Allows you to select a print job to be sent to the top of the queue.

Shift-F7 (Print)

4 – Control Printer

2 Rush Job

<any key>

F7 (Exit)

To move a print job to the head of the queue, select the Rush Job option (**4** or **C**) from the Control Printer screen. WordPerfect will prompt you for the number of the job to rush. Enter the job number and press ←┘. If you answer **Y** to the Interrupt prompt, WordPerfect will immediately print your rush job and then resume printing the job it was working on. If you answer **N**, it will print the rush job as soon as the current job is finished.

If the job you want to rush is a new print job that you haven't yet sent to the printer, first send it to the printer in the normal way; then select the Rush Job option and enter the job number for that job.

SEE ALSO

Print Job, Cancel
Print Job, Display

Print Options

See **Binding, Print Quality,** *and* **Printer, Select**.

Print Quality

Allows you to specify the print quality to be used for text and graphics as well as to print graphics separate from the text in your document.

KEY SEQUENCE

To change the graphics print quality or to print text only:

Shift-F7 (Print)

—▭—

G – **G**raphics Quality

—▭—

1 Do **N**ot Print; **2** Draft; **3** Medium; **4** High

To change the text print quality or to print graphics only:

Shift-F7 (Print)

———⊏▭⊐———

T – **Text** Quality

———⊏▭⊐———

1 Do **N**ot Print; **2 D**raft; **3 M**edium; **4 H**igh

USAGE

The Graphics Quality and Text Quality options on the Print menu control the quality of document printing (draft, medium, and high) for the text and graphic images in your document. You can use these options to prepare rough drafts of documents and to print graphics, which take longer to print, separately from document text. You can select a different print quality for both text and graphics. WordPerfect prints color graphics in black and white, using shading for the color areas.

Your printer may be capable of printing both text and graphics, but not at the same time. If this is the case, you can use the Do Not Print option (**1** or **N**) after selecting the Graphics Quality option to print just the text. Then reinsert the paper in the printer and print just the graphics by selecting the Do Not Print option after choosing the Text Quality option.

Print Quality settings apply to every print job until you change them again or quit WordPerfect.

Note: If your graphics do not print completely on a laser printer, you may need additional memory. Graphic images take up a large amount of memory.

Printer Command

Inserts special printer formatting commands that are sent to the printer when your document is printed.

KEY SEQUENCE

Shift-F8 (Format)

———□———

4 – Other

———□———

6 – Printer Functions

———□———

2 – Printer Command

———□———

1 Command; **2 F**ilename

———□———

<printer command codes or filename> ↵

———□———

F7 (Exit)

USAGE

You can use the Other option (**4** or **O**) on the Format menu (Shift-F8) to display the Printer Functions menu and insert special printer codes, turning on special effects that your printer is capable of producing. However, WordPerfect 5.0 can provide most common printer features directly.

To use special printing effects that WordPerfect does not support directly, you must insert a code that WordPerfect sends to your printer to tell it what to do. These codes are specific to each printer, and you must consult your printer manual for a list of the codes used.

To issue a printer command, enter the ASCII code for the printing effect you want. You cannot enter ASCII codes less than 32 or greater than 126 directly from the keyboard, but instead must enter their decimal equivalents, enclosed in angle brackets. ASCII codes are case-sensitive: Uppercase *A* (ASCII code 065) is not the same as lowercase *a* (ASCII code 097), for example.

For example, to enter the sequence *Esc #* for your printer, you do not enter the letters *esc* or press the Esc key. Instead, you enter the decimal ASCII equivalent of Esc, 27, enclosed in angle brackets and followed by the # symbol. To do this, you select the Command option as indicated in the key sequence and then enter **<27>#** after the Cmnd: prompt. The format code entered for this printer command (visible only when you use Reveal Codes) will appear as

[Cmnd:<27>#]

You will not see printer commands on the screen, but they will be sent to the printer when you print your document.

Printer Control

Allows you to examine and make modifications to the jobs in the printer queue, as well as to start and stop printing.

KEY SEQUENCE

Shift-F7 (Print)

4 – Control Printer

1 Cancel Job(s); **2 R**ush Job; **3 D**isplay Jobs; **4 G**o (start printer); **5 S**top

USAGE

To control the printing process as it is going on, you select the Control Printer option (**4** or **C**) from the Print menu. Doing this brings you to the Control Printer screen (Figure 11), where you may cancel specific print jobs, start a rush print job, display print jobs, restart the printer after it has been stopped, or stop the printer without canceling print jobs.

```
Print: Control Printer

Current Job

Job Number: None                              Page Number:  None
Status:     No print jobs                     Current Copy: None
Message:    None
Paper:      None
Location:   None
Action:     None


Job List

Job  Document               Destination          Print Options



Additional Jobs Not Shown: Ø


1 Cancel Job(s); 2 Rush Job; 3 Display Jobs; 4 Go (start printer); 5 Stop: Ø
```

Figure 11: Control Printer screen

After you have temporarily stopped the printer, you can start it again by using the Go option (**4** or **G**) on this menu.

SEE ALSO

Print Job, Cancel

Print Job, Display

Print Job, Rush

Printing, Stop

Printer Functions

See **Justification, Kerning, Printer Command,** *and* **Word/ Letter Spacing**.

Printer, Select

Allows you to install a printer, edit a printer definition, or select a new printer.

KEY SEQUENCE

To select a new printer:

Shift-F7 (Printer)

S – **S**elect Printer

[highlight the name of the printer]

1 Select

F7 (Exit)

To install a new printer:

Shift-F7 (Printer)

S – **S**elect Printer

2 Additional Printers

1 Select; **2 O**ther Disk; **3 H**elp; **4 L**ist Printer Files;
N Name Search

F7 (Exit)

To edit a printer definition:

Shift-F7 (Printer)

—▭—

S – **S**elect Printer

—▭—

[highlight of the name of the printer]

—▭—

3 Edit

—▭—

1 – **N**ame
2 – **P**ort
3 – **S**heet Feeder
4 – **F**orms
5 – **C**artridges and Fonts
6 – **I**nitial Font
7 – Path for **D**ownloadable
        Fonts and Printer
        Command Files

—▭—

F7 (Exit)

USAGE

WordPerfect saves the printer selection you have made for each document with that document. To select a printer for the document,
press Shift-F7 (Print) and choose the Select Printer option (**1** or **S**).
The program will display a list of printers that you have installed,
and an asterisk (★) will appear next to the name of the currently
selected printer. You can move the highlighting to the printer you
want to use and press ◄─┘ to select it, or select an option from the following menu:

1 Select; **2 A**dditional Printers; **3 E**dit; **4 C**opy; **5 D**elete;
6 Help:1

Installing a New Printer

If the printer you want to use is not displayed, use the Additional Printers option (**2** or **A**) to install it. If the program cannot find the additional printer files, use the Other Disk option (**2** or **O**) to direct it to the drive or directory containing the additional printer files. The printer drivers are on Printer disks 1 through 4. The program will display a list of the printer drivers on each disk. When you see the printer you want to install, move the cursor to highlight its name; then press ←. The Name Search option (**N**) allows you to search for a specific printer's name. When you select a printer, WordPerfect will display the printer definition file (with the .PRS extension) used by this printer. Press ← again to have the program copy this file (see **Establishing a Printer Definition**).

Viewing Installed Printers

As you are selecting new printers, you may want to review the list of printers you have already installed. The List Printer Files option (**4** or **L**) on the Additional Printers submenu allows you to view a list of the printers that you have already installed. WordPerfect keeps information about printer drivers in files with an .ALL extension. Once a printer file is created, its definition is kept in a file with a .PRS extension, which is what you see listed on this screen.

Establishing a Printer Definition

After you have selected a new printer, you will see the Printer Helps and Hints screen, which contains information about the specific printer you are installing. Press F7 (Exit) to go to the next menu (Figure 12), where you can change the printer's name, specify which port it is connected to, select a sheet feeder, select forms, specify cartridges and fonts, set the default font that the printer is to use, and specify a path for downloadable fonts and printer command files.

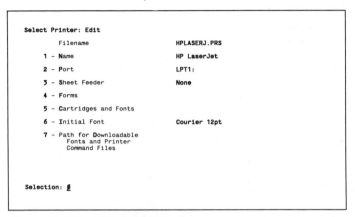

```
Select Printer: Edit

            Filename                    HPLASERJ.PRS

        1 - Name                        HP LaserJet

        2 - Port                        LPT1:

        3 - Sheet Feeder                None

        4 - Forms

        5 - Cartridges and Fonts

        6 - Initial Font                Courier 12pt

        7 - Path for Downloadable
            Fonts and Printer
            Command Files



Selection: ▌
```

Figure 12: Select Printer: Edit menu

Establishing Printer Settings

The Name option (**1** or **N**) allows you to change the name that appears on the Printer Selection menu. You can enter up to 36 characters for a new name.

The Port option (**2** or **P**) is used to indicate the port your printer is connected to. The default setting is LPT1, the first parallel printer port. If the printer whose definition you just chose is connected to another parallel port, select option 2. You will see a menu listing LPT ports 1 through 3 and COM ports 1 through 4. If your printer is connected to a different port, select the Other option (**8** or **O**) and specify the device name.

When defining a printer that uses a serial port, you will see a screen similar to the one in Figure 13. It indicates the baud rate, parity, number of stop bits, character length, and type of hardware handshaking (XON/XOFF) that your printer normally uses. If you are using different settings, select them and change them. All of the settings possible for your printer should be in your printer manual.

Use the Sheet Feeder option (**3** or **S**) if you are using a sheet feeder to feed paper into your printer. Select the sheet feeder that you are using; then choose the Select option (**1** or **S**). A Helps and Hints screen will appear after you have selected the sheet feeder, and the sheet feeder definition will be copied into the .PRS file that is being created for your printer definition.

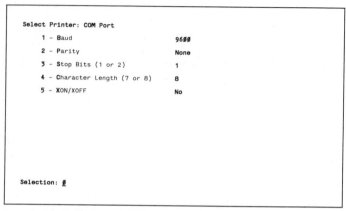

```
Select Printer: COM Port

    1 - Baud                        9600

    2 - Parity                      None

    3 - Stop Bits (1 or 2)          1

    4 - Character Length (7 or 8)   8

    5 - XON/XOFF                    No




Selection: 0
```

Figure 13: Defining a COM port

The Forms option (**4** or **F**) indicates the location of the paper sizes and types you intend to use with the printer (see **Forms**). The Cartridges and Fonts option (**5** or **C**) indicates the fonts and cartridges you plan to use with the printer (see **Cartridges and Fonts**). The Initial Font option (**6** or **I**) indicates the current default font to be used with that printer. The font selected as the initial font will be used each time you start a new document. To override it, you can use the Initial Font option on the Document Format menu (see **Initial Settings**) or change it through the Base Font option (see **Base Font**). The last option (**7** or **D**) is used to indicate the path name for the subdirectory in which you are storing downloadable fonts or printer command files (see **Cartridges and Fonts** and **Printer Command**).

Editing Printer Definitions

The Edit and Copy options (options **3** or **E** and **4** or **C**) of the Select Printers menu allow you to copy and then modify an existing printer definition. For example, you might want to set up the same physical printer with two different definitions under different names. The first definition might specify a different default font or sheet feeder from the second definition, and you could quickly choose either "printer" by selecting its name from the list of installed printers.

You also use the Select Printer option to delete a printer from the list of installed printers by choosing the Delete option (**5** or **D**). However, you cannot delete the printer definition that is currently selected; to delete it, select a different printer first. To get additional help about the specific printers you have installed, use the Help option (**6** or **H**). To get help with a sheet feeder, press Shift-F3 (Switch) when you are viewing the Printer Help screen.

SEE ALSO

Cartridges and Fonts

Forms

Printing

Printing

Prints all or part of a document using the selected printer.

KEY SEQUENCE

To print the current page or entire document on your editing screen:

Shift-F7 (Print)

1 – **F**ull Document
2 – **P**age

To print a document on disk:

Shift-F7 (Print)

3 – **D**ocument on Disk

Document on disk: *<file name>* ←

Page(s): ← *(to print all) or*
<range or selected page numbers> ←

To print a document on disk from the List Files menu:

F5 (List Files) ←

[highlight name of file to be printed]

4 Print

Page(s): ← *(to print all) or*
<range or selected page numbers> ←

| USAGE |

WordPerfect allows you to print documents in a variety of ways, as summarized in Table 8. You can print the document that is currently in RAM (displayed on the screen) or you can print a saved document through the Control Printer screen. In addition, you can print through the List Files screen (F5), or you can print a block of text that you have marked with Block (Alt-F4).

When you press Shift-F7, the Print menu appears (Figure 14). (You can also press Ctrl-PrtSc to bring up this menu.) To print the text of the entire document on the screen, select the Full Text option (**1** or **F**). To print the current page, select the Page option (**2** or **P**).

TO PRINT	KEY SEQUENCE
A saved document from the Control Printer screen	Shift-F7 3 *or* D *<file name>* ⏎ ⏎
A range of pages	Shift-F7 3 *or* D *<file name> <page numbers to print separated by commas, range of page numbers to print separated by dashes>* ⏎
A document on the List Files screen	F5 ⏎ *[highlight document]* 4
A group of documents on the List Files screen	F5 ⏎ *[highlight each document]* * (*to mark it*) 4 Y
The entire document on the screen	Shift-F7 1 *or* F
The page on the screen	Shift-F7 2 *or* P
The text on the screen	Shift-PrtSc
A block of text	Alt-F4 *[highlight block]* Shift-F7 Y

Table 8: WordPerfect's Printing Methods

To print a document that has been saved on disk, you select the Document on Disk option (**3** or **D**), from the Print menu and enter the file name of the saved document. Press ⏎ to print the whole document, or enter the pages you want to print. To enter the page range, you type the starting and ending page numbers, separated by a dash, over the *(All)* that appears after the Page(s) prompt. To print from a specific page to the end of the document, you enter the starting page number followed by a dash. To print from the beginning of the document up to and including a specific page, you enter a dash followed by the ending page number. When entering any of these combinations, be sure not to enter any spaces between the numbers and the dash or commas used.

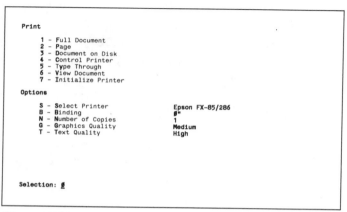

Figure 14: Print menu

Table 9 shows the various combinations that can be entered at the Page(s) prompt and the results of each.

Note that if you have used the Fast Save option to save a document, you cannot print it from disk unless you moved the cursor to the end of the document before you saved it. You must retrieve the document to the screen and then print it.

If you did not select a printer when you installed WordPerfect, when you print a document for the first time, you will need to select the printer you want to use. WordPerfect saves the printer selection you have made for each document with that document. To select a printer for the document, press Shift-F7 and choose the Select Printer option. When you select a different printer for a document, it is reformatted for that printer. To print a document formatted for a printer other than the one that is attached to your computer, select the printer you want the document to be formatted for. Then print it from disk (using the Document on Disk option on the Print menu or the Print option on the List Files screen) without retrieving it to the screen. This technique lets you get a hard copy of a document formatted for a printer that is not available—for example, if you are working at home with a dot matrix printer but will print a final draft of your document on a laser printer at work.

If the document you are retrieving has been formatted for a printer that you have not installed (for example, if you are exchanging files with other WordPerfect users), you will see a message indicating that WordPerfect cannot find that particular printer (.PRS) file. It will format the document for your default printer in that case.

ENTRY	RESULT
Page(s): 4	Prints only page 4 of the document.
Page(s): 6,12	Prints pages 6 and 12 of the document.
Page(s): 2–6,17	Prints pages 2 through 6 and page 17 of the document.
Page(s): 10–	Prints from page 10 to the end of the document.
Page(s): –5	Prints from the beginning of the document through page 5.
Page(s): x–xii	Prints Roman numeral pages 10 through 12.
Page(s): iv,2–5,iv–x	Prints the first Roman numeral page iv, Arabic numeral pages 2 through 5, and finally the second Roman numeral pages iv through x.

Table 9: Entering Pages to be Printed

Other Print Options

If your printer supports type-through printing, you can also use the Print menu's Type Through feature (**5** or **Y**) to print as though your keyboard were a typewriter, either one character or one line at a time.

The View Document option (**6** or **V**) lets you preview your document by pages to see how it will appear when printed. Headers, footers, notes, graphics, and page numbers will be displayed on the previewed pages.

The Initialize Printer option (**7** or **I**) is used when you download soft fonts. When you choose this option, the fonts you have marked as present when the print job begins (using ★) with the Cartridges and Fonts option are downloaded to the printer you have selected.

All of these options are discussed in separate sections. Refer to the See Also list at the end of this entry.

Changing Print Options

Before you print a document, you can temporarily modify the print options that control the printer used, the number of copies printed, the binding width, and the quality of text and graphics. To do this, you select one of the options from the lower half of the Print menu:

S - **S**elect Printer

B - **B**inding Width

N - **N**umber of Copies

G - **G**raphics Quality

T - **T**ext Quality

(Note: The Select Printer and Binding options are discussed in their own separate sections, and the Graphics Quality and Text Quality options are discussed in the Print Quality section.)

Use the Number of Copies option (**N**) to specify the number of copies of a document to be printed while you work on other documents or begin a new one.

Printing from the List Files Screen

To print a document listed on the List Files screen, move the cursor highlight to the document's name and select the Print option (**4** or **P**) on the List Files menu.

To have WordPerfect consecutively print (batch-print) a group of documents listed on this screen, you must mark each document to be printed by highlighting it and then typing an asterisk (★) to mark it.

After you have marked all of the document files you wish to print, select the Print option. When you respond **Y** to the prompt to print the marked files, WordPerfect begins printing the documents in the order in which they were marked. The program places all marked files in its print queue in the order they were marked.

If you need to use printer control at any time, you can press Shift-F7 and enter **4** or **C** to go to the Control Printer screen.

To print documents in other subdirectories, highlight the directory name and press ⏎ twice, then highlight the document file you want to print and select the Print option. Again, if you want to print a group of files listed in this subdirectory, mark all of the files with an asterisk. To return to the current directory, highlight .. <*PAR-ENT*> <*DIR*> and press ⏎.

SEE ALSO

Cartridges and Fonts

Fast Save: Unformatted

Fonts

Printer Control

Printer, Select

Type Through

View Document

Printing, Stop

Halts the current printing job.

KEY SEQUENCE

Shift-F7 (Print)

4 − Control Printer

5 Stop

[fix printing problem]

4 Go (start printer)

F7 (Exit)

USAGE

You may need to stop the printer temporarily to insert a new ribbon or clear a paper jam. To do so, choose the Stop option (**5** or **S**) from the Control Printer screen. This interrupts printing but does not cancel the job. After you have stopped the printer, select the Go option (**4** or **G**) to start it again. If printing does not resume as soon as you type **4** or **G**, check the message area of the Control Printer screen. You may need to reposition the paper in the printer, for example.

SEE ALSO

Print Job, Cancel

Printing to Disk

Saves a copy of the document on disk in DOS text or ASCII format.

KEY SEQUENCE

Shift-F7 (Print)

—◻—

S – **S**elect Printer

—◻—

[highlight printer name]

—◻—

3 – **E**dit

—◻—

2 – **P**ort

—◻—

8 Other

—◻—

Device or filename: <*name of text file*> ↵

—◻—

F7 (Exit) *twice*

—◻—

1 – **F**ull Document

USAGE

WordPerfect can output a document file to a new disk file rather than to your printer; this is known as printing to a disk. The new disk file created with this operation is essentially a DOS text (ASCII) file that also contains all of the printing control codes required to print it as it was formatted by WordPerfect. To save a file as a DOS text file without the formatting codes, you use the Text In/Out key (Ctrl-F5).

When you follow the key sequence shown above, the DOS text file can be printed from the DOS operating system without having a copy of WordPerfect running. This allows you to print WordPerfect documents on a printer attached to another computer that does not even have WordPerfect on it.

As indicated in the key sequence, you need to select the printer name that represents the type of printer that will be used to print the file. Remember that the correct printer definition may differ from the one you use to print documents on the printer (or printers) attached to your computer.

After you specify the printer port, you will need to select the Other option (**8** or **O**) and then type a file name under which the DOS text file version of your document will be stored. If you do not specify a new path name, WordPerfect will save the document in the default directory. When naming the file, you can use the same file name and add the extension .TXT to differentiate it from the original document file.

To obtain a hard copy of the DOS text file, you can use the DOS COPY or PRINT command. (Use COPY if you have temporarily exited from WordPerfect to DOS.)

SEE ALSO

Text In/Out

Redline/Strikeout

Allows you to mark text that has been added to the document with redlining and text that has been deleted from it with strikeout.

KEY SEQUENCE

To redline or strike out text as you type it:

Ctrl-F8 (Font)

2 – Appearance

8 – Redln
9 – Stkout

<text> →

To redline or strike out existing text:

Alt-F4 (Block)

[highlight text]

Ctrl-F8 (Font)

2 Appearance

8 – Redln
9 – Stkout

To select a new redline method:

Shift-F8 (Format)

3 – Document

3 – Redline Method

1 Printer Dependent; **2 L**eft; **3 A**lternating

F7 (Exit)

To removing redline markings and strikeout text from the document:

Alt-F5 (Mark Text)

───▭───

6 – Generate

───▭───

1 Remove Redline Markings and Strikeout Text from Document

───▭───

F7 (Exit)

USAGE

Redlining and strikeout are useful features for marking sections of text that have been altered so that others can review the changes quickly without having to check the entire document.

To mark text for redlining (most printers do this by placing a vertical bar in the left margin), you select the Redline option. When you have finished typing the text you wish to highlight, press the → key to move beyond the second [redln] format code, or press Ctrl-F8 (Font) and select the Normal option (**3** or **N**) to turn off redlining.

To redline text you have already typed, mark the text as a block before you turn on redlining. The way WordPerfect represents red·· lining on the screen varies according to the type of monitor you are using. It may not be the same way that it will appear in the printed document.

To strike out existing text, mark the text as a block and then select the Strikeout option (**9** or **S**) from the Appearance submenu of Font.

Changing the Redlining Method

You can choose Printer Dependent, Left, or Alternating as the method of redlining. If you choose Printer Dependent, redlining will appear as your printer has defined it; you can test-print a red-lined paragraph to see how this appears. The Left option marks redlined text with a horizontal bar in the left margin. The Alternating option marks redlined text on even pages in the left margin and redlined text on odd pages in the right margin.

Deleting Struck-Out Text and Removing Redlining

Before you issue the final version of a document, you will probably want to delete text that has been struck out and remove redlining marks. To do so, press Alt-F5 (Mark Text), choose the Generate option (**6** or **G**) and choose the Remove Redline Markings and Strikeout Text from Document option (**1** or **R**). When you type **Y** in response to the prompt, all text between the [STKOUT] and [stkout] codes will be deleted, and the Redline and Strikeout codes will be removed from the document.

SEE ALSO

Document Compare

Renaming a Document

See **Move/Rename File**.

Repeat Value

See **Esc Key**.

Retrieve

Retrieves a document on disk or the last text that was cut or copied.

To retrieve a document while in the editing screen:

Shift-F10 (Retrieve)

Document to be retrieved: *<document name>* ←

To retrieve the text most recently cut or copied from the current document:

Shift-F10 (Retrieve)

Document to be retrieved: ←

To retrieve a document from the List Files menu:

F5 (List Files) ←

[highlight name of file to be retrieved]

1 Retrieve

Retrieve (Shift-F10) is used to retrieve a saved document. Press Shift-F10 and enter the name of the document; then press ←.

If you do not enter a document name but instead press ← at the prompt, the last text you moved or copied from a document you have been working on in the current session will be inserted at the cursor position, so you can paste a selection several times by using this feature.

You can also retrieve documents from the List Files menu, by selecting its Retrieve option (**1** or **R**). If you retrieve a document while you are working on another document, you see the prompt

Retrieve into current document? (Y/N) No

If you type **Y**, the retrieved document will be inserted at the current cursor position, *added to* the current document.

To retrieve a DOS text file, use Text In/Out (Ctrl-F5).

| SEE ALSO |

Text In/Out

Reveal Codes

See **Codes**.

Rewrite, Screen

Turns off and on automatic screen rewriting.

KEY SEQUENCE

Ctrl-F3 (Screen)

0 Rewrite *or* ⏎ *or* **Ctrl-F3** (Screen)

USAGE

WordPerfect normally rewrites the screen as you enter and edit text so that what you see on the screen resembles what you get in your printed documents. You can temporarily turn off automatic screen formatting to speed up the program's operation if you are working with graphics or complex screen displays.

When you have turned automatic formatting off, you can rewrite the screen by simply pressing Screen (Ctrl-F3) twice.

SEE ALSO

Display, Setup: Automatically Format and Rewrite

Ruler, On-Screen

See **Windows**.

Save

Saves a document on disk under the name you assign to it.

F10 (Save)

Document to be saved: <*file name*> ←

USAGE

To save a file you are working on and then return to it, press Save (F10). WordPerfect will prompt you for a file name if you have not saved the file before. Enter a name of up to eight characters with an optional three-character extension (include a directory and drive designation if you want to save the file somewhere other than the current drive and/or directory); then press ←.

If you have saved the file previously, WordPerfect will provide its file name when you press Save. To save the file under the same name, press ← and respond **Y** to the prompt

Replace <*file name*>? (Y/N)No

to indicate that you *do* want to replace the original version of the file with the edited version you are now saving. The default setting is No, which allows you to leave the existing file intact and save the new version under another name. If you want to rename the file in order to keep two versions of a document, press ← to accept the No setting. WordPerfect will allow you to enter a new file name. Enter the new name (including a drive and directory designation, if you do not want to use the current ones) or edit the existing name; then press ←.

To cancel a save sequence, use the Cancel key (F1).

SEE ALSO

Exit: Saving and Exiting

Text In/Out

Screen Key

See **Line Draw**; **Rewrite, Screen**; and **Windows**.

Search

Locates the next occurrence in the document of specified text or formatting codes.

KEY SEQUENCE

To perform a forward search:

F2 (→Search)

– > Srch: < *search text or function keys* >

F2 (→Search)

To perform a backward (reverse) search:

Shift-F2 (←Search) *or* **F2** ↑

< – Srch: < *search text or function keys* >

F2 (→Search)

USAGE

When you press Forward Search (F2), the prompt

 -> Srch:

appears at the bottom of your screen. The rightward direction of the arrow indicates that WordPerfect will search for your string of characters from the cursor's present position to the end of the document. After you have entered the search string, press F2 or Esc to carry out the search.

You can include up to 59 characters in the search string. WordPerfect ignores case (capitalization) differences in a search as long as the search string is entered in all lowercase letters. To make a search case-sensitive, enter it using the appropriate capital letters. If you enter characters in uppercase, WordPerfect will search for those characters only as capital letters.

If WordPerfect does not find a match for your search string, it will display the message ⋆ *Not Found* ⋆, and the cursor will not move from its original position. In such a case, you can press F2 again and retype or edit the search string.

After WordPerfect finds the first occurrence of your search string, you must repeat the Search command to locate any subsequent occurrences. To reissue the command without changing the search string, press F2 twice. To edit the search string before performing the search again, press F2 once, make your changes, and then press F2 again.

For example, if you enter

 file list

WordPerfect will find all occurrences of *File List*, *file list*, *file List*, and *File list*. If you do not enter a space before *file* and after *list*, WordPerfect will also return any occurrences of the two words together within other words, such as "re*file list*ings." To have WordPerfect search for an entire word by itself, enter a space before and after it.

If you enter

 FILE LIST

WordPerfect will search for *FILE LIST* in uppercase letters only.

Canceling a Search Operation

To abort a search operation after entering the search string, press F1 (Cancel). To return to the place in your document where you were before you began a search operation, press Ctrl-Home (Go To) twice.

Using Wild Cards in a Search

You can substitute Ctrl-X for any character when searching for words or phrases in your documents. For example, a search for

noCtrl-X

returns *now, not, nor, non,* and so forth. It also returns words that contain *now, not, nor, non,* and so forth, such as *nowadays, notable, nonapplicable, enormous, denoted,* and *anonymous.* To enter the wild card (Ctrl-X), press Ctrl-V first. Also note that you cannot use Ctrl-X at the beginning of a search string. Using Ctrl-X as a wild card is useful if you do not remember the exact spelling of the word you wish to find. If you want to limit WordPerfect's search to complete words, you must enter spaces before and after the search string. However, note that this method will not locate words that have a punctuation mark immediately following them.

Extended Searches

When WordPerfect performs a standard search operation, it does not look for matches to your search string in any headers, footers, footnotes, endnotes, graphics box captions, or text boxes that you have added to the document. However, you can perform an extended search operation to include these elements. To do this, press Home before you press F2 to perform a forward search.

Searching in Reverse

You can instruct WordPerfect to search backward through your document to the beginning by pressing Shift-F2 instead of F2 (or by pressing ↑ when the Search prompt is displayed). When you press Shift-F2, WordPerfect responds with this prompt:

   < – Srch:

The leftward direction of the arrow shows you that WordPerfect will search from the cursor's present position toward the beginning of the document. After you enter your search string, press Search (F2) to initiate the reverse search. To perform the reverse search operation to locate a previous occurrence, press Shift- F2. To change directions and perform a forward search using the same search string, press the ↓ key when the Search prompt is displayed. You can always change the direction of a search by pressing ↓ or ↑ when you see this prompt.

   You can also have WordPerfect perform an extended reverse search by pressing Home before you press Shift-F2 and enter your search string.

Searching for Format Codes

You can also use WordPerfect's Search feature to locate a particular formatting code. (This feature also works while you are using Reveal Codes.) To indicate the code to be searched for, press the appropriate function key or key combination (including, if applicable, the number of the menu option) instead of typing an alphanumeric search string in response to the Search prompt. For instance, to perform a forward search to find the first occurrence of a hard page break, press F2 and then press Ctrl- ↵. In response, the program will display the format code as the search string:

   – > Srch: [HPg]

   When the code is located, the cursor will be positioned immediately after it.

You can also use this technique to find format codes that require the use of menu options. For example, to search for a [Col On] code, press F2, then press Alt-F7 (Math/Columns) and type **C**.

If you press twice the key that generates a paired code, the Search function will locate the second formatting code of a pair, such as the [undrln] in [UNDRLN][undrln] or the [bold] in [BOLD][bold], so that, for example, you can replace an underlined word or phrase with a boldfaced version of that same word or phrase. If you perform a regular search for one of these paired codes, WordPerfect locates the first (uppercase) code. However, if you press the key for the code twice, the program will locate the second (lowercase) code, which allows you to locate the beginning of a bold word or phrase, mark it as a block, locate its end, and change it to another style or attribute, such as underline or italics.

For example, to search for an [undrln] code, you press F2 and then press Underline (F8) twice. Press ← twice; then press Del to remove the [UNDRLN] code. (If you do not delete the first code, the program will locate only codes with no text between them.)

For a list of the codes that WordPerfect uses, see Appendix B.

SEE ALSO

Search and Replace

Search and Replace

Locates the next occurrence of specified text or formatting codes and replaces them with new text or codes.

KEY SEQUENCE

Alt-F2 (Replace)

w/Confirm? (Y/N) **Y** *or* **N**

Srch: <*search text or codes*> **F2** (→Search)

Replace with: <*replacement text or codes*> **F2** (→Search)

USAGE

You can search for words or phrases and replace them with substitute words or phrases that you specify. You can search for up to 59 characters and replace them with as many as 59 characters, including spaces. In version 5.0, you can search and replace backward by pressing ↑ before entering the search string.

To perform a search-and-replace operation, press Replace (Alt-F2). For an extended replacement that includes headers, footers, endnotes, footnotes, graphics box captions, and text boxes, press Home before you press Alt-F2. WordPerfect then asks you whether you want to confirm each replacement:

w/Confirm? (Y/N) N

If you enter **Y**, WordPerfect will ask you to confirm whether you want to make the replacement each time it finds the word or phrase you specified (the *search string*). If you press ◄━┘ to accept the No default selection, WordPerfect will replace each occurrence of the search string without prompting you.

After you select whether to confirm, you are prompted to enter the search string. Press F2 after you enter it. WordPerfect then prompts you to enter the replacement string. You can enter text as well as the following formatting codes if you want them to be inserted in your document:

Appearance	Left-Right Indent
Center	Page Margin Release

Center	Math On/Off
Columns On/Off	Math Operators
Font	Merge Code
Hard Space	Size
Hyphen	Soft Hyphen
Hyphenation Cancel	Tab
Indent	Tab Align
Justification On/Off	Widow/Orphan On/Off

If you do not enter a replacement, WordPerfect will delete all occurrences of the phrase or codes you are searching for.

After you have entered the replacement string, press F2 to begin the search-and-replace operation.

Press Cancel (F1) to end a search-and-replace operation.

SEE ALSO

Search

Setup

Allows you to customize the way WordPerfect works by changing many of its default settings.

KEY SEQUENCE

Shift-F1 (Setup)

1 – Backup
2 – Cursor Speed
3 – Display
4 – Fast Save
5 – Initial Settings
6 – Keyboard Layout
7 – Location of Auxiliary Files
8 – Units of Measure

USAGE

You use Setup (Shift-F1) to customize the way WordPerfect works for your own particular needs. Changes you make by using this key remain in effect each time you use WordPerfect. To change settings temporarily as you use the program, use the Format key (Shift-F8).

All of the Setup options are discussed in their own separate sections in this reference.

NOTE

The Setup options associated with Shift-F1 take the place of the WP/S startup command in version 4.2.

SEE ALSO

Backup, Timed and Original Document

Beep Options

Colors/Fonts/Attributes

Cursor Speed

Display, Setup

Document Comments

Fast Save (Unformatted)

Initial Settings
Keyboard Layout
Location of Auxiliary Files
Units of Measure

Sheet Feeders

See **Printer, Select**.

Shell

See **Go To DOS/Shell**.

Sort and Select

Allows you to select and sort lines of text, paragraphs, or secondary merge file records.

KEY SEQUENCE

Ctrl-F9 (Merge/Sort)

2 – Sort

Input file to sort: ← *(for screen) or*
       <file name> ←

Output file for sort: ← *(for screen) or*
       <file name> ←

1 Perform Action; **2 V**iew; **3 K**eys; **4 S**elect; **5 A**ction;
6 Order; **7 T**ype

USAGE

WordPerfect's Sort feature allows you to perform three kinds of sorting. Each kind calls for its own special formatting:

- For a line sort, data is organized into columns and rows, as in a spreadsheet. Each row forms a record, and each column is separated by a tab.

- For a paragraph sort, the data to be sorted is separated by two (or more) hard returns or a hard page break (Ctrl-←).

- For a merge sort, the data is in a secondary merge file. Each field is terminated by a Merge R code (^R), and each record in the file is terminated by a Merge E code (^E).

To sort a file by any of these three methods, you press Ctrl-F9 (Merge/Sort) and select the Sort option (**2** or **S**). You will then be prompted for the name of the input file to sort. If you press ← to accept the default selection (Screen), WordPerfect will sort the file that's in RAM. To sort a file that's on disk, enter the complete file name and press ←.

You are then prompted to indicate where you want the sorted data output. WordPerfect will suggest (Screen) as the output destination.

If you wish to save the data in a disk file, enter the file name.
You can also mark a block of text and sort the items in it.

Selecting the Type of Sort

You are then presented with the Sort by Line screen. Sort by Line is
the default sort type. To perform a different kind of sort, select the
Type option (**7** or **T**). When you do, you are presented with these
options:

Sorting Type: **1** Merge; **2** Line; **3** Paragraph: 0

To select Merge Sort, enter **1** or **M**. To select Paragraph Sort, enter **3**
or **P**.

Defining the Sort Order

The default sorting order used by WordPerfect is ascending. To
change the sort order, select the Order option (**6** or **O**) from the Sort
menu. When you do, you are presented with these options:

Sorting Order: **1** Ascending; **2** Descending: 0

Defining the Sort Keys

To sort data in a file, you must designate the key, or keys, on which to
sort it. WordPerfect lets you define up to nine keys for any one sorting operation.

To define the sort key, or keys, to be used, you select the Keys
option (**3** or **K**) from the Sort menu. You then define the type of data
that will be sorted (alphanumeric or numeric), indicate the field
and/or word to be used as the key (fields and words are numbered
beginning with 1 from left to right, with words being separated by
spaces), and specify the line number to be used (for a paragraph or
merge sort).

When you have defined the type of sort, the sort order, and the
sort keys to be used, you select Perform Action (**1** or **P**) to sort your

data. As soon as WordPerfect has sorted your data, the Sort window will disappear, and you will be returned to the full-screen document window.

Selecting the Records to Be Sorted

WordPerfect also allows you to set up conditions that select only certain records. To use the Select feature, you must first define the sort keys that you wish to use. Then choose the Select option (**4** or **S**) from the Sort menu. Enter the condition that must be met, followed by the number of the key to which the condition is applied. When entering the condition, you type the appropriate logical operator after the key number (see Table 10), followed by a value. For example:

Key1 > = 650.00*Key1 < = 2500.00

specifies those records in which Key1 (an amount-due field) is between $650.00 and $2500.00. The asterisk (*) indicates the logical AND operator.

SYMBOL	FUNCTION	EXAMPLE
=	Equal to	key1 =IL
< >	Not equal to	key1 < >CA
>	Greater than	key1 >M
<	Less than	key2 <50.00
> =	Greater than or equal to	key1 > =74500
< =	Less than or equal to	key2 < =H
*	Logical AND	key1 =IL * key2 <60600
+	Logical OR	key1 =IL + key3 >1000.00
g	Global selection	keyg =Mary

Table 10: Symbols and Logical Operators Used in Sorting Records

After you enter your selection condition, press Exit (F7) to return to the Sort menu. Select Perform Action (**1** or **P**) to have Word-Perfect select and sort your records.

WordPerfect also lets you select records without sorting them. To do this, you still must define the necessary keys and enter the selection condition as previously described. However, before you select Perform Action, select the Action option (**5** or **A**). When you do this, WordPerfect presents these options:

Action: **1** Select and Sort; **2** Select Only: 0

Select the Select Only option (**2** or **O**). When you choose the Perform Action option, WordPerfect will eliminate all records that do not meet the selection condition, although their arrangement will be unchanged from the order in which they were originally entered.

Changing the Sorting Sequence

To change the sorting sequence, press Ctrl-F9 and select Sort Order (**3** or **O**). You are then presented with these options:

Sort Order: **1** US/European; **2** Scandinavian: 0

To select the Scandinavian sorting sequence, which contains more than 26 letters, press **2** or **S**. To return to the US/European sorting sequence (the normal dictionary sort order for languages using the Roman alphabet without any foreign-language characters), press **1** or **U**.

SEE ALSO

Merge Operations

Speller

Allows you to check the spelling of a word, a block of text, or an entire document.

KEY SEQUENCE

Ctrl-F2 (Spell)

1 Word; **2** Page; **3** Document; **4** New Sup. Dictionary; **5** Lookup; **6** Count

USAGE

WordPerfect's Speller key (Ctrl-F2) allows you to check your documents for typographical errors and misspellings. Its main dictionary contains over 100,000 words, and it automatically creates a supplemental dictionary that contains all the words you add to the dictionary as you write.

If you are using the Speller on a floppy disk system, you must first insert the Speller disk into drive B.

You can choose whether to check the word the cursor is on, the current page, or the entire document. You can also check the spelling in text you have marked with Block (Alt-F4).

Checking a Word

To check the spelling of the word the cursor is on, press Spell (Ctrl-F2) and select Word (**1** or **W**). If the cursor moves to the next word, the current word is spelled correctly. If the spelling is incorrect, WordPerfect will present a list of any possible alternatives. Press the letter corresponding to the word you wish to use or, if the correct alternative is not displayed, press → to begin editing the word manually.

Checking a Page

To check for misspellings and typographical errors only on the page on which the cursor appears, use the Page option (**2** or **P**). You may want to do this if you have checked the entire document and then made corrections or additions to a certain page.

Checking a Document

The Document option (**3** or **D**) allows you to check your entire document, including headers, footers, footnotes, and endnotes.

Changing Dictionaries

By selecting the New Sup. Dictionary option (**4** or **N**), you can specify that WordPerfect check a custom dictionary that you have created. To create a new supplemental dictionary, you simply create a new document containing the words you want to include, each separated by a hard return. *Make sure that the words are spelled correctly.* When you save the document, give it a name, such as LEGAL.SUP, that helps you remember that it is a supplemental dictionary. Then enter that name when you are prompted for the name of a supplemental dictionary after selecting this option.

To create custom main dictionaries, you use the Speller Utility, a separate program that is available on the Speller/Thesaurus disk.

You can specify the directory in which your dictionaries are stored by using the Location of Auxiliary Files option on the Setup menu.

Looking Up an Alternative Spelling

To look up alternative spellings of a word, select the Lookup option (**5** or **L**) and type a word or word pattern at the prompt. WordPerfect then presents all the close combinations of that pattern it can find in its dictionaries.

When you look up a word, you can use the question mark (?) and asterisk (*) wild-card characters in place of letters you are unsure of. The question mark stands for any one letter, and the asterisk represents a sequence of letters. For example, type **rec??ve** to see whether *receive* is spelled as *receive* or *recieve*.

Getting a Word Count

To obtain a quick count of the number of words in a document, use the Count option (**6** or **C**) of the Speller menu. This option works without spell-checking the document. A count is also given after each spell check.

Using the Speller

When you use the Speller, WordPerfect checks your document for words it does not recognize. When it encounters one of these, it presents the message *Not Found* and displays a list of possible spellings (if it finds any near matches). You can simply press the letter corresponding to the correct word; WordPerfect inserts it into the document for you.

The Speller ignores numbers, but it will query alphanumeric words, such as *F3*.

WordPerfect's Speller also locates words that occur twice in a row and presents the following menu:

Double word: **1 2 S**kip; **3** Delete 2nd; **4** Edit; **5** Disable Double Word Checking

You can press **3** to delete the second occurrence, or you can leave the words in place (press **1** or **2**). Disable Double Word Checking (**5**) allows you to turn this feature off so that the program does not query you at double words.

Once you've selected the Page or Document option of the Speller, the standard menu you see when a word is being queried contains five options:

1 Skip Once; **2** Skip; **3** Add Word; **4** Edit; **5** Look Up

Skipping a Word

If you instruct the Speller to skip a word once (option 1), it will query you the next time it locates the pattern in your document. Use Skip (option 2) if you want to keep a certain spelling in this document but do not want to add it to the dictionary. You will not be queried on that spelling again during the current session with the Speller.

Adding a Word

To add a word that is being queried—such as a proper name or a specialized term—to the dictionary as you are correcting a document, select Add Word (option 3). WordPerfect will then add it to the supplemental dictionary that is automatically created as you use the Speller.

You can also add words to the supplemental dictionary directly by retrieving the file WP{WP}EN.SUP and typing each word that you wish to add, separated by a hard return. Be sure to save the file under the same name after you have added words to it. (While you have the file on the screen, you can also correct any misspelled words that may have been inadvertently added to the supplemental dictionary.)

Editing a Word

If you choose Edit (option 4), you may edit the word that is presented or simply use the → or ← key to move from that word to the part of the sentence or paragraph that you wish to edit. While you are working with the Speller, only the → and ← keys, along with

Backspace and Del, are available as cursor movement keys. You cannot use most of the other cursor movement techniques, such as Go To (Ctrl-Home), or End. You can change from Insert to Typeover mode, however.

After you have edited a word in your document, press Exit (F7) to return to the Speller.

Looking Up a Word

By selecting this option while you are checking a document, you can enter a word that you wish WordPerfect to look up. Type a word or word pattern at the prompt. WordPerfect then presents all of the close matches to the word that it can find in its dictionaries.

Exiting from the Speller

To exit from the Speller, press Cancel (F1). The program will present a count of the text it has checked up to that point. Save your document if you want the changes introduced with the Speller to be incorporated into the saved version.

SEE ALSO

Location of Auxiliary Files

Thesaurus

Styles

You can store sets of formatting commands that can be applied to various parts of your document.

To create or edit a style:

Alt-F8 (Style)

3 Create *or* **4 E**dit

1 – **N**ame
2 – **T**ype
3 – **D**escription
4 – **C**odes
5 – **E**nter

F7 (Exit)

To apply a style in the document:

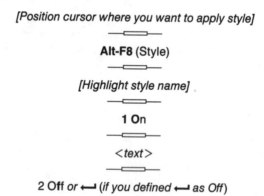

[Position cursor where you want to apply style]

Alt-F8 (Style)

[Highlight style name]

1 On

<text>

2 Off *or* ⏎ (*if you defined* ⏎ *as Off*)

With version 5.0 of WordPerfect, you can set up styles for each element in your document and use the style instead of formatting text
as you type. For example, you can use one style for quotations, and
you can define other styles for each level of heading you are using in
your documents. For instance, if you want all level-1 headings to be
boldfaced and centered, you can define that style. Then, when you

are typing a level-1 heading in your text, you can simply turn on the style instead of pressing F6 for bold and Shift-F6 for center. If you work with complex design elements, such as multicolumn formats and a variety of type styles, this feature can save you many keystrokes throughout a document.

Style Types

You can use two different types of styles in WordPerfect: *paired* and *open*. In a paired style, the codes are turned on and then turned off at the end of the text element, such as turning off bold at the end of the heading or returning to normal size after a quotation in smaller type. Open styles are not turned off, so they are appropriate for setting the style of an entire document, such as margins, justification, line spacing, and so forth.

Creating a Style

To create a style:

1. Press Alt-F8 (Style). You will see the Style menu as illustrated in Figure 15.

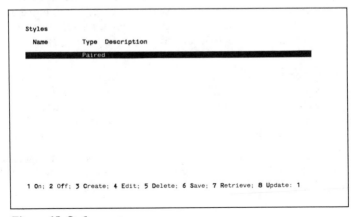

```
Styles
  Name        Type  Description
                Paired




 1 On; 2 Off; 3 Create; 4 Edit; 5 Delete; 6 Save; 7 Retrieve; 8 Update: 1
```

Figure 15: Style menu

2. Select the Create option (**1** or **C**); then select Name (**1** or **N**).

3. Enter a descriptive name for the style, such as **1 head** (for level-1 headings). You can use up to 11 characters.

4. To select whether the style is to be paired or open, select Type (**2** or **T**); then select Open or Paired.

5. To enter a description of the style you are creating, select Description (**3** or **D**); then enter a short description (up to 54 characters) of the style.

6. You can use both text and codes in a style. To indicate to Word-Perfect which codes you want generated when you use this style, select Codes (**4** or **C**) and press the appropriate keys to generate the codes. For example, if you want level-1 heads to be centered and boldfaced, press Center (Shift-F6) and Bold (F6). If you are defining a paired style, type the codes that are to be used when the style is turned on *before* the [Comment] on the screen. Move the cursor past the comment and then type the codes that you want WordPerfect to generate when the style is turned off *after* the [Comment]. For example, to insert bold-facing codes, press Bold (F6), to generate the [BOLD] code; then press → to move past the [Comment]. Press F6 again to generate the [bold] code. If the style is being used to mark text—as for an index or table of contents heading, for example—press Block (Alt-F4) before the [Comment], move the cursor past the [Comment], and then press the appropriate keys to generate the correct Mark Text code. For example, to mark a heading for a level-1 table of contents entry, you would press Alt-F5, choose ToC, and enter **1** for level 1. Press Exit (F7) when you have defined the style.

7. If you are creating a paired style, you can assign it to the ← key by choosing Enter (**5** or **E**) and selecting an option for the way the ← key is to function. You can choose to have the ← key turn off the style, or you can have it turn the style on and then turn it off again. Press Exit (F7) to return to the Style menu.

For a quick way to create a style in an existing document, mark as a block (Alt-F4) the codes that generate the style you want to define; then press Alt-F8 (Style) and select the Create option (**3** or **C**). When you type **4** or **C** for Codes, you will see that WordPerfect has created a paired style from the codes you have highlighted. You can then edit these codes. Be sure to name your new style so that you can remember what it does.

Editing a Style

After you have created a style, you can use the Style menu's Edit option (**4** or **E**) to edit it:

1. Press Style (Alt-F8) and highlight the style you want to change.
2. Choose Edit (**4** or **E**) and edit the style.
3. Press Exit (F7) when you have finished editing the style.

WordPerfect automatically changes the codes in your document to conform to the edited style after you have changed it.

To delete a style, highlight it and select Delete (**5** or **D**); then type **Y** to confirm the deletion.

Applying a Style

To use an open style you have created, press Style (Alt-F8), use the arrow keys to move the cursor to the style, and select On (**1** or **O**). Then type the text that you want to appear in that style. When you apply an open style, it will affect the entire document from the cursor's position forward.

If you are applying a paired style, press Style (Alt-F8), use the arrow keys to move the cursor to the style, then select On. When you reach the end of the text you want to have in that style, press Alt-F8 and select Off. Or, if you have assigned the Off or Off/On option to the ⏎ key, press ⏎ to turn off the style.

If you are using a paired style, you can also block the text you want to apply the style to and then apply the style as described above. WordPerfect automatically inserts the Style On and Style Off codes around the blocked text.

Saving and Retrieving Styles

The styles you define for a document are saved with the document. You can save the styles as a separate document, however, so that you can apply them to several different documents without having to define styles in each one. To do this, choose Save (**6** or **S**) from the Style menu and enter a name for the list of styles displayed on the screen. Then, to retrieve those styles into another document, choose the Retrieve option (**7** or **R**) from the Style menu and enter the name of the style list.

If you retrieve a style list into a document that already has a list of styles, you will be prompted as to whether you want to replace the document's existing styles with the new ones that you are retrieving. Type **N** to retrieve only the styles that have different names from the ones in the current document, or type **Y** to replace the list on the screen with the list you are retrieving.

Creating a Style Library

You can create a library of all the different styles you use. If you press Style (Alt-F8) and you have not defined specific styles for a document, WordPerfect retrieves the style library. To create the style library, you must first use Setup (Shift-F1) to indicate its path name by using the Location of Auxiliary Files option. Then, after you have created a list of styles for the style library, select option 6 (Save) from the Style menu and enter the path name of the style library.

Once you have created a style library, you can update it with new styles by selecting Update (**7** or **U** on the Style menu), adding new styles or editing existing ones, and selecting Save (**6** or **S**) to save it again.

SEE ALSO

Setup

Superscript/Subscript

See **Font**.

Suppress Page Format

Allows you to suppress the printing of page numbers or headers and footers for the current page.

KEY SEQUENCE

Shift-F8 (Format)

2 – Page

9 – Suppress (this page only)

1 – Suppress **A**ll Page Numbers, Headers, and Footers
2 – **S**uppress Headers and Footers
3 – Print Page Numbers at **B**ottom Center
4 – Suppress **P**age Number
5 – Suppress **H**eader A
6 – Suppress He**a**der B
7 – Suppress **F**ooter A
8 – Suppress Fo**o**ter B

F7 F7 (Exit)

To suppress headers, footers, and/or page numbers on a single page, position the cursor at the top of the page (just under the dashed line that marks the page break on your screen). Then press Shift-F8 and select the Page option (**2** or **P**) followed by Suppress for Current Page Only (**9** or **U**). Then select the features (or the combination of features) you want to suppress.

To restore a suppressed format, locate the page with the [Suppress] code and delete that code.

Headers and Footers

Page Numbering

Switch Document

Switches between the Doc 1 and Doc 2 editing screens.

Shift-F3 (Switch)

If the "Block on" message is displayed (indicating that text has not been marked as a block), pressing Switch (Shift-F3) switches you to a second document window. Pressing it a second time returns you to the original document window. You can work with another document or another version of the same document in each window.

NOTE

If you have marked text as a block, pressing Switch displays the Conversion menu so that you can switch to uppercase or lowercase.

SEE ALSO

Case Conversion

Windows

Tab Align

Aligns text on or around the next tab stop using the decimal/align character in effect.

KEY SEQUENCE

Ctrl-F6 (Tab Align)

USAGE

The Tab Align command (Ctrl-F6) aligns text on or around a tab setting using the alignment character that is in effect. WordPerfect uses the period as the alignment character unless you specify another character or symbol. You can use the Tab Align command with any tab stop that is in effect.

Characters that you type after pressing Tab Align are inserted to the left of the cursor, and the cursor remains stationary at the tab stop until you type the alignment character.

To change the alignment character from the period to another character—for example, the colon (:)—follow these steps:

1. Press Format (Shift-F8) and choose the Other option (**4** or **O**).

2. Choose Decimal/Align Char (**3** or **D**) and enter the character you want to use as the alignment character—in this case, the colon (:). Press ◄─┘, then press Exit (F7) to return to your document.

3. To then align your text on the colon, press the Tab key until you are only one tab stop away from where you want the text aligned.

4. Press Ctrl-F6. The cursor will advance to the next tab stop, and you will see this message at the bottom of the screen:

   Align Char = :

As you type your text, it will be entered from right to left, just as it is when you use a right-justified or decimal tab. As soon as you type the alignment character—in this case, the colon— the *Align Char = :* message disappears, and any text you then type is entered from left to right as though you were using a left- justified tab. Pressing Tab again or pressing ◄─┘ leaves text aligned and simply moves the cursor.

To return text that was aligned with the Tab Align command to the previous tab stop, access the Reveal Codes screen (Alt-F3) and delete the [Align] or [C/A/Flrt] formatting codes that surround the aligned text. If you press Backspace when the cursor is located on one of these codes, you will see a message asking you to confirm the deletion. If you wish to retain the current alignment, press ◄─┘. If you do not, type **Y**.

SEE ALSO

Decimal/Align Character

Tables of Authorities

Allows you generate in a legal document a list of citations that is automatically maintained by WordPerfect.

KEY SEQUENCE

To mark the full form for the table:

Alt-F4 (Block)

[highlight text to be cited]

Alt-F5 (Mark Text)

4 To**A**

ToA Section Number (Press Enter for Short Form only):
 <section number between 1 and 16>↵

[edit blocked text] F7

Short Form: *<short form name>* ↵

To define the style of the table of authorities:

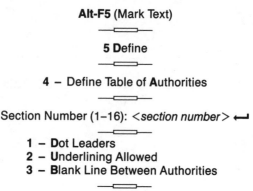

Alt-F5 (Mark Text)

5 Define

4 – Define Table of **A**uthorities

Section Number (1–16): *<section number>* ↵

   1 – **D**ot Leaders
   2 – **U**nderlining Allowed
   3 – **B**lank Line Between Authorities

F7 (Exit)

To generate a table of authorities:

Alt-F5 (Mark Text)

6 Generate

5 – **G**enerate Tables, Indexes, Automatic References, etc.

Existing tables, lists, and indexes will be replaced.
Continue? (Y/N) ↵ *or any key except N*

Tables of authorities are used in legal documents as lists of citations. Creating them involves essentially the same three steps as creating tables of contents: (1) marking the citations, (2) defining the style, and (3) generating the table.

You can divide a table of authorities into 16 sections, such as statutes, regulations, treaties, and so forth. Within each section, WordPerfect sorts the authorities alphanumerically.

Marking Citations for a Table of Authorities

To mark citations for inclusion in a table of authorities:

1. Move to the beginning of the document. You can press Search (F2) or Extended Search (Home F2) and specify the citation you wish to find in the document, or simply move to the first occurrence of the citation.

2. Mark the first occurrence of the citation in its full form by pressing Block (Alt-F4) and highlighting the entire citation.

3. Press Alt-F5 (Mark Text) and select the ToA option (**4** or **A**).

4. The following prompt appears:

   ToA Section Number (Press Enter for Short Form Only):

   For the first occurrence of the citation, enter the number of the section in which you want the citation to be listed in the table of authorities. If this is not the first occurrence and you have already defined a short form, simply press ← to have Word-Perfect mark the citation and its section number for you.

5. For the first occurrence of the citation, WordPerfect presents you with an editing screen in which you can edit the full form of the citation. The text can be up to 30 lines long, and you can use different character styles (bold, italics, and so forth), different fonts, and formats such as indentation.

6. When you have edited the full form of the citation, press Exit (F7). WordPerfect then presents you with a suggested short form (the first 40 characters of the full form) on the prompt line. You can shorten the short form even further or accept the program's suggestion by simply pressing ←. The short form must be unique for each citation.

7. Search for the next occurrence of the citation by using Search (F2) to move directly to it.

8. When the program stops at the next occurrence of the citation, press Mark Text (Alt-F5) and select ToA Short Form (**4** or **A**). The program displays the short form you have defined. Press ← to accept it and mark the citation in the document.

Defining the Style of a Table of Authorities

To define the style of a table of authorities:

1. Move the cursor to the location where you want the table of authorities to be generated, usually at the beginning of the document.

2. Press Ctrl-◄┘ to insert a hard page break. Renumber the first text page as page 1 so that references will be accurate. Position the cursor on the new page and type the heading you want for the table, such as **Table of Authorities**; press ◄┘ twice to move to a new line.

3. Define each section as you want it to be included in the table. Enter the section name (such as **CASES** or **STATUTES**). Press Alt-F6 (Flush Right) to align the heading *Page:* at the right margin and enter **Page:**. Press ◄┘ to move to a new line to separate the heading from the entries that will be generated. Then press Mark Text (Alt-F5) and select Define (**5** or **D**). Select Define Table of Authorities (**4** or **A**), enter the section number at the prompt, and press ◄┘.

4. Select the style you wish to use in that section from the options that appear. You can choose whether to use dot leaders, allow underlining, and allow space between citations. Press ◄┘ to return to the document.

5. Repeat steps 3 and 4 for each section.

If you don't start with a new page number between the definition of the table of authorities and the first text that has been marked for inclusion in the table, your page number references may not be accurate, and WordPerfect will warn you if it does not find a New Page Number code.

Generating a Table of Authorities

After you have marked text for your table of authorities and defined the style of the sections, you can generate the table itself, as shown in the key sequence.

The table will be generated at the [Def Mark] code where you defined the document. If your computer does not have sufficient RAM to hold the entire table in memory, you may be asked to close the Doc 2 window so that WordPerfect can use more memory for generating the table.

To delete a table of authorities, be sure to delete both the [Def Mark] code and the [End Def] code marking the end of the table. If WordPerfect finds a [Def Mark] code but no [End Def] code, it will continue to generate a table of authorities each time you generate your tables and lists.

Editing a Table of Authorities

To edit the full form of a citation in a table of authorities after you have generated the table, position the cursor to the right of the code for the full form in the Reveal Codes screen. Then select Define (**5** or **D**) from the Mark Text menu (Alt-F5), and select Edit Table of Authorities Full Form (**5** or **E**).

The citation will be displayed on the screen. After you have edited it, press Exit (F7). Then enter the section number to which this citation belongs and press ←┘.

You must then generate a new table of authorities to update the changes you have made.

SEE ALSO

Mark Text

Page Numbering

Tables of Contents

Allows you to generate from entries in your document a table of contents that is automatically maintained by WordPerfect.

KEY SEQUENCE

To mark an entry for the table of contents:

Alt-F4 (Block)

[highlight text to be included]

Alt-F5 (Mark Text)

1 ToC

ToC Level: *<level number between 1 and 5>* ⟵

To define the style of the table of contents:

Alt-F5 (Mark Text)

5 Define

1 – Define Table of **C**ontents

1 – **N**umber of Levels
2 – **D**isplay Last Level in Wrapped Format
3 – **P**age Number Position – Level 1
                                Level 2
                                Level 3
                                Level 4
                                Level 5

F7 (Exit)

To generate a table of contents:

Alt-F5 (Mark Text)

6 Generate

5 – Generate Tables, Indexes, Automatic References, etc.

Existing tables, lists, and indexes will be replaced.
Continue? (Y/N) ↵ *or any key except N*

USAGE

Creating a table of contents consists of three basic steps: (1) marking the headings, (2) defining the style, and (3) generating the table.

Marking Text for a Table of Contents

You can mark up to five levels of headings to be included in a table of contents. For each heading you want included in the table of contents, follow these steps:

1. Press Alt-F4 to mark the heading as a block.

2. Press Mark Text (Alt-F5). The following prompt appears:

    Mark for: **1** ToC; **2** List; **3** Index; **4** ToA: 0

3. Select the ToC option (**1** or **C**). The following prompt appears:

    ToC Level:

4. Enter the level of the heading (from 1 to 5).

5. Repeat steps 1 through 4 for each item you want to include in the table of contents.

WordPerfect inserts [Mark] and [End Mark] codes around each entry as you mark it. To remove the markings so that an item will not be included in the table of contents, delete the [Mark] code.

Defining the Style of a Table of Contents

When you define the style of a table of contents, WordPerfect creates the table at that point in your document. For this reason, go to the beginning of your document, press Ctrl-← to create a new, blank page, and type any heading you may want for the contents page, such as **Contents**. Then press ← to add space between the heading and the table entries that will be generated at that point.

To define the format of the contents page (required before you can generate a table of contents):

1. Press Mark Text (Alt-F5) and select the Define option (**5** or **D**).

2. Select Define Table of Contents (**1** or **C**). The Table of Contents Definition screen appears.

3. Select Number of Levels (**1** or **N**) and enter the number of heading levels you are using in the table of contents (1–5).

4. Select Display Last Level in Wrapped Format (**2** or **D**) and type **Y** if you want the last level of entries to be wrapped on one line, rather than listed vertically. If you enter **Y**, WordPerfect displays the headings with the last level as one wrapped line and the headings and page numbers separated by semicolons. The default is No.

5. Select Page Number Position (**3** or **P**) and enter a numbering style for each level.

Choose option **1** or **N** to print headings only, with no page numbers. If you choose option **2** or **3** (or **P** or (), page numbers will occur next to headings, and with option **3** or (, they will be in parentheses. Options **4** and **5** (or **F** and **L**) place page numbers flush right, with or without dot leaders.

Generating a Table of Contents

After you have marked text for your table of contents, created a page for it, and defined its style, you can generate the table itself, as shown in the key sequence.

The table will be generated at the [Def Mark] code where you defined the document. If your computer does not have sufficient RAM to hold the entire table in memory, you may be asked to close the Doc 2 window so that WordPerfect can use more memory for generating the table.

To delete a table of contents, be sure to delete both the [Def Mark] code and the [End Def] code marking the end of the table. If Word-Perfect finds a [Def Mark] code but no [End Def] code, it will continue to generate a table of contents each time you generate your tables and lists.

If you edit your document so that page breaks change, be sure to generate a new table of contents. WordPerfect does not automatically update tables of contents as page changes occur.

SEE ALSO

Automatic Reference

Lists

Mark Text

Tabs

Allows you to change the tab settings in your document.

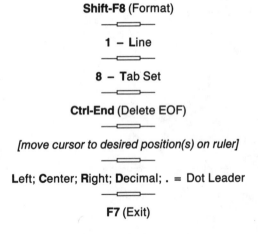

To enter equally spaced tabs:

Shift-F8 (Format)

1 – Line

8 – Tab Set

<start position>, *<increment spacing>* ←┘

F7 F7 (Exit)

To clear all tabs and set different kinds of tabs individually:

Shift-F8 (Format)

1 – Line

8 – Tab Set

Ctrl-End (Delete EOF)

[move cursor to desired position(s) on ruler]

Left; **C**enter; **R**ight; **D**ecimal; **.** = Dot Leader

F7 (Exit)

WordPerfect is preset with left-justified tabs every ½ inch up to position 8.5". To move to the next tab setting, use the Tab key.

To set individual tabs, press Format (Shift-F8) and select the Line option (**1** or **L**). Select Tab Set (**8** or **T**), and the Tab Set menu illustrated in Figure 16 will appear. To select a new tab stop, move the cursor to the position on the ruler line where you want the new tab and type **L** for a left-justified tab, **R** for a right-justified tab, **C** for a centered tab, **D** for a decimal tab, or **.** (period) for a dot-leader tab. You can indicate that dot leaders be used with left, right, or decimal tabs by moving the cursor to the L, R, or C tab that has already been set and typing a period. As you type, when you press Tab and the next tab has been set as a dot-leader tab, you will see the dot leaders appear on your screen.

```
L....L....L....L....L....L....L....L....L....L....L....L....L....L....L...
!    ^    !    ^    !    ^    !    ^    !    ^    !    ^    !    ^    !    ^
1"        2"        3"        4"        5"        6"        7"        8"
Delete EOL (clear tabs); Enter number (set tab); Del (clear tab);
Left; Center; Right; Decimal; .= Dot leader; Press EXIT when done.
```

Figure 16: Tab Set menu

Table 11 illustrates the various types of tabs you can set.

TAB TYPE	HOW SET	EXAMPLE
Left-justified	L	First Quarter .....L............
Right- justified	R	First Quarter ....R............

Table 11: Types of Tabs

TAB TYPE	HOW SET	EXAMPLE
Centered	C	First Quarter ....C.............
Decimal	D	$1,256.00 ....D.............
Dot-leader left	L	Benefits..............Section 1.11 L....................L...........
Dot-leader right	R	Benefits...Section 1.11 L....................R...........
Dot-leader decimal	D	Benefits.....Section 1.11 L....................D...........

Table 11: Types of Tabs (continued)

You may use the space bar or the → key to position the cursor on the tab ruler line to see where these tabs appear in relation to your text. You can also type the number of the position where you want a tab and press ←. For example, to set a tab at the 6.3" mark, type **6.3** and press ←.

To delete the existing tabs and set new ones, press Home Home ← to move to the beginning of the line; then press Ctrl-End to delete the existing tab settings. You do not need to delete old tab settings before you set new ones, however.

To delete a single tab, move to the setting on the line; then press Backspace or Delete.

To return to your document without setting tabs after you have displayed the Tab Set menu, press Cancel (F1).

Setting Evenly Spaced Tabs

You can also specify that WordPerfect set tabs in evenly spaced increments. To do this, press Shift-F8, type **1** or **L**, type **8** or **T**, move the cursor to the beginning of the line, and press Ctrl-End to delete the existing tab settings. Then move the cursor to the first tab stop that you want to set and type **L**, **R**, **C**, or **D** to establish the style of the evenly spaced tabs you are setting (left, right, centered, or decimal). If you are using the default of left-justified tabs, you do not have to take this step.

Then type the number of the character position where you want tabs to start, type a comma, then type the increment by which you want them to be spaced. Finally, press Exit (F7) twice to return to the document.

For example, to set decimal tabs every inch starting one inch from the left margin, you would type **D** at the 1" position and then type

1,1

and press ←┘.

SEE ALSO

Tab Align

Text In/Out

Allows you to retrieve a DOS text (ASCII) file into WordPerfect; to save a document as a DOS text, generic, or WordPerfect 4.2 file; to create document comments; and to assign passwords to documents.

KEY SEQUENCE

To retrieve or save a DOS text file:

Ctrl-F5 (Text In/Out)

—▭—

1 – DOS Text

—▭—

1 Save; **2 R**etrieve (CR/LF to [HRt]); **3 R**etrieve (CR/LF to [SRt] in HZone)

—▭—

<file name> ⏎

To retrieve a DOS text file from List Files:

F5 (List Files) ⏎

—▭—

[highlight file to be retrieved]

—▭—

5 Text In

—▭—

(DOS) Retrieve *<file name>*? (Y/N) **Yes**

To save a document as a generic or WordPerfect 4.2 file:

Ctrl-F5 (Text In/Out)

—▭—

3 – Save Generic *or*
4 – Save WP 4.2

—▭—

<file name> ⏎

USAGE

The Text In/Out key (Ctrl-F5) allows you to bring DOS text files into WordPerfect, to save WordPerfect documents in DOS text file format, to assign password protection to files (see **Locking a File**), to save

WordPerfect 5.0 files in WordPerfect 4.2 format, to save WordPerfect documents in a generic word processor format, and to create document comments (see **Document Comments**).

Importing and Exporting DOS Text Files

To convert a document to DOS text file (ASCII) format within WordPerfect or to retrieve a document in DOS text format, you use the DOS Text option (**1** or **T**) on the Text In/Out menu (Ctrl-F5). When you select this option, the following menu will appear:

1 **S**ave; 2 **R**etrieve (CR/LF to [HRt]); 3 Retrieve (CR/LF to [SRt] in HZone): 0

If you select Save (**1** or **S**), your current WordPerfect document is converted to a DOS text file. In this format, most of the codes that Word-Perfect uses to control formatting are removed. Some WordPerfect codes that control indenting, centering, paragraph numbering, and the Date function are converted to ASCII codes, however. All of your document except footnotes and endnotes will be converted.

To retrieve a document that is in DOS text file format, use option **2** or **3** (or **R** or **e**) instead of using the Retrieve command (Shift-F10). When you press **2** or **R**, carriage returns and line feeds in the DOS text document are converted to hard returns in WordPerfect, so you get a line-for-line conversion. If you are bringing in data from programs such as Lotus 1-2-3 or dBASE III or lines of programming code for which you want to use WordPerfect as a text editor, choose this option, which preserves the column and row format. You may also want to set your margins wider before you import the document to make sure that wide rows are kept intact.

If you use option 3, carriage returns and line feeds in the DOS text document are converted to soft returns when they occur in the hyphenation zone, so hard returns will not occur in the middle of a paragraph in the imported document. You should use this option for word-wrapped text. You may want to set your margins in Word-Perfect as close as possible to those of the DOS text file so that the same line breaks occur.

Retrieving a DOS Text file from List Files

You can also use the Text In option (**5** or **T**) on the List Files menu (F5) to retrieve DOS text files. It is the same as the Retrieve (CR/LF to [HRt]) option on the Text In/Out key.

Converting Documents to a Generic Word Processor Format

You can convert a WordPerfect document to a generic word processor format by using the Save Generic option (**3** or **G**) on the Text In/Out menu. In this format, special WordPerfect format codes are not saved, but the overall text format is maintained. Footnotes and endnotes are not converted, however. In place of the codes that indicate centering, indenting, flush-right text, and soft returns, spaces are inserted, and <CR><LF> (carriage return–line feed) codes are inserted in place of hard returns.

Converting Documents to WordPerfect 4.2 Format

In addition, you will notice on this menu that you can use Save WP 4.2 (**4** or **W**) to convert documents you create in WordPerfect 5.0 into WordPerfect 4.2 format so that they can be used by others who do not have version 5.0. You will be asked to enter a name for the new document; use a different name from that of the current document so that you do not overwrite it.

However, some 4.2 codes, such as font change codes, do not have equivalents in version 5.0. If you have such codes in your 5.0 document, you can use a special file called STANDARD.CRS, located on the Conversion disk, to manually change the codes.

SEE ALSO

Document Comments
List Files
Locking a File
Printing to Disk

Thesaurus

Allows you to look for synonyms for any word in the text of your document.

KEY SEQUENCE

[position cursor on word to be looked up]

Alt-F1 (Thesaurus)

1 Replace Word; **2** View Doc; **3** Look Up Word; **4** Clear Column

USAGE

On a floppy disk system, you must first insert the Thesaurus disk into drive B. Since WordPerfect normally looks for the Thesaurus on the default drive, this means you must also change the Thesaurus default drive to B by using the Setup menu. When you have finished using the Thesaurus, replace your data disk in drive B and save any changes. On a hard disk system, the Thesaurus is installed in the default directory during the installation process, and no special instructions are needed.

There are several ways to look up a word:

- Move the cursor to the word in your document and press Thesaurus (Alt-F1).

- If you are already in the Thesaurus, select View Doc (option 2), move the cursor to the word you want to look up, and press Thesaurus (Alt-F1).

- If the word you want to look up is not displayed on the screen, press Alt-F1 (to start the Thesaurus), select Look Up Word (option 3), and then enter the word.

While you are using the Thesaurus, you will see a few lines of your document at the top of the screen, along with three columns of alternatives, grouped into nouns, verbs, adjectives, and adverbs, as well as antonyms—words of opposite meaning. Any word preceded by a dot is a *headword,* which indicates that you can look up further references to that word by pressing the accompanying letter. At the bottom of the screen is a menu that allows you to replace words, view more of your document, and look up other words.

Replacing a Word

Replace Word (option **1**) allows you to replace the highlighted word in your document with any of the suggested words (with accompanying letters) that appear on the Thesaurus screen. Enter **1** followed by the letter corresponding to the word you wish to use. You can move between the columns of words by using the ← and → keys; the letters will follow the cursor, allowing you to select more words. The ↑ and ↓ keys as well as the PgUp and PgDn keys scroll the columns vertically. The Home Home ↑ and Home Home ↓ key combinations take you to the beginning and end of the Thesaurus entry.

To view groups of related words, type the letter corresponding to any of the headwords (those with dots to their left).

Viewing a Document

The View Doc option (**2**) allows you to return to view your document—for example, to get a better idea of the context in which the word was used. When you are in the document, you can use the cursor movement keys to scroll through the text. After using View Doc, you can return to the Thesaurus screen you were viewing before by pressing Exit (F7), or you can press Alt-F1 again to look up another word in the Thesaurus.

Looking Up a Word

Look Up Word (option **3**) directs the Thesaurus to look up a word. After you press **3**, WordPerfect will prompt you to enter the word you want to look up.

Clearing a Column

If your screen becomes cluttered with too many alternative words, you can use the Clear Column option (**4**) to clear the column the cursor is in to make room for more synonyms of another headword.

SEE ALSO

Speller

Typeover

Toggles between the default Insert mode and Typeover mode.

KEY SEQUENCE

Ins

USAGE

WordPerfect is preset for Insert mode, which means that characters you type are inserted on the screen, with existing characters being pushed to the right of the cursor. To use Typeover mode, in which characters you type replace the characters on the screen, press Ins. A *Typeover* message appears at the bottom of the screen when Typeover is on. To return to Insert mode, press Ins again.

Pressing Tab in Typeover mode does not insert a tab but simply moves the cursor to the next tab stop.

To define a macro in which the typing mode changes, use Word-Perfect's Forced Typeover mode (Home Ins) or Forced Insert mode (Home Home Ins). Otherwise, each time you execute the macro, WordPerfect will use the mode you were in when you recorded the macro.

Type Through

Allows you to use your printer as a typewriter so that any character or line you type is immediately printed.

KEY SEQUENCE

Shift-F7 (Print)

—▭—

5 – Type Through

—▭—

1 Line; **2 C**haracter

—▭—

<characters or line>

—▭—

F7 (Exit)

USAGE

WordPerfect's Type Through feature allows you to use your keyboard as you would a typewriter. The text you type is not saved, however, but is sent directly to the printer, so you need to position the paper so that the printhead is on the first line to be printed.

To use the Type Through feature, press Shift-F7 and choose Type Through (**5** or **Y**). Then select By Line (**1** or **L**) or By Character (**2** or **C**). Use the By Line option if you want the characters you type to be sent to the printer only when you press ↵. Choose the By Character option if you want each character to go to the printer as it is typed; remember, however, that you cannot correct characters if you use this option.

When you use Type Through, you are placed in a special Type Through screen. The line at the top of the screen displays the previously typed line. You cannot edit it, but if you press Move (Ctrl-F4) it will be copied to the bottom line, which can be edited. You can enter up to 200 characters per line; lines that are too wide to be displayed on the screen will move to the left as you type.

While in Type Through mode, you can use the space bar to move the cursor to the right. You can also use the arrow keys to move the cursor right or left, and Home with the → or ← key moves the cursor to the beginning or end of a line. Pressing Format (Shift-F8) allows you to insert printer command codes. Press Exit (F7) or Cancel (F1) to return to the regular editing screen.

Undelete

Restores any of the last three deletions at the cursor's position.

KEY SEQUENCE

F1 (Cancel)

1 Restore; **2** Previous Deletion

USAGE

If WordPerfect is not carrying out a command, the Cancel key (F1) functions as an Undelete key. The following prompt appears along with the most recently deleted text:

Undelete: **1** Restore; **2** Previous Deletion: 0

Entering **1** or **R** restores the displayed text to your document; entering **2** or **P** displays the text that was deleted prior to that deletion. Three levels of deletions can be displayed and restored. After the third most recently deleted text is displayed, pressing **2** or **P** displays the first deletion again. Pressing **1** or **R** restores the displayed deletion to your document.

SEE ALSO

Cancel

Underline

Underscores selected portions of text.

KEY SEQUENCE

To underline new text:

F8 (Underline)

⎯⎯◻⎯⎯

<text to be underlined>

⎯⎯◻⎯⎯

F8 (Underline) or →

To underline existing text:

F4 (Block)

⎯⎯◻⎯⎯

[highlight text to be underlined]

⎯⎯◻⎯⎯

F8 (Underline)

USAGE

To underline new text, press F8 before you type. After you press F8, the Pos indicator appears underlined, indicating that text you type will be underlined. To turn underlining off, press F8 again. You can also indicate a block of existing text to be underlined (by pressing Alt-F4 and marking the block).

You can also underline text by pressing Font (Ctrl-F8), selecting Appearance (**2** or **A**), and selecting Undrln (**2** or **U**).

WordPerfect is preset to underline spaces between words but not spaces created by pressing the Tab key. To change these settings, choose Other (**4** or **O**) from the Format menu (Shift-F8); then select Underline (**7** or **U**).

To use double underlining in a document, press Font (Ctrl-F8), select Appearance (**2** of **A**), and then select Double Underline (**3** or **D**). You will not see the double underline on the screen unless you have a graphics card such as the Hercules Graphics Card Plus, but it will appear in your document when it is printed.

SEE ALSO

Font: Changing the Appearance of the Font

Units of Measure

Allows you to choose the basic unit of measure used by WordPerfect.

KEY SEQUENCE

Shift-F1 (Setup)

⎯◻⎯

8 – **U**nits of Measure

⎯◻⎯

1 – **D**isplay and Entry of Numbers for Margins, Tabs, etc.
2 – **S**tatus Line Display

⎯◻⎯

F7 (Exit)

USAGE

WordPerfect 5.0 is preset to display measurements in inches, but you can change the default unit of measurement to centimeters, points, or "WordPerfect 4.2 units," which means that vertical measurements will be in terms of lines and horizontal measurements will be in terms of columns. (The size of a line or a column will vary with the font you are using.) After you have set a default unit of measurement, the program will convert any values you enter in other units of measurement to the default units. (If you enter measurements in WordPerfect 4.2 units, indicate vertical measurements with v (as in **8v** for 8 lines) and horizontal measurements with h (as in **8h** for 8 columns).

You can also choose a different style for the way information is displayed on the status line. WordPerfect is preset to display the cursor's vertical and horizontal location in inches, but you can specify points (especially useful for many desktop publishing applications), centimeters, or "WordPerfect 4.2 units" (lines and columns).

To change the default units of measure, press Setup (Shift-F1), then select Units of Measure (**8** or **U**). You will see the menu shown in Figure 17. For each option that you want to change, select it; then type **i** or **"** for inches, **c** for centimeters, **p** for points, or **u** for WordPerfect 4.2 units. Then press Exit (F7).

After you have changed the default units of measure, they will be used each time you start WordPerfect.

```
Setup: Units of Measure

        1 - Display and Entry of Numbers        "
            for Margins, Tabs, etc.

        2 - Status Line Display                 u

   Legend:

        " = inches
        i = inches
        c = centimeters
        p = points
        u = WordPerfect 4.2 Units (Lines/Columns)




   Selection: 0
```

Figure 17: Units of Measure menu

View Document

Allows you to preview the way the document will appear when printed.

KEY SEQUENCE

Shift-F7 (Print)

6 – **V**iew Document

1 100%; **2** 200%; **3** Full Page; **4** Facing Pages

F7 (Exit)

USAGE

Choosing View Document (**6** or **V**) from the Print menu (Shift-F7) allows you to see how your document will appear when it is printed, complete with text elements that are not normally visible on the screen, such as page numbers and headers. You can select the 100% option (**1**) to view the document in its actual size, 200% (**2**) to see it at twice its actual size, or Full Page (**3**) to view the page. If you select the Facing Pages option (**4**), you will see odd-numbered pages on the right and even-numbered pages on the left.

Once you have displayed a page or pages, you can use the cursor movement keys to scroll through the document, or use the PgUp, PgDn, Screen Up, and Screen Down keys.

To see the previewed pages in reverse video, press Switch (Shift-F3) while you are in the View Document screen.

To return to your document after previewing it, press Exit (F7).

SEE ALSO

Graphics

Widow/Orphan Protection

Prevents either the first or last line of a paragraph from being separated from the rest of the paragraph by a soft page break.

KEY SEQUENCE

Shift-F8 (Format)

1 – Line

9 – Widow/Orphan Protection **Y or **N**

F7 (Exit)

USAGE

Widow/Orphan protection instructs the program not to leave the first line of text in a paragraph by itself as the last line of a page (a widow) or the last line of a paragraph as the first line of a page (an orphan). Widow lines are forced to the next page, while orphan lines get one more line added from the previous page.

To turn on Widow/Orphan protection for an entire document, move the cursor to the beginning. Then press Format (Shift-F8) and select the Line option (**1** or **L**). Select Widow/Orphan Protection (**9** or **W**) and enter **Y**. This option is a toggle; to turn off Widow/Orphan protection, type **N**.

Windows

Allows you to split the editing screen into two windows to view the text in the Doc 1 and Doc 2 editing areas simultaneously.

KEY SEQUENCE

Ctrl-F3 (Screen)

1 Window

Number of lines in this window: *<number>* ⏎ *or* ↑ ⏎

USAGE

To split the screen into two windows, select Window (**1** or **W**) from the Screen key menu (Ctrl-F3). WordPerfect will prompt you for the number of lines of text you want to see in the current window. The screen can display up to 24 lines, so you can enter any combination that adds up to 24. For example, to see 12 lines in each window, enter **12**; to see 18 lines in one window and 6 in the other, enter **18**.

You can also use the ↑ and ↓ keys to move the cursor to the position where you want the split to occur and then press ⏎. The window will be split at the cursor position.

To move back and forth between windows, press Switch (Shift-F3). To remove the split screen and return to a full-screen display, press Ctrl-F3, select Windows, and this time enter **0** or **24** as the number of lines you want displayed. The second document will still be in memory, and you can return to it at any time by pressing Switch (Shift-F3).

You can view the same document in each of the two windows by retrieving it into both windows—for example, if you want to see the beginning and end of a long document at the same time. Both documents will have the same file name, however, so you will have to keep track of which version you want to have as the final saved version.

SEE ALSO

Switch

Word Count

See **Speller**.

Word/Letter Spacing

Allows you to adjust the spacing between letters of a word and/or between words in a line.

KEY SEQUENCE

Shift-F8 (Format)

——⬚——

4 – Other

——⬚——

6 – Printer Functions

——⬚——

3 – Word Spacing
Letter Spacing

——⬚——

Word Spacing: **1 N**ormal; **2 O**ptimal; **3 P**ercent of Optimal; **4 Set**
Pitch
Letter Spacing: **1 N**ormal; **2 O**ptimal; **3 P**ercent of Optimal; **4
Set Pitch**

——⬚——

F7 (Exit)

USAGE

WordPerfect's Word/Letter Spacing option allows you to adjust the spacing between words and between letters within words. When you justify text, for example, you may want to adjust the amount of space that the program adds between words to make the line of text come out even with the right margin. Letter spacing is normally used to add spaces between letters, creating a visual effect that is widely seen in company logos and on business cards, for example.

To change the word or letter spacing, press Format (Shift-F8) and select Other (**4** or **O**). Then select Printer Functions (**6** or **P**) and choose Word Spacing/Letter Spacing (**3** or **W**) from the menu that appears (Figure 18). You can then select a setting for word spacing, letter spacing, or both.

The Normal setting (**1** or **N**) sets spacing between words as well as letters to the amount recommended by the manufacturer of your printer. Optimal (**2** or **O**), which is the default, produces the setting that appears best according to the manufacturer of WordPerfect.

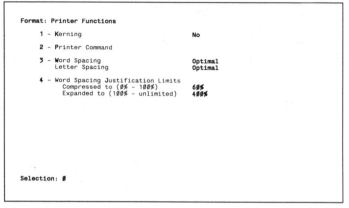

Figure 18: Printer Functions menu

The Optimal and Normal settings are often, but not always, the same.

If you want to specify the amount of space to be used between words and letters, choose Percent of Optimal (**3** or **P**) and enter a percentage. Percentages less than 100% reduce the amount of space, while percentages greater than 100% enlarge it. Normally, you will not want to change the default setting unless you want to create special typographic effects.

If you want to adjust the spacing between words and letters in terms of pitch (characters per inch), use the Set Pitch option (**4** or **S**) and enter the pitch you want to use. WordPerfect then calculates the correct Percent of Optimal setting needed to generate that pitch in the font you are currently using.

SEE ALSO

Justification

Kerning

WordPerfect Startup Options

Allows you to start WordPerfect with a specific document on the editing screen or to start the program using any of its startup options.

KEY SEQUENCE

To start WordPerfect and retrieve a document:

$$\textbf{WP} \ <\textit{file name}> \longleftarrow$$

To start WordPerfect with a specific startup option:

$$\textbf{WP/}<\textit{startup option}> \longleftarrow$$

USAGE

WordPerfect has various setup options that you can add to the basic **WP** startup command.

Retrieving a Document at Startup

If you want to start working on a particular document immediately, you can include its file name as part of the startup command. For example, to edit a document named RPT87 located in a directory named \WP\FILES, give the startup command as

    WP \WP\FILES\RPT87

If the file is in your default directory, you do not have to give its full path name.

Invoking a Macro at Startup

You can also start WordPerfect and have it invoke a macro as soon as the program starts. For example, if you know that the first thing you need to do when WordPerfect is loaded is to change the current directory and you have created a change-directory macro named CD, you can enter the startup command as

WP/M-CD

You can start WordPerfect with any macro that has been saved in the directory that WordPerfect uses on startup. If the macro is an Alt-key macro, enter its name exactly as it is saved in your data directory. For example, to invoke a macro named Alt-Y when you start WordPerfect, enter the startup command as

WP/M-ALTY

Resetting Default Values

The /X startup option tells WordPerfect to restore all the default values that can be changed through the Setup key (Shift-F1). If you are sharing a workstation with other users, you may want to start WordPerfect with this option to make sure that the regular default values are in effect.

Redirecting Overflow Files

Overflow files, which are temporary files containing parts of the document you are currently working on, are normally saved in the drive or directory that WordPerfect uses at startup. You can instruct WordPerfect to save them in a new drive or directory by appending /D- (followed by the drive letter and path names, if required), to the WordPerfect startup command. For example, to save overflow files in the same directory (named SALESUM) as the document you are working on, you can start WordPerfect with this command:

```
WP/D-C:\WP\SALESUM
```

This instructs WordPerfect to save overflow files in a subdirectory named SALESUM under the WP directory on drive C.

Not only overflow files but also buffers and temporary macros will be redirected to this new drive and/or directory. Practically, this means that if you are using WordPerfect on a system with two disk drives and start it using both the /D- and /R options (as discussed in the following section), you can remove the WordPerfect System disk from drive A as you work with the program and replace it with a second data disk. In such a case, you would give the startup command as:

```
A:WP/D-B/R
```

Overflow files will then be saved on the data disk in drive B along with the documents you are creating and editing. The disk in drive A could then hold macros that you wish to use during the work session, for example.

Using the RAM Option

If your computer has at least 300K of unused expanded memory, you can run WordPerfect with the RAM option. When this option is specified as a part of the startup command, WordPerfect loads all of its menus, error messages, and overlay files from the WordPerfect System disk into RAM. Because the program does not have to read these files from the System disk, it runs faster.

To start the program on a hard disk system using this option, you would enter

```
WP/R
```

If you use the /R option with the /D option on a system with two disk drives, you can even remove the WordPerfect System disk during operation, as discussed in the previous section.

Setting Timed Backups for One Session

You can start WordPerfect with a timed backup feature that will be in effect only for the current session. For example, to start Word-Perfect and specify a timed backup at 10-minute intervals, enter

WP/B-10

and press the ◄─┘ key.

The optimal number of minutes between backups depends on your location and the frequency of power interruptions in your area. If an electrical storm is threatening, you may want to set a very small interval between backups, such as 5 or 10 minutes. The inconvenience caused when WordPerfect interrupts your work to save the document is slight compared to the time it takes to retype a long section of text.

Using the Non-flash Option

There are two circumstances under which you use this option:

- If you are using an IBM-compatible computer.
- If you have loaded WordPerfect from a window program.

If you are using an IBM-compatible computer and your screen goes blank from time to time, start WordPerfect with this option. Likewise, use it in the startup command that the window program uses to load WordPerfect if you have any screen difficulties when using a window program. To start WordPerfect with the Non-flash option, enter the startup command as

WP/NF

Starting WordPerfect When TSR's Are Running

Some TSR (terminate and stay resident) programs such as SideKick may conflict with WordPerfect's operation. Three startup options may be used if you are having difficulty running WordPerfect concurrently with a TSR program.

- **/NC** disables the cursor speed feature. If WordPerfect does not start when you are running a TSR program, try starting it with this option.

- **/NE** restricts the use of expanded memory so that more memory is available to the TSR program.

- **/NK** disables certain keyboard functions that several TSR programs do not recognize. If WordPerfect starts but locks up when you are running a TSR program, try starting it with this option.

Setting the Screen Size

The /SS option allows you to set the screen size. WordPerfect normally detects the screen size of the monitor you are using, but if for some reason it doesn't, try starting it with this option and setting the actual screen size.

Combining Startup Options

You can combine all startup options. For example, if you want to speed up the program by using the /R option and set a timed backup interval of 10 minutes while retrieving a document named REPORT89 at the same time, you would enter the command as **WP/R/B-15 REPORT89**. Just remember not to enter spaces between the slashes and to enter a hyphen between the option letter and any particular required entry such as a macro name or number of minutes. The command

    WP/R/B-15/M-CD

starts WordPerfect with the RAM option, specifies a timed backup at 15-minute intervals, and invokes a macro named CD.

Restoring Setup Defaults

Starting WordPerfect with the /X option restores the program's initial default setup values for the current session only. When you exit WordPerfect, any changes you have made through the Setup key (Shift-F1) are restored.

SEE ALSO

Setup

Word Search

Locates all of the files in the current directory that contain a specified word or phrase.

KEY SEQUENCE

To perform a word search:

F5 (List Files) ⏎

━━⬚━━

9 Word Search

━━⬚━━

1 Doc Summary; **2** First Page; **3 E**ntire Doc

━━⬚━━

Word Pattern: *<word(s) or phrase(s)>* ⏎

To set the search conditions:

F5 (List Files) ⏎

━━⬚━━

9 Word Search

━━⬚━━

4 Conditions

━━⬚━━

1 – **P**erform Search on
2 – **U**ndo Last Search
3 – **R**eset Search Conditions
4 – File **D**ate
      From (MM/DD/YY):
      To (MM/DD/YY):
5 – **F**irst Page
6 – **E**ntire Doc
7 – Document **S**ummary
      Creation Date (e.g. Nov)
      Descriptive Name
      Subject/Account
      Author
      Typist
      Comments

━━⬚━━

F7 (Exit)

| USAGE | |

The Word Search option (**9** or **W**) of the List Files menu (F5) allows you to search through all the files in one directory or through the files you have explicitly marked with an asterisk (*) to find a specific word or phrase (up to 20 characters).

After WordPerfect locates the files that contain what you are searching for, it marks them with an asterisk on the List Files screen. You can use the Look option to view their contents and determine which of them are the documents you are seeking. You can also retrieve a marked file to the editing screen.

To return to the List Files screen with the marked files still displayed after using the Look option, press Exit (F7). To return to List Files with the marked files displayed after retrieving a file, press List Files (F5) twice.

Setting Search Options

After you select Word Search, you will see the following menu:

1 Document Summary; **2** First Page; **3** Entire Document; **4** Conditions:0

Select Document Summary (**1** or **D**) for a word, phrase, or pattern only in the document summaries of the files you have marked or of all the files in the directory, if you haven't marked any particular ones.

Select First Page (**2** or **F**) to search through only the first page or the first 4000 characters of each file.

Select Entire Document (**3** or **E**) to search through all the files you have marked or all the files in the directory.

Select Condition (**4** or **C**) to enter specialized search conditions, as discussed below.

Setting Search Conditions

If you select Conditions, you will see the Conditions menu illustrated in Figure 19. You can then choose the conditions that the files must meet.

```
Word Search

   1 - Perform Search on              All 190 File(s)

   2 - Undo Last Search

   3 - Reset Search Conditions

   4 - File Date                      No
          From (MM/DD/YY):            (All)
          To   (MM/DD/YY):            (All)

                    Word Pattern(s)

   5 - First Page
   6 - Entire Doc
   7 - Document Summary
          Creation Date (e.g. Nov)
          Descriptive Name
          Subject/Account
          Author
          Typist
          Comments

   Selection: 1
```

Figure 19: Conditions menu

The Perform Search On option (**1** or **P**) lists the number of files that will be searched. After the search has finished, this number changes to the number of files that the search located. To start a search after selecting other search conditions, select this option.

To repeat a search on the same group of files, select Undo Last Search (**2** or **U**). Normally, if you were searching through ten files and WordPerfect located what you were searching for in two files, the next search you carried out would be on the two files that it located. Selecting this option changes the number of files that are to be included in the search to the previous level—in this example, ten files.

Use the Reset Search Conditions option (**3** or **R**) to clear the search conditions and enter new ones for the next search.

File Date (**4** or **D**) allows you to specify that files created on or between certain dates be included in the search. You can enter the date with or without leading zeroes—as **01/02/89** or as **1/2/89**, for example. To enter a single month or an entire year, use the form **1//89** or **//89**.

Options 5 through 7 are the same as the options on the Word Search menu; they are presented here to allow you to specify searches and carry them out from the same screen.

Entering Patterns for Word Searches

When you search a directory for a file containing a specific word or phrase that contains spaces, you must enter the word or phrase to be searched for in quotation marks.

You can search for an exact phrase by adding a blank space after the last letter and before the last quotation mark. You can also enter an exact phrase to be searched for by pressing Ctrl-◄⎯┘ before typing the phrase.

You can also use wild cards to enlarge the search pattern. For example, if you are searching for a file containing an address for a company and you are sure that its name began with *South* but do not remember whether its full name is *Southwestern, Southeastern,* or *Southern,* you can enter the word pattern as **South★**.

To search for a phrase beginning with one pattern and ending with another, enter it as **"South★Industries"**. This will locate all phrases starting with *South* and ending with *Industries,* such as *Southern Industries, Southwestern Industries, south of the industries,* and so forth. Uppercase and lowercase are considered to be the same.

Using Logical Operators with Word Search

You can further expand or restrict a word search by using semicolons and blank spaces (which stand for *and*) or commas (which stand for *or*). For example, to search for files that contain both the word *invoice* and the phrase *past due,* you enter

    invoice;"past due"

To search for files that contain either the word *invoice* or the phrase *past due,* enter

    invoice,"past due"

To search for files that contain either the word *invoice* or the phrase *past due* in combination with the word *October,* enter

    invoice,"past due";October

SEE ALSO

Document Summary
Name Search

APPENDIX A
Installing WordPerfect

The following installation procedures are for IBM and IBM-compatible computers that operate under PC-DOS and MS-DOS.

Installation on a
Two-Disk-Drive System

To install WordPerfect on a two-disk-drive system:

1. Take the copy of the DOS system disk you use to start your computer and place it in drive A.

2. Get a directory listing to make sure that this disk contains a file called CONFIG.SYS by entering

    DIR CONFIG.SYS ←

    at the A> prompt.

3. If this file exists, you need to examine its contents. This file must contain a FILES = statement that sets the number of files equal to at least 20 files. At the DOS prompt, enter

    TYPE CONFIG.SYS ←

    and read the contents from the screen.

4. If your DOS disk doesn't have a CONFIG.SYS file or this file doesn't contain the correct FILES = statement, you need to rectify this situation by entering

```
COPY CON:CONFIG.SYS ←—
FILES = 20 ←—
^Z ←—
```

Note that you enter the last line, ^Z, by pressing the Ctrl key and Z before pressing ←—. If the CONFIG.SYS file already exists and you are recreating it just so that it will have the correct FILES = statement, enter all of the other statements from the original CONFIG.SYS. before you enter the last line and press ←—. (You may want to make a copy of the original CONFIG.SYS file to compare with, in case you make typos.)

5. If your computer uses 5¼" floppy disks, format 12 disks to be used as the working copies of your program disks, plus a data disk—13 disks in all. If your computer uses 3½" disks, format 7 disks for the program plus a data disk—8 in all. With your DOS disk still in drive A, place a blank disk in drive B, and at the A > prompt enter the command

   FORMAT B:

   Follow the on-screen prompts. Format the remaining disks in this way.

6. Place the original WordPerfect 1 disk (labeled WordPerfect 1/ WordPerfect 2 in the 3½" disk version) in drive A and enter

   COPY A:*.* B:

7. Repeat the process, copying each original disk to a blank formatted disk in drive B. Label each disk so that you can keep track of them. Also label the blank formatted disk that you will be using as a data disk.

8. Place your new WordPerfect 1 disk in drive A and the data disk in drive B.

You can now run WordPerfect by entering the command **WP**. When prompted to do so, replace the WordPerfect 1 disk with the disk marked WordPerfect 2 (5¼" disks only). Before trying to print any documents you create with WordPerfect 5.0, install your printer according to the instructions contained in the **Printer, Select** reference entry in this book.

Installation on a Hard Disk System

To install WordPerfect on a hard disk, you can use the Install program found on the Learning disk. This program creates a WordPerfect directory called WP50 and copies all of the program files into it. It also adds a FILES=20 statement to your CONFIG.SYS file, if necessary. To run this program, have all of your WordPerfect program disks available, turn on your computer, and follow these steps:

1. Place the Learning disk in drive A.

2. At the C> prompt, enter

   A: ←

3. At the A> prompt, type

   INSTALL ←

4. Follow the prompts as they appear on your screen.

You can now run WordPerfect by entering the command **WP**. When you start WordPerfect in future work sessions, you must remember to change to the WP50 directory before entering the WP startup command. To automate the startup procedure, you can create a batch file by following these steps:

1. At the C> prompt, type

   CD\ ←

2. Then, type

   COPY CON:WP5.BAT ←
   CD\WP50 ←
   WP ←
   ^Z ←

Note that you enter the last line, ^Z, by pressing the Ctrl key and Z before pressing ←. You can now start WordPerfect 5.0 simply by entering **WP5** and pressing ← after you boot your computer. Before trying to print any documents you create with WordPerfect 5.0, install your printer according to the instructions contained in the **Printer, Select** reference entry in this book.

APPENDIX **B**
WordPerfect's Formatting Codes

Code	Meaning
_	Cursor Position
[ ]	Hard Space
[-]	Hyphen
-	Soft Hyphen
[/]	Cancel Hyphenation
!	Formula Calculation
+	Calculate Subtotal
=	Calculate Total
★	Calculate Grand Total
[AdvDn]	Advance Down
[AdvLft]	Advance Left
[AdvRgt]	Advance Right
[AdvToLn]	Advance to Line
[AdvToPos]	Advance to (Column) Position
[AdvUp]	Advance Up
[Align]	Tab Align
[Block]	Beginning of Block
[Block Pro]	Block Protection
[Bold]	Bold
[Box Num]	Caption in Graphics Box (inserted inside of Box code)

Code	Meaning
[C/A/Flrt]	End of Tab Align or Flush Right
[Center Pg]	Center Page Top to Bottom
[Cndl EOP]	Conditional End of Page
[Cntr]	Center
[Col Def]	Column Definition
[Col Off]	End of Text Columns
[Col On]	Beginning of Text Columns
[Color]	Print Color
[Comment]	Document Comment
[Date]	Date/Time Function
[Dbl Und]	Double Underline
[Decml Align Char]	Decimal Character or Thousands Separator
[Def Mark:Index]	Index Definition
[Def Mark:List]	List Definition
[Def Mark:ToC]	Table of Contents Definition
[EndDef]	End of Index, List, or Table of Contents
[Endnote]	Endnote
[Endnote Placement]	Endnote Placement
[End Opt]	Endnote Options
[Ext Large]	Extra Large Print
[Fig Opt]	Figure Box Options
[Figure]	Figure Box
[Fine]	Fine Print
[Flsh Rt]	Flush Right
[Font]	Base Font
[Footer]	Footer
[Footnote]	Footnote

Code	Meaning
[Force]	Force Odd/Even Page
[Form]	Form (Printer Selection)
[Form Typ]	Form Type
[Ftn Opt]	Footnote/Endnote Options
[Full Form]	Table of Authorities, Full Form
[Header]	Header
[HLine]	Horizontal Line
[HPg]	Hard Page Break
[HRt]	Hard Return
[Hyph Off]	Hyphenation Off
[Hyph On]	Hyphenation On
[HZone]	Hyphenation Zone
[→Indent]	Indent
[→Indent←]	Left/Right Indent
[Index]	Index Entry
[ISRt]	Invisible Soft Return
[Italc]	Italics
[Just Lim]	Word/Letter Spacing Justification Limits
[Just Off]	Left-Justified/Ragged-Right
[Just On]	Right Justification
[Kern]	Kerning
[Lang]	Language
[Large]	Large Print
[Line Height]	Leading
[Ln Num]	Line Numbering
[L/R Mar]	Left and Right Margins
[Mark:List]	List Entry
[Mark:ToC]	Table of Contents Entry

Code	Meaning
[←Mar Rel]	Left Margin Release
[Math Def]	Definition of Math Columns
[Math Off]	End of Math
[Math On]	Beginning of Math
[New End Num]	New Endnote Number
[New Fig Num]	New Figure Box Number
[New Ftn Num]	New Footnote Number
[New Tab Num]	New Table Box Number
[New Txt Num]	New Text Box Number
[New Usr Num]	New User-Defined Box Number
[Note Num]	Footnote/Endnote Reference (inserted inside of Footnote or Endnote code)
[Ovrstk]	Overstrike Preceding Character
[Paper Sz/Typ]	Paper Size and Type
[Par Num]	Paragraph Number
[Par Num Def]	Paragraph Numbering Definition
[Pg Num]	New Page Number
[Pg Numbering]	Page Number Position
[Ptr Cmnd]	Printer Command
[RedLn]	Redline
[Ref]	Reference (Automatic Reference)
[Shadw]	Shadow
[Small]	Small Print
[Sm Cap]	Small Caps
[SPg]	Soft Page Break
[SRt]	Soft Return
[StkOut]	Strikeout
[Style Off]	Style Off
[Style On]	Styles On

Code	Meaning
[Subdoc]	Subdocument (Master Documents)
[SubScrpt]	Subscript
[Suppress]	Suppress Page Format
[SuprScrpt]	Superscript
[t]	Subtotal Entry
[T]	Total Entry
[Tab]	Tab
[Table]	Table Box
[Tab Set]	Tab Set
[Target]	Target (Auto Reference)
[T/B Mar]	Top and Bottom Margins
[Tbl Opt]	Table Box Options
[Text Box]	Text Box
[Txt Opt]	Text Box Options
[Und]	Underlining
[Usr Box]	User Box
[Usr Opt]	User Box Options
[VLine]	Vertical Line
[Vry Large]	Very Large Print
[W/O Off]	Widow/Orphan Off
[W/O On]	Widow/Orphan On
[Wrd/Ltr Spacing]	Word and Letter Spacing

APPENDIX C
WordPerfect's Macro Commands

WordPerfect 5.0 includes a powerful macro command language. You can access these macro commands by pressing Ctrl-PgUp (Macro Commands) when in the Macro Editor. To access the Macro Editor, you must first have defined a macro. You then take the steps to redefine the same macro, which presents you with the option of replacing or editing it. When you select the Edit option (**2** or **E**), you are placed in the Macro Editor.

To enter a macro command in the Macro Editor, select the Action option (**2** or **A**) and then press Ctrl-PgUp. This opens a window in the upper right corner of the screen. The macro commands in this window are listed in alphabetical order. To select a particular command, position the highlight cursor on the name of the command and press ◄─┘. You can use any of WordPerfect's cursor movement commands to scroll through the list until you find the command you wish to insert into the current macro. To quickly locate a particular command, just type the first letter or letters of its name (Name Search is automatically active). To exit the list of macro commands without selecting one of them, press Cancel (F1).

Most of these macro commands require arguments that specify how they are to operate in the macro. Arguments are separated and terminated in a macro command by a tilde (˜). When you select a command in the Macro Editor that uses arguments, only the command word is inserted into your macro. You must then type in the values you wish to assign to arguments as well as the required tildes.

List of WordPerfect 5.0 Macro Commands

{;} <*comment*>˜   Allows you to add comments to your macro. Any text between {;} and ˜ is ignored during macro execution.

{ASSIGN} <*variable*>˜ <*value*>˜   Initializes a variable between 0 and 9 with the value given.

{BELL}   Sounds the bell one time.

{BREAK}   Terminates the execution of an IF statement. Execution resumes after the IF statement or at the end of the macro if there is no IF statement.

{CALL} <*label*>˜   Calls the subroutine identified by the <*label*> variable. This routine must be located in the same macro.

{CANCEL OFF}   Suppresses the Cancel (F1) function during the macro's execution until a {CANCEL ON} command is encountered or the macro terminates.

{CANCEL ON}   Turns the Cancel (F1) function back on.

{CASE} <*value*>˜ <*case1*>˜ <*label1*>˜ <*case2*>˜ <*label2*>˜ ... <*casen*>˜ <*labeln*>˜ ˜   Executes the commands listed after a particular label (indicated by the <*label*n> argument) if the case value (indicated by <*case*n>) is the equivalent of the value of the variable (listed by the <*value*> argument). If no match is found between the value of the variable and any of the case numbers, the macro continues to execute the keystrokes and commands listed after the {CASE} command.

{CASE CALL} <*value*>˜ <*case1*>˜ <*label1*>˜ <*case2*>˜ <*label2*>˜ ...<*casen*>˜ <*labeln*>˜ ˜   Executes the subroutine at a particular label (indicated by the <*label*n> argument) if the case value (indicated by <*case*n>)

is the equivalent of the value of the variable (listed by the <*value*> argument). If no match is found between the value of the variable and any of the case numbers, the macro continues to execute the keystrokes and commands listed after the {CASE CALL} command.

{**CHAIN**}<*macro*>˜   Executes the macro named in the <*macro*> argument when the current macro is finished executing.

{**CHAR**}<*variable*>˜ <*message*>˜   Pauses the macro and displays the contents of the <*message*> argument on the status line. When the user enters a single character, it assigns this character to the number between 0 and 9 entered as the <*variable*> argument.

{**DISPLAY OFF**}   Freezes the display of WordPerfect menus until a {DISPLAY ON} command is encountered or the macro terminates.

{**DISPLAY ON**}   Unfreezes the display of WordPerfect menus.

{**ELSE**}   Used in IF statements. The keystrokes and commands listed after {ELSE} are executed only if the IF condition is false.

{**END IF**}   Terminates an IF statement. (*See* {IF}.)

{**Enter**}   Inserts a hard return [HRt] into the document via the macro. Press Ctrl-V and ⬅ to insert this command in the macro.

{**GO**}<*label*>˜   Directs the execution of the macro to a new set of keystrokes or commands following the <*label*> argument in the macro. (*See* {LABEL}.)

{**IF**}<*condition*>˜ <*command*>   Executes the command(s) and/or keystrokes entered as the <*command*> argument if the condition is found to be true. (*See also* {ELSE} *and* {END IF} *commands.*)

{**IF EXISTS**}<*variable*>˜<*command*>   Executes the command(s) and/or keystrokes entered as the <*command*> argument if the variable (indicated by the <*variable*> argument) contains a value—that is, is not empty.

{**LABEL**}<*name*>˜   Identifies a command or group of commands by the name indicated in the <*name*> argument. It is used with the {GO}, {CALL}, {CASE}, and {CASE CALL} commands. The label you assign can consist of any characters and be as long as you want.

{**LOOK**}<*variable*>˜   Checks to see if a character has been typed by the user. If it has, it assigns that character to the variable number indicated by the <*var*> argument.

{**NEST**}<*macro*>˜   Immediately executes the macro whose name is given as the <*macro*> argument. After the program has finished executing the nested macro, it resumes execution of the macro that contains the {NEST} command.

{**ON CANCEL**}<*command*>˜   Indicates what command is to be executed if the Cancel function is encountered after the {ON CANCEL} command in the macro is executed. The <*command*> argument can be any of the following macro commands:

> {RETURN CANCEL} − the default
> {RETURN ERROR}
> {RETURN NOT FOUND}
> {BREAK}
> {GO}
> {CALL}
> {RETURN}
> {RESTART}
> {QUIT}

{ON ERROR} *<command>* ˜   Indicates what command is to be executed if an error is encountered after the {ON ERROR} command in the macro is executed. The *<command>* argument can be any command that can be used with the {ON CANCEL} command. The default command is {RETURN ERROR}. (*See* {ON CANCEL}.)

{ON NOT FOUND} *<command>* ˜   Indicates what command is to be executed if a search fails after the {ON NOT FOUND} command in the macro is executed. The *<command>* argument can be any command that can be used with the {ON CANCEL} command. The default command is {RETURN NOT FOUND}. (*See* {ON CANCEL}.)

{ORIGINAL KEY}   Returns the original value of the last key that the user pressed at the keyboard—that is, the last key before the macro began.

{PAUSE}   Pauses the execution of the macro until ⟵ is pressed.

{PROMPT} *<message>* ˜   Pauses the macro and displays the contents of the *<message>* argument on the status line. When the user presses ⟵, the message disappears and the macro resumes execution.

{QUIT}   Immediately terminates the execution of the macro.

{RESTART}   Terminates the execution of the macro as soon as the keystrokes and commands in the current subroutine or macro are finished executing.

{RETURN}   Immediately terminates the current subroutine and resumes execution at the command just after the subroutine call statement. If {RETURN} is used with the {CASE} or {CASE CALL} command, it terminates the macro.

{RETURN CANCEL}   Immediately terminates the current subroutine and issues Cancel before resuming execution at the command just after the subroutine call statement.

{RETURN ERROR} Immediately terminates the current subroutine and indicates an error before resuming execution at the command just after the subroutine call statement.

{RETURN NOT FOUND} Immediately terminates the current subroutine and issues a Not Found condition before resuming execution at the command just after the subroutine call statement.

{SPEED} *<hundredths of a second>* ˜ Slows down the macro's execution by waiting the amount of time expressed as hundredths of a second between each keystroke or command execution.

{STATE} Can be used with an IF condition to test for the current state of WordPerfect. When performing such a test, you enter an ampersand (**&**) before the number representing the state tested for. This is placed after the {STATE} command, according to the following list:

1,2,3	Current Document Number
4	Main Editing Screen
8	Editing (Other than Main Document)
16	Macro Definition
32	Macro Execution (always set)
64	Merge Execution
128	Block on
256	Typeover on
512	Reveal Codes operative
1024	Yes/No question operative

{STEP ON} Turns on Step mode, in which each macro keystroke and command is executed in a single step. The next step in the macro is indicated on the status line. To step through the macro keystrokes and commands, you must press a key (not necessarily the key required by the macro). The macro returns to normal execution if it encounters a {STEP OFF} command.

{STEP OFF}   Turns off Step mode.

{Tab}   Inserts a [Tab] code into the document via the macro. Press Ctrl-V and the Tab key to insert this command in the macro.

{TEXT} *<variable>* ˜ *<message>* ˜   Pauses the macro and displays the contents of the *<message>* argument on the status line. When the user enters a response up to 120 characters and presses ←┘, this character is assigned to the variable number between 0 and 9 entered as the *<variable>* argument.

{WAIT} *<tenths of a second>* ˜   Pauses execution of the macro for the amount of time specified in tenths of a second.

Using Control Characters in a Message String

The following Ctrl-letter key codes can be entered as part of the *<message>* arguments for the {CHAR}, {PROMPT}, and {TEXT} commands:

^ H   Positions the message in the upper left corner of the screen. It is displayed by {Home} in the macro.

^ J   Enters a new line. It is displayed by {Enter} in the macro.

^ K   Clears to the end of the line. It is displayed by {Del to EOL} in the macro.

^ L   Clears a full screen. It is displayed by {Del to EOP} in the macro.

^ M   Positions the message at the beginning of the line. It is displayed by { ^ M} in the macro.

^ N   Turns on the display attribute specified by an attribute character after the ^ N. It is displayed by { ^ N} in the macro.

^O   Turns off the display attribute previously used. It is displayed by { ^O} in the macro.

^P   Positions the cursor at the column and row specified by the column number (1–80) and row number (1–25). It is displayed by { ^P} in the macro. Enter the column and row number immediately after the { ^P}.

^Q   Turns off all display attributes previously used. It is displayed by { ^Q} in the macro.

^R   Turns on reverse (or inverse) video. It is displayed by { ^R} in the macro.

^S   Turns off reverse (or inverse) video. It is displayed by { ^S} in the macro.

^T   Turns on underlining. It is displayed by { ^T} in the macro.

^U   Turns off underlining. It is displayed by { ^U} in the macro.

^V   Turns on the menu letter (mnemonic) attribute. It is displayed by {V} in the macro

^W   Positions the cursor one line up on the document editing screen. It is displayed by {Up} in the macro.

^X   Positions the cursor one character to the right on the document editing screen. It is displayed by {Right} in the macro.

^Y   Positions the cursor one character to the left on the document editing screen. It is displayed by {Left} in the macro.

^Z   Positions the cursor one line down on the document editing screen. It is displayed by {Down} in the macro.

^\   Turns off bold. It is displayed by {^\} in the macro.

^]   Turns on bold. It is displayed by {^]} in the macro.

The following control characters can be entered after the display-attribute-on character (^O) and the display-attribute-off character (^Q):

^A   Very large print attribute. It is displayed by {^A} in the macro.

^B   Large print attribute. It is displayed by {^B} in the macro.

^C   Small print attribute. It is displayed by {^C} in the macro.

^D   Fine print attribute. It is displayed by {^D} in the macro.

^E   Superscript attribute. It is displayed by {^E} in the macro.

^F   Subscript attribute. It is displayed by {^F} in the macro.

^G   Outline print attribute. It is displayed by {^G} in the macro.

^H   Italics attribute. It is displayed by {Home} in the macro.

^I   Shadow print attribute. It is displayed by {Tab} in the macro.

^J   Redline attribute. It is displayed by {Enter} in the macro.

^K   Double underline print attribute. It is displayed by {Del to EOL} in the macro.

^M   Strikeout print attribute. It is displayed by {^M} in the macro.

^N   Underline print attribute. It is displayed by {^N} in the macro.

^O   Small caps print attribute. It is displayed by {^O} in the macro.

^P   Blink attribute. It is displayed by {^P} in the macro.

^Q   Reverse video attribute. It is displayed by {^Q} in the macro.

Assigning Values to Variables in Macros

You can assign values to up to ten variables, designated by numbers between 0 and 9, for use in macros. This can be done in a number of ways. In addition to using the {ASSIGN} command from within the Macro Editor, you can also assign values to variables from the regular editing screen. When Block is not on or you are not in the process of defining a macro and you press Ctrl-PgUp (Macro Commands), the prompt

Variable:

appears in the lower left corner of the status line. You then enter a number between 0 and 9. When you do, the prompt changes to

Value:

and you enter the value you wish to assign. This value can consist of a literal number, text string, or a calculation (see the Advanced Macros section of your WordPerfect 5.0 documentation for a list of the types of operations you can assign). After assigning a value to a variable, you can enter it into the text of your document or macro simply by pressing the Alt key plus the variable number. For example, if you assign the text string *Confidential* as the value for the variable 0, WordPerfect will enter *Confidential* into the text whenever you press Alt-0.

You can also assign a value to a variable by using the Block (Alt-F4) feature. After you mark a block, press Ctrl-PgUp, and type the number of the variable, WordPerfect automatically assigns the contents of the block as the value of the variable named.

Finally, you can assign a value to a variable during macro definition. To do this, you press Ctrl-PgUp after beginning the macro definition (by pressing Ctrl-F10 and entering a name and optional description for the macro). When you do, the program displays the following menu

1 Pause; **2** Display; **3** Assign; **4** Comments: 0

When you select the Assign option (**3** or **A**), you are prompted to enter the variable number and value just as you are when you press Ctrl-PgUp in the normal editing screen (that is, when Block is not on and you aren't defining a macro).

Selections from The SYBEX Library

WORD PROCESSING

Visual Guide to WordPerfect
Jeff Woodward

457pp. Ref. 591-3

This is a visual hands-on guide which is ideal for brand new users as the book shows each activity keystroke-by-keystroke. Clear illustrations of computer screen menus are included at every stage. Covers basic editing, formatting lines, paragraphs, and pages, using the block feature, footnotes, search and replace, and more. Through Version 5.

The ABC's of WordPerfect 5
Alan R. Neibauer

283pp. Ref. 504-2

This introduction explains the basics of desktop publishing with WordPerfect 5: editing, layout, formatting, printing, sorting, merging, and more. Readers are shown how to use WordPerfect 5's new features to produce great-looking reports.

The ABC's of WordPerfect
Alan R. Neibauer

239pp. Ref. 425-9

This basic introduction to WordPefect consists of short, step-by-step lessons—for new users who want to get going fast. Topics range from simple editing and formatting, to merging, sorting, macros, and more. Includes version 4.2

Mastering WordPerfect 5
Susan Baake Kelly

709pp. Ref. 500-X

The revised and expanded version of this definitive guide is now on WordPerfect 5 and covers wordprocessing and basic desktop publishing. As more than 200,000 readers of the original edition can attest, no tutorial approaches it for clarity and depth of treatment. Sorting, line drawing, and laser printing included.

Mastering WordPerfect
Susan Baake Kelly

435pp. Ref. 332-5

Step-by-step training from startup to mastery, featuring practical uses (form letters, newsletters and more), plus advanced topics such as document security and macro creation, sorting and columnar math. Through Version 4.2.

Advanced Techniques in WordPerfect 5
Kay Yarborough Nelson

586pp. Ref. 511-5

Now updated for Version 5, this invaluable guide to the advanced features of Word-Perfect provides step-by-step instructions and practical examples covering those specialized techniques which have most perplexed users—indexing, outlining, foreign-language typing, mathematical functions, and more.

WordPerfect 5 Desktop Companion
SYBEX Ready Reference Series
Greg Harvey/Kay Yarborough Nelson

1006pp. Ref. 522-0

Desktop publishing features have been added to this compact encyclopedia. This title offers more detailed, cross-referenced entries on every software feature including page formatting and layout, laser printing and word processing macros. New users of WordPerfect, and those new to Version 5 and desktop publishing will find this easy to use for on-the-job help.

WordPerfect Tips and Tricks (Third Edition)
Alan R. Neibauer

650pp. Ref. 520-4

This new edition is a real timesaver. For on-the-job guidance and creative new uses, this title covers all versions of WordPerfect up to and including 5.0—covers stream-lining documents, automating with macros, new print enhancements, and more.

WordPerfect Instant Reference
SYBEX Prompter Series
Greg Harvey/Kay Yarborough Nelson
254pp. Ref. 476-3, 4 ¾" × 8"
When you don't have time to go digging through the manuals, this fingertip guide offers clear, concise answers: command summaries, correct usage, and exact key-stroke sequences for on-the-job tasks. Convenient organization reflects the struc-ture of WordPerfect. Through Version 4.2.

WordPerfect 5 Macro Handbook
Kay Yarborough Nelson
488pp. Ref. 483-6
Readers can create macros custom-tailored to their own needs with this excel-lent tutorial and reference. Nelson's expertise guides the WordPerfect 5 user through nested and chained macros, macro libraries, specialized macros, and much more.

The ABC's of Microsoft Word
(Third Edition)
Alan R. Neibauer
461pp. Ref. 604-9
This is for the novice WORD user who wants to begin producing documents in the shortest time possible. Each chapter has short, easy-to-follow lessons for both keyboard and mouse, including all the basic editing, formatting and printing functions. Version 5.0.

Mastering Microsoft Word
on the IBM PC
(Fourth Edition)
Matthew Holtz
680pp. Ref.597-2
This comprehensive, step-by-step guide details all the new desktop publishing developments in this versatile word pro-cessor, including details on editing, for-matting, printing, and laser printing. Holtz uses sample business documents to dem-onstrate the use of different fonts, graph-ics, and complex documents. Includes Fast Track speed notes. For Versions 4 and 5.

Advanced Techniques in
Microsoft Word (Second Edition)
Alan R. Neibauer
462pp. Ref. 615-4
This highly acclaimed guide to WORD is an excellent tutorial for intermediate to advanced users. Topics include word pro-cessing fundamentals, desktop publish-ing with graphics, data management, and working in a multiuser environment. For Versions 4 and 5.

Mastering DisplayWrite 4
Michael E. McCarthy
447pp. Ref. 510-7
Total training, reference and support for users at all levels—in plain, non-technical language. Novices will be up and running in an hour's time; everyone will gain com-plete word-processing and document-management skills.

Mastering MultiMate Advantage II
Charles Ackerman
407pp. Ref. 482-8
This comprehensive tutorial covers all the capabilities of MultiMate, and highlights the differences between MultiMate Advantage II and previous versions—in pathway support, sorting, math, DOS access, using dBASE III, and more. With many practical examples, and a chapter on the On-File database.

The Complete Guide
to MultiMate
Carol Holcomb Dreger
208pp. Ref. 229-9
This step-by-step tutorial is also an excel-lent reference guide to MultiMate features and uses. Topics include search/replace, library and merge functions, repagina-tion, document defaults and more.

Advanced Techniques
in MultiMate
Chris Gilbert
275pp. Ref. 412-7
A textbook on efficient use of MultiMate for business applications, in a series of self-contained lessons on such topics as multiple columns, high-speed merging, mailing-list printing and Key Procedures.

Introduction to WordStar
Arthur Naiman

208pp. Ref. 134-9

This all time bestseller is an engaging first-time introduction to word processing as well as a complete guide to using WordStar—from basic editing to blocks, global searches, formatting, dot commands, SpellStar and MailMerge. Through Version 3.3.

Practical WordStar Uses
Julie Anne Arca

303pp. Ref. 107-1

A hands-on guide to WordStar and MailMerge applications, with solutions to comon problems and "recipes" for day-to-day tasks. Formatting, merge-printing and much more; plus a quick-reference command chart and notes on CP/M and PC-DOS. For Version 3.3.

Mastering WordStar Release 5
Greg Harvey/David J. Clark

450pp. Ref. 491-7

This book is the ultimate reference book for the newest version of WordStar. Readers may use Mastering to look up any word processing function, including the new Version 5 and 5.5 features and enhancements, and find detailed instructions for fundamental to advanced operations.

WordStar Instant Reference
SYBEX Prompter Series
David J. Clark

314pp. Ref. 543-3, 4 ¾" × 8"

This quick reference provides reminders on the use of the editing, formatting, mailmerge, and document processing commands available through WordStar 4 and 5. Operations are organized alphabetically for easy access. The text includes a survey of the menu system and instructions for installing and customizing WordStar.

Understanding WordStar 2000
David Kolodney/Thomas Blackadar

275pp. Ref. 554-9

This engaging, fast-paced series of tutorials covers everything from moving the cursor to print enhancements, format

files, key glossaries, windows and MailMerge. With practical examples, and notes for former WordStar users.

DESKTOP PUBLISHING

The ABC's of Ventura
Robert Cowart/Steve Cummings

390pp. Ref. 537-9

Created especially for new desktop publishers, this is an easy introduction to a complex program. Cowart provides details on using the mouse, the Ventura side bar, and page layout, with careful explanations of publishing terminology. The new Ventura menus are all carefully explained. For Version 2.

Mastering Ventura
(Second Edition)
Matthew Holtz

613pp. Ref. 581-6

A complete, step-by-step guide to IBM PC desktop publishing with Xerox Ventura Publisher. Practical examples show how to use style sheets, format pages, cut and paste, enhance layouts, import material from other programs, and more. For Version 2.

Ventura Tips and Techniques
Carl Townsend/Sandy Townsend

424pp. Ref. 559-X

Packed with an experienced Ventura user's tips and tricks, this volume is a time saver and design booster. From crop marks to file management to using special fonts, this book is for serious Ventura users. Covers Ventura 2.

Ventura Instant Reference
SYBEX Prompter Series
Matthew Holtz

320pp. Ref. 544-1, 4 ¾" × 8"

This compact volume offers easy access to the complex details of Ventura modes and options, commands, side-bars, file management, output device configuration, and control. Written for versions through Ventura 2, it also includes standard procedures for project and job control.

Ventura Power Tools
Rick Altman
318pp. Ref. 592-1

Renowned Ventura expert, Rick Altman, presents strategies and techniques for the most efficient use of Ventura Publisher 2. This includes a power disk with DOS utilities which is specially designed for optimizing Ventura use. Learn how to soup up Ventura, edit CHP files, avoid design tragedies, handle very large documents, and improve form.

Mastering PageMaker on the IBM PC (Second Edition)
Antonia Stacy Jolles
384pp. Ref. 521-2

A guide to every aspect of desktop publishing with PageMaker: the vocabulary and basics of page design, layout, graphics and typography, plus instructions for creating finished typeset publications of all kinds.

Understanding Professional Write
Gerry Litton
400pp. Ref. 656-1

A complete guide to Professional Write that takes you from creating your first simple document, into a detailed description of all major aspects of the software. Special features place an emphasis on the use of different typestyles to create attractive documents as well as potential problems and suggestions on how to get around them.

Understanding PFS: First Publisher
Gerry Litton
310pp. Ref. 616-2

This complete guide takes users from the basics all the way through the most complex features available. Discusses working with text and graphics, columns, clip art, and add-on software enhancements. Many page layout suggestions are introduced. Includes Fast Track speed notes.

Mastering Ready, Set, Go!
David A. Kater
482pp. Ref. 536-0

This hands-on introduction to the popular desktop publishing package for the Macintosh allows readers to produce professional-looking reports, brochures, and flyers. Written for Version 4, this title has been endorsed by Letraset, the Ready, Set, Go! software publisher.

Understanding PostScript Programming (Second Edition)
David A. Holzgang
472pp. Ref. 566-2

In-depth treatment of PostScript for programmers and advanced users working on custom desktop publishing tasks. Hands-on development of programs for font creation, integrating graphics, printer implementations and more.

Your HP LaserJet Handbook
Alan R. Neibauer
564pp. Ref. 618-9

Get the most from your printer with this step-by-step instruction book for using LaserJet text and graphics features such as cartridge and soft fonts, type selection, memory and processor enhancements, PCL programming, and PostScript solutions. This hands-on guide provides specific instructions for working with a variety of software.

SPREADSHEETS AND INTEGRATED SOFTWARE

Visual Guide to Lotus 1-2-3
Jeff Woodward
250pp. Ref. 641-3

Readers match what they see on the screen with the book's screen-by-screen action sequences. For new Lotus users, topics include computer fundamentals, opening and editing a worksheet, using graphs, macros, and printing typeset-quality reports. For Release 2.2.

The ABC's of 1-2-3 Release 2.2
Chris Gilbert/Laurie Williams
340pp. Ref. 623-5
New Lotus 1-2-3 users delight in this book's step-by-step approach to building trouble-free spreadsheets, displaying graphs, and efficiently building data-bases. The authors cover the ins and outs of the latest version including easier calculations, file linking, and better graphic presentation.

The ABC's of 1-2-3 Release 3
Judd Robbins
290pp. Ref. 519-0
The ideal book for beginners who are new to Lotus or new to Release 3. This step-by-step approach to the 1-2-3 spreadsheet software gets the reader up and running with spreadsheet, database, graphics, and macro functions.

The ABC's of 1-2-3
(Second Edition)
Chris Gilbert/Laurie Williams
245pp. Ref. 355-4
Online Today recommends it as "an easy and comfortable way to get started with the program." An essential tutorial for novices, it will remain on your desk as a valuable source of ongoing reference and support. For Release 2.

Mastering 1-2-3 Release 3
Carolyn Jorgensen
682pp. Ref. 517-4
For new Release 3 and experienced Release 2 users, "Mastering" starts with a basic spreadsheet, then introduces spreadsheet and database commands, functions, and macros, and then tells how to analyze 3D spreadsheets and make high-impact reports and graphs. Lotus add-ons are discussed and Fast Tracks are included.

Mastering 1-2-3
(Second Edition)
Carolyn Jorgensen
702pp. Ref. 528-X
Get the most from 1-2-3 Release 2 with this step-by-step guide emphasizing advanced features and practical uses. Topics include data sharing, macros,

spreadsheet security, expanded memory, and graphics enhancements.

The Complete Lotus 1-2-3
Release 2.2 Handbook
Greg Harvey
750pp. Ref. 625-1
This comprehensive handbook discusses every 1-2-3 operating with clear instructions and practical tips. This volume especially emphasizes the new improved graphics, high-speed recalculation techniques, and spreadsheet linking available with Release 2.2.

The Complete Lotus 1-2-3
Release 3 Handbook
Greg Harvey
700pp. Ref. 600-6
Everything you ever wanted to know about 1-2-3 is in this definitive handbook. As a Release 3 guide, it features the design and use of 3D worksheets, and improved graphics, along with using Lotus under DOS or OS/2. Problems, exercises, and helpful insights are included.

Lotus 1-2-3 Desktop Companion
SYBEX Ready Reference Series
Greg Harvey
976pp. Ref. 501-8
A full-time consultant, right on your desk. Hundreds of self-contained entries cover every 1-2-3 feature, organized by topic, indexed and cross-referenced, and supplemented by tips, macros and working examples. For Release 2.

Advanced Techniques
in Lotus 1-2-3
Peter Antoniak/E. Michael Lunsford
367pp. Ref. 556-5
This guide for experienced users focuses on advanced functions, and techniques for designing menu-driven applications using macros and the Release 2 command language. Interfacing techniques and add-on products are also considered.

Lotus 1-2-3 Tips and Tricks
Gene Weisskopf
396pp. Ref. 454-2

A rare collection of timesavers and tricks for longtime Lotus users. Topics include macros, range names, spreadsheet design, hardware considerations, DOS operations, efficient data analysis, printing, data interchange, applications development, and more.

Lotus 1-2-3 Instant Reference Release 2.2
SYBEX Prompter Series
Greg Harvey/Kay Yarborough Nelson
254pp. Ref. 635-9, 4 ¾" × 8"
The reader gets quick and easy access to any operation in 1-2-3 Version 2.2 in this handy pocket-sized encyclopedia. Organized by menu function, each command and function has a summary description, the exact key sequence, and a discussion of the options.

Lotus 1-2-3 Instant Reference
SYBEX Prompter Series
Greg Harvey/Kay Yarborough Nelson
296pp. Ref. 475-5; 4 ¾" × 8"
Organized information at a glance. When you don't have time to hunt through hundreds of pages of manuals, turn here for a quick reminder: the right key sequence, a brief explanation of a command, or the correct syntax for a specialized function.

Mastering Symphony (Fourth Edition)
Douglas Cobb
857pp. Ref. 494-1
Thoroughly revised to cover all aspects of the major upgrade of Symphony Version 2, this Fourth Edition of Doug Cobb's classic is still "the Symphony bible" to this complex but even more powerful package. All the new features are discussed and placed in context with prior versions so that both new and previous users will benefit from Cobb's insights.

The ABC's of Quattro
Alan Simpson/Douglas J. Wolf
286pp. Ref. 560-3
Especially for users new to spreadsheets, this is an introduction to the basic concepts and a guide to instant productivity through editing and using spreadsheet formulas and functions. Includes how to print out graphs and data for presentation. For Quattro 1.1.

Mastering Quattro
Alan Simpson
576pp. Ref. 514-X
This tutorial covers not only all of Quattro's classic spreadsheet features, but also its added capabilities including extended graphing, modifiable menus, and the macro debugging environment. Simpson brings out how to use all of Quattro's new-generation-spreadsheet capabilities.

Mastering Framework III
Douglas Hergert/Jonathan Kamin
613pp. Ref. 513-1
Thorough, hands-on treatment of the latest Framework release. An outstanding introduction to integrated software applications, with examples for outlining, spreadsheets, word processing, databases, and more; plus an introduction to FRED programming.

The ABC's of Excel on the IBM PC
Douglas Hergert
326pp. Ref. 567-0
This book is a brisk and friendly introduction to the most important features of Microsoft Excel for PC's. This beginner's book discusses worksheets, charts, database operations, and macros, all with hands-on examples. Written for all versions through Version 2.

Mastering Excel on the IBM PC
Carl Townsend
628pp. Ref. 403-8
A complete Excel handbook with step-by-step tutorials, sample applications and an extensive reference section. Topics include worksheet fundamentals, formulas and windows, graphics, database techniques, special features, macros and more.

Excel Instant Reference
SYBEX Prompter Series
William J. Orvis
368pp. Ref.577-8, 4 ¾" × 8"

This pocket-sized reference book contains all of Excel's menu commands, math operations, and macro functions. Quick and easy access to command syntax, usage, arguments, and examples make this Instant Reference a must. Through Version 1.5.

Understanding PFS: First Choice
Gerry Litton
489pp. Ref. 568-9

From basic commands to complex features, this complete guide to the popular integrated package is loaded with step-by-step instructions. Lessons cover creating attractive documents, setting up easy-to-use databases, working with spreadsheets and graphics, and smoothly integrating tasks from different First Choice modules. For Version 3.0.

Mastering Enable
Keith D. Bishop
517pp. Ref. 440-2

A comprehensive, practical, hands-on guide to Enable 2.0—integrated word processing, spreadsheet, database management, graphics, and communications—from basic concepts to custom menus, macros and the Enable Procedural Language.

Mastering Q & A (Second Edition)
Greg Harvey
540pp. Ref. 452-6

This hands-on tutorial explores the Q & A Write, File, and Report modules, and the Intelligent Assistant. English-language command processor, macro creation, interfacing with other software, and more, using practical business examples.

Mastering SuperCalc5
Greg Harvey/Mary Beth Andrasak
500pp. Ref. 624-3

This book offers a complete and unintimidating guided tour through each feature. With step-by-step lessons, readers learn about the full capabilities of spreadsheet, graphics, and data management functions. Multiple spreadsheets, linked spreadsheets, 3D graphics, and macros are also discussed.

DATABASE MANAGEMENT

The ABC's of Paradox
Charles Siegel
300pp. Ref.573-5

Easy to understand and use, this introduction is written so that the computer novice can create, edit, and manage complex Paradox databases. This primer is filled with examples of the Paradox 3.0 menu structure.

Mastering Paradox (Fourth Edition)
Alan Simpson
636pp. Ref. 612-X

Best selling author Alan Simpson simplifies all aspects of Paradox for the beginning to intermediate user. The book starts with database basics, covers multiple tables, graphics, custom applications with PAL, and the Personal Programmer. For Version 3.0.

Quick Guide to dBASE: The Visual Approach
David Kolodney
382pp. Ref. 596-4

This illustrated tutorial provides the beginner with a working knowledge of all the basic functions of dBASE IV. Images of each successive dBASE screen tell how to create and modify a database, add, edit, sort and select records, and print custom labels and reports.

The ABC's of dBASE IV
Robert Cowart
338pp. Ref. 531-X

This superb tutorial introduces beginners to the concept of databases and practical dBASE IV applications featuring the new menu-driven interface, the new report writer, and Query by Example.

Understanding dBASE IV (Special Edition)
Alan Simpson
880pp. Ref. 509-3

This Special Edition is the best introduction to dBASE IV, written by 1 million-reader-strong dBASE expert Alan Simpson. First it gives basic skills for creating and manipulating efficient databases. Then the author explains how to make reports, manage multiple databases, and build applications. Includes Fast Track speed notes.

Mastering dBASE IV Programming
Carl Townsend

496pp. Ref. 540-9

This task-oriented book introduces structured dBASE IV programming and commands by setting up a general ledger system, an invoice system, and a quotation management system. The author carefully explores the unique character of dBASE IV based on his in-depth understanding of the program.

dBASE IV User's Instant Reference
SYBEX Prompter Series
Alan Simpson

349pp. Ref. 605-7, 4 ¾" × 8"

This handy pocket-sized reference book gives every new dBASE IV user fast and easy access to any dBASE command. Arranged alphabetically and by function, each entry includes a description, exact syntax, an example, and special tips from Alan Simpson.

dBASE IV Programmer's Instant Reference
SYBEX Prompter Series
Alan Simpson

544pp. Ref.538-7, 4 ¾" × 8"

This comprehensive reference to every dBASF. command and function has everything for the dBASE programmer in a compact, pocket-sized book. Fast and easy access to adding data, sorting, performing calculations, managing multiple databases, memory variables and arrays, windows and menus, networking, and much more. Version 1.1.

dBASE IV User's Desktop Companion
SYBEX Ready Reference Series
Alan Simpson

950pp. Ref. 523-9

This easy-to-use reference provides an exhaustive resource guide to taking full advantage of the powerful nonprogramming features of the dBASE IV Control Center. This book discusses query by example, custom reports and data entry screens, macros, the application generator, and the dBASE command and programming language.

dBASE IV Programmer's Reference Guide
SYBEX Ready Reference Series
Alan Simpson

1000pp. Ref. 539-5

This exhaustive seven-part reference for dBASE IV users includes sections on getting started, using menu-driven dBASE, command-driven dBASE, multiuser dBASE, programming in dBASE, common algorithms, and getting the most out of dBASE. Includes Simpson's tips on the best ways to use this completely redesigned and more powerful program.

The ABC's of dBASE III PLUS
Robert Cowart

264pp. Ref. 379-1

The most efficient way to get beginners up and running with dBASE. Every 'how' and 'why' of database management is demonstrated through tutorials and practical dBASE III PLUS applications.

Understanding dBASE III PLUS
Alan Simpson

415pp. Ref. 349-X

A solid sourcebook of training and ongoing support. Everything from creating a first database to command file programming is presented in working examples, with tips and techniques you won't find anywhere else.

Mastering dBASE III PLUS: A Structured Approach
Carl Townsend

342pp. Ref. 372-4

In-depth treatment of structured programming for custom dBASE solutions. An ideal study and reference guide for applications developers, new and experienced users with an interest in efficient programming.

Also:

Understanding dBASE III
Alan Simpson
300pp. Ref. 267-1

Advanced Techniques in dBASE III PLUS
Alan Simpson
454pp. Ref. 369-4
A full course in database design and structured programming, with routines for inventory control, accounts receivable, system management, and integrated databases.

Simpson's dBASE Tips and Tricks (For dBASE III PLUS)
Alan Simpson
420pp. Ref. 383-X
A unique library of techniques and programs shows how creative use of built-in features can solve all your needs—without expensive add-on products or external languages. Spreadsheet functions, graphics, and much more.

dBASE III PLUS Programmer's Reference Guide
SYBEX Ready Reference Series
Alan Simpson
1056pp. Ref. 508-5
Programmers will save untold hours and effort using this comprehensive, well-organized dBASE encyclopedia. Complete technical details on commands and functions, plus scores of often-needed algorithms.

dBASE Instant Reference
SYBEX Prompter Series
Alan Simpson
471pp. Ref. 484-4; 4 ¾" × 8"
Comprehensive information at a glance: a brief explanation of syntax and usage for every dBASE command, with step-by-step instructions and exact keystroke sequences. Commands are grouped by function in twenty precise categories.

Understanding R:BASE
Alan Simpson/Karen Watterson
609pp. Ref.503-4

This is the definitive R:BASE tutorial, for use with either OS/2 or DOS. Hands-on lessons cover every aspect of the software, from creating and using a database, to custom systems. Includes Fast Track speed notes.

Power User's Guide to R:BASE
Alan Simpson/Cheryl Currid/Craig Gillett
446pp. Ref. 354-6
Supercharge your R:BASE applications with this straightforward tutorial that covers system design, structured programming, managing multiple data tables, and more. Sample applications include ready-to-run mailing, inventory and accounts receivable systems. Through Version 2.11.

Understanding Oracle
James T. Perry/Joseph G. Lateer
634pp. Ref. 534-4
A comprehensive guide to the Oracle database management system for administrators, users, and applications developers. Covers everything in Version 5 from database basics to multi-user systems, performance, and development tools including SQL*Forms, SQL*Report, and SQL*Calc. Includes Fast Track speed notes.

COMPUTER-AIDED DESIGN AND DRAFTING

Visual Guide to AutoCAD
Genevieve Katz
325pp. Ref. 627-8
A visual step-by-step tutorial for AutoCAD beginners, this book gives the reader at a quick glance, the graphically presented information needed to understand and respond to commands. It covers more than 90 commands, from getting started to drawing composites using multiple commands. Through Release 10.

The ABC's of AutoCAD (Second Edition)
Alan R. Miller
375pp. Ref. 584-0

This brief but effective introduction to AutoCAD quickly gets users drafting and designing with this complex CADD package. The essential operations and capabilities of AutoCAD are neatly detailed, using a proven, step-by-step method that is tailored to the results-oriented beginner.

Mastering AutoCAD (Third Edition)
George Omura
825pp. Ref. 574-3

Now in its third edition, this tutorial guide to computer-aided design and drafting with AutoCAD is perfect for newcomers to CADD, as well as AutoCAD users seeking greater proficiency. An architectural project serves as an example throughout.

Advanced Techniques in AutoCAD (Second Edition)
Robert M. Thomas
425pp. Ref. 593-X

Develop custom applications using screen menus, command macros, and AutoLISP programming—no prior programming experience required. Topics include customizing the AutoCAD environment, advanced data extraction techniques, and much more.

AutoCAD Desktop Companion SYBEX Ready Reference Series
Robert M. Thomas
1094pp. Ref.590-5

This is a complete reference work covering all the features, commands, and user options available under AutoCAD Release 10, including drawing basic and complex entities, editing, displaying, printing, plotting, and customizing drawings, manipulating the drawing database, and AutoLISP programming. Through Release 10.

AutoCAD Instant Reference SYBEX Prompter Series
George Omura

390pp. Ref. 548-4, 4 ¾" × 8"

This pocket-sized reference is a quick guide to all AutoCAD features. Designed for easy use, all commands are organized with exact syntax, a brief description, options, tips, and references. Through Release 10.

The ABC's of Generic CADD
Alan R. Miller
278pp. Ref. 608-1

This outstanding guide to computer-aided design and drafting with Generic CADD assumes no previous experience with computers or CADD. This book will have users doing useful CADD work in record time, including basic drawing with the keyboard or a mouse, erasing and unerasing, making a copy of drawings on your printer, adding text and organizing your drawings using layers.

The ABC's of AutoLISP
George Omura
300pp. Ref. 620-0

This book is for users who want to unleash the full power of AutoCAD through the AutoLISP programming language. In non-technical terms, the reader is shown how to store point locations, create new commands, and manipulate coordinates and text. Packed with tips on common coding errors.

Mastering VersaCAD
David Bassett-Parkins
450pp. Ref. 617-0

For every level of VCAD user, this comprehensive tutorial treats each phase of project design including drawing, modifying, grouping, and filing. The reader will also learn VCAD project management and many tips, tricks, and shortcuts. Version 5.4.

SYBEX Computer Books
are different.

Here is why . . .

At SYBEX, each book is designed with you in mind. Every manuscript is carefully selected and supervised by our editors, who are themselves computer experts. We publish the best authors, whose technical expertise is matched by an ability to write clearly and to communicate effectively. Programs are thoroughly tested for accuracy by our technical staff. Our computerized production department goes to great lengths to make sure that each book is well-designed.

In the pursuit of timeliness, SYBEX has achieved many publishing firsts. SYBEX was among the first to integrate personal computers used by authors and staff into the publishing process. SYBEX was the first to publish books on the CP/M operating system, microprocessor interfacing techniques, word processing, and many more topics.

Expertise in computers and dedication to the highest quality product have made SYBEX a world leader in computer book publishing. Translated into fourteen languages, SYBEX books have helped millions of people around the world to get the most from their computers. We hope we have helped you, too.

For a complete catalog of our publications:

SYBEX, Inc. 2021 Challenger Drive, #100, Alameda, CA 94501
Tel: (415) 523-8233/(800) 227-2346   Telex: 336311
Fax: (415) 523-2373